The Mismanagement
of America, Inc.

The Mismanagement of America, Inc.

Lawrence G. Hrebiniak, Ph.D.

The Wharton School

Author of Making Strategy Work

iUniverse, Inc.

New York Lincoln Shanghai

The Mismanagement of America, Inc.

iUniverse books may be ordered through booksellers or by contacting:

iUniverse
2021 Pine Lake Road, Suite 100
Lincoln, NE 68512
www.iuniverse.com
1-800-Authors (1-800-288-4677)

Because of the dynamic nature of the Internet, any Web addresses or links contained in this book may have changed since publication and may no longer be valid.

The views expressed in this work are solely those of the author and do not necessarily reflect the views of the publisher, and the publisher hereby disclaims any responsibility for them

ISBN: 978-0-595-48434-8 (pbk)
ISBN: 978-0-595-71874-0 (cloth)
ISBN: 978-0-595-60530-9 (ebk)

Printed in the United States of America

To Laura and Justin

Contents

Preface

This is a serious book that focuses on serious issues. It identifies a host of problems resulting from gross mismanagement by leaders in the White House and Congress. The problems are real, huge, and, left unaddressed, their costs and consequences will soon exact a heavy toll on the nation and its citizens. The book is a call to action and its warnings simply cannot be ignored much longer.

My motivation to write this book is driven by a number of factors or conditions. Basically, I'm fed up with costly mismanagement and excessive waste at the highest levels of our government, in the White House and Congress.

I'm sick and tired of hearing that devastating mismanagement and poor organizational design can't be corrected because "that's politics" or "that's the way things are done in Washington."

I'm deathly afraid of the dangers and severe consequences of allowing management abuses or neglect to continue, especially in critical areas like financial and fiscal management and vital planning and intelligence activities.

I'm weary of hearing from dedicated government employees that the value and impact of their efforts are hampered or negated by organizational problems and the ineffective or incompetent management by their bosses in the White House and on Capitol Hill.

Most of all, I'm worried that the U.S. is heading for a big fall, much like other great empires in history, and I'm hoping that something can be done to forestall or avoid it.

The U.S. is in danger, not just from terrorists, evil governments, and growing global economic powers, but sadly from horrendous mismanagement and the wasteful policies of its own leaders, Democrats and Republicans alike, and I find this to be deplorable. People must be made aware of the problems and dangers U.S. leadership in the White House and Congress has been engendering and supporting over the years before misfortune strikes and real damage is done. My book is dedicated to this task.

There are many facts and data to support the statements and accusations made in this book. There are many facts and numbers presented that are disconcerting and irritating, and some that are downright scary. There are prognostications whose validity is difficult to rebuke. I have tried to collect and check the facts and numbers presented in the book in a careful and painstaking manner, as many of them are indeed shocking, even unbelievable.

Beyond the facts or the numbers, I have also tried to show the thrust and impact of trends suggested by the data. Some of the facts and figures surely will change before this book is published, but the data are still important primarily because of what they suggest or imply for the well-being of the country. It's shocking, for example, to learn that total military spending plus the interest payment on a huge national debt consumes roughly 60% of any year's tax receipts. Whether the actual number is 58% or 62% makes little difference—these expenses are sucking up massive amounts of money and creating huge opportunity costs, as many other programs—health, education, infrastructure repairs, science and medicine, etc.—cannot be funded adequately, causing the country to fall behind in many areas in an increasingly competitive world. Similar trends, problems, or thrusts are suggested by yet other numbers and facts, and they all spell trouble if our leaders in the White House and Congress continue to ignore them. I'm hoping that this book will make it increasingly difficult to do so.

This book takes a managerial and organizational design perspective, not the "shout-in-your-face" attack mode so common today in the political arena. It defines "America, Inc." and shows why it is a valid and useful concept and why mismanagement by America, Inc.'s leaders can no longer be tolerated. It argues that change is desperately needed and cannot be put off much longer.

As a professor for over three decades in the Department of Management of the Wharton School, University of Pennsylvania, I have often tackled problems of dysfunctional management practices and poor organizational design. I teach, consult, and do research in the area of strategic management and have numerous publications, including a recent book, *Making Strategy Work*, which contains useful information to address many of the problems identified in *The Mismanagement of America, Inc.* A brief overview of my work and experience can be found at: http://www-management.wharton.upenn.edu/hrebiniak, along with my contact information should anyone need to get in touch with me to debate a point or clarify an issue.

In a huge undertaking like this one, many people play important roles or perform critical jobs that, in total, determine the utility and success of a project. Of course, I alone assume responsibility for the book's content, the interpretation of data, presentation of facts, and any conclusions or recommendations for action the book may offer. Still, while the ultimate responsibility is mine, there are people who helped me immensely in my work and I would like to recognize them for their contributions. Laura Marmar was a tireless researcher and discoverer of many of the critical data and facts upon which I relied heavily in my analysis. Her ability to find important research and source materials and integrate them with other findings and facts was remarkable. More than this, she was truly my muse and often a source of inspiration and encouragement when the project seemed to be bogged down and going nowhere. A valuable friend and companion, her support was a constant element of motivation for me. Cecilia Atoo of Wharton was tireless and professional in her work. She typed and formatted the manuscript, helped create understandable figures and exhibits, found time for last-minute but "critical" revisions, and always kept a pleasant demeanor, regardless of the problems at hand. My son, Justin, proved as always to be a good buddy and sounding board when I needed one. He also knew when to hand me a fly rod or get me on the golf course, away from the work, to help my mental state and allow me to keep things in perspective. I owe these people a great deal and I hope they know how helpful they have been.

Introduction

THE MISMANAGEMENT OF AMERICA, INC.

The U.S. is heading toward major trouble and certain distress. There are problems or threats on the horizon that soon will have a significant negative impact on the country and many of its citizens. Serious financial, fiscal, organizational, and power-or dependency-related issues are coming to a head, with potentially devastating results. If unaddressed, these problems will soon wreak havoc on the country's financial health, social fabric, standing in the global community, and even its vulnerability in an increasingly hostile and dangerous world. There can be no doubt that this is true, as I'll show in this book.

It's troublesome and sad to note that most of these problems and threats are due to gross mismanagement by U.S. leaders in the White House and Congress. They are the result of major management failings that have been ignored or swept under the carpet for years because "government is different," or "that's the way things are done in Washington." The American public has long accepted politics, the foibles of politicians, and even horrendous crimes and violations of the public trust with a shoulder shrug. After all, that's the nature of politics and the normal behavior of the elected denizens of the White House and the politically turbid and turgid confines of Capitol Hill.

This passive, permissive attitude simply cannot persist. Severe mismanagement by U.S. leaders is creating huge problems that can no longer be ignored. Management shortcomings, poor organizational design, and inadequate leadership can no longer be tolerated or brushed aside because of the looming negative consequences and debilitating costs.

These statements and other criticisms in this book are not part of a rant against any single administration or political party. The focus is on long-standing mismanagement by U.S. leaders in the White House and Congress, including those currently in power. This assessment is based on my experience with scores of organizations as a consultant and professor at one of the nation's top schools of business over a span of more than three decades. These organizations have included well-known government agencies, and not just private sector companies. The problems being referred to are real and dangerous, and they result from gross mismanagement and poor organizational design, issues I am well qualified to address. These debilitating problems include, but are not limited to:

- *Financial and fiscal mismanagement of the worst kind* that is creating a mountain of debt and a projected fiscal shortfall that, if unaddressed, will lead to economic turbulence of major proportions. A financial earthquake is looming that will challenge the economic foundations and stability of the country and injure both our institutions and the man in the street. Financial and fiscal problems related to massive debt, wasteful spending, earmarks and "pork-barrel" projects, a complex and unfair tax structure, and leaders' short-term thinking and "head-in-the-sand" policies are real and must finally be addressed before it's too late.

- *Unintelligent design of the Intelligence Community* that is hurting the country's intelligence and planning capabilities. A large, complex, and unwieldy system of intelligence simply cannot do the job adequately and is putting the country at serious risk. Major organizational design and management changes are sorely needed to allow more effective performance before intelligence lapses lead to unspeakable results.

- *A power structure based on lobbying, money, and influence peddling* that is creating a management oligarchy that favors the few and actually disenfranchises many U.S. citizens in the current political system. A malevolent balance of power and influence threatens the nation. Witness, for example, how a dysfunctional oil dependency and a reliance on Arab countries, none of which is a democracy or real ally, has created a powerful oil lobby whose influence has run unconstrained for decades, at high cost and, increasingly, at high risk for the nation. This dependency and U.S. vulnerability are growing stronger, suggesting that major negative consequences are never far off.

- *Leadership of the worst kind.* U.S. leaders in the White House and Congress, overall, comprise an ineffectual bunch. When benchmarked against the qualities and capabilities of effective leaders or managers, they fall short. Inability to plan and think strategically; appointment or election based on cronyism, restrictive gerrymandering, or access to the money of narrow, specialized interests; no incentive to focus on real problems plaguing Americans (e.g. Social Security and healthcare); a proliferation of earmarks and wasteful spending; approval of costly bills, without even reading them; a stealthy approach to legislation in a process designed to avoid public scrutiny and analysis; and many other questionable behaviors, in total, define the inadequate and costly leadership in the country's top-management executive and legislative ranks. Political party doesn't matter—horrendous leadership is shared equally by the two major parties.

There are other problems facing the country, and the few just mentioned are highlights (or "lowlights") of what's to come in later discussions. Mismanagement and poor organization abound and the cumulative effect of bad policies, inaction, and concerted action in the wrong directions will soon take its disastrous toll, affecting the country negatively, in a host of areas—financial, political, and social. This position is certainly consistent with the dire warnings of David Walker, Comptroller General of the U.S., who stressed emphatically in 2007 that the country is on a *"burning platform" of mismanagement, financial and fiscal irresponsibility, and a host of other ominous and potentially devastating problems.* To avoid disaster and a collapse of the U.S. republic, he argues, major changes are needed, a point emphasized repeatedly in the pages below.

The purpose of this book is to sound the alarm, identify the threats and dangerous consequences of mismanagement that are becoming more certain and imminent, and move our leaders and citizens to do something about them, finally. The book takes a management and organizational perspective, not the typical, inside-the-beltway political view, although the relationship between power/politics and management is duly explored. It assumes a high-level, strategic view and details the problems, costs, and dangers of poor management by U.S. leaders in the White House, Cabinet, and Congress. It details how gross mismanagement by U. S. leaders is hurting the country and its citizens, and shows how poor management is leading inexorably to disastrous results in a number of important areas. The book also discusses the negative consequences of poor organizational structure or "unintelligent design" at the highest levels, e.g. in the White House and Intelligence Community. It represents a long-overdue wake-up call and a plea for needed corrective action, while also presenting viable steps or actions to confront the problems at hand.

The central underlying and organizing theme of the book is threefold:

a. Poor management is the norm at the highest levels of leadership in the U.S., especially in the White House and Congress;

b. Mismanagement and unintelligent or dysfunctional organizational design are creating debilitating costs and real political, social, and economic dangers for the country and its citizens that can no longer be ignored; and

c. "America, Inc." can be depicted and treated as an entity that shares many of the characteristics of large global corporations, and thus can benefit from benchmarking and importing proven management processes and organizational design characteristics from them. America, Inc. certainly is not a business, nor are all business practices worthy of emulation. The book simply argues that the country can benefit from a subset of useful management knowledge gleaned from the business community and other large global organizations.

Poor management at the highest levels is leading to big trouble, and something must be done soon to improve management and organization and ward off the looming threats. This is the thrust of the present work. It identifies the threats, details the costs and dangers, and lays out the necessary steps to reduce or eliminate them. The time has come for serious management change and this book provides a roadmap for action.

Identifying and Solving Real Problems

The present work is different, timely, and important, given the economic and political realities currently facing the country. The current climate in the U.S. after the 2006 mid-term elections and in anticipation of 2008 seems ripe for change and for finally tackling the issues laid out in this book. Let's look briefly at these critical issues, chapter by chapter.

Chapter 1 introduces "America, Inc." and explains why this is an apt title and concept. It lists a host of similarities between America, Inc. and the large global corporation. While certainly not arguing that America, Inc. is a business or that it should abandon or change its commonweal goals, it develops a convincing picture of the management and organizational concerns America, Inc. shares with other large global organizations. The main conclusion is that America, Inc. can emulate and learn from proven practices and improve its management and organizational capabilities before real and devastating problems take their toll.

Chapter 2 looks at problems of management and organization at the White House and Cabinet level. The theme is how poor management and organization at the very top can obfuscate decisions and important actions and trickle down to create additional problems of unclear responsibility, accountability, and authority at lower levels. The problems and issues identified in this chapter aren't as potentially debilitating as many of those laid out in subsequent chapters, but the discussion sets the stage to begin to understand and correct the more serious problems that are to follow.

Chapter 3 details the reasons for the poor performance of the Intelligence Community, a dangerous situation in an increasingly hostile and terrorist world. It shows clearly and forcefully how poor management and a large, unwieldy organizational structure will *never allow the Intelligence Community to perform effectively.* It discusses how size, culture, unclear responsibility and accountability, and a lack of coordination or integration are negatively impacting intelligence performance and why the situation, left alone, will never improve. The chapter also debunks recent management-related actions in the Intelligence Community, e.g. the appointment of an Intelligence Czar, and shows why these steps or actions are only worsening the capabilities of the entire intelligence system. These revelations are memorable and frightening.

The chapter also presents one possible reorganization of the Intelligence Community to detail the types of managerial and organizational changes that must be made before calamity strikes again. It shows how to confront the severe problems identified, as they are too important to be simply railed against and then ignored. This chapter underscores the main theme and purpose of this book, as it identifies management and organizational problems and needed areas of change for present and future U.S. leaders in the White House and Congress to analyze and consider for remedial action.

Chapter 4 details carefully why *a looming economic earthquake is highly likely* because of horrific financial and fiscal management by U.S. leaders in the White House and Congress. It discusses the severe negative problems of debilitating debt, pork-barrel legislation, negative savings, an ever-widening fiscal gap, and the impact of a complex and unfair tax structure on the country and the man in the street. It shows how the country and most U.S. citizens are being hurt badly by this poor financial management and fiscal policy, and how mismanagement is even creating a type of "financial apartheid" in the U. S. It lays out what can be done to forestall or eliminate the economic problems that are looming ever closer.

This chapter raises grave concerns for all readers to ponder. It shows how critical economic problems are being ignored and exacerbated by "head-in-the-sand" policies by U.S. leaders and how myopic management policies and practices will strike a horrible blow to our economic well being. It raises serious questions about U. S. leaders' financial and fiscal policies and suggests how poor financial and fiscal management can hurt the power and economic position of the U.S. in a changing, threatening, and increasingly competitive world. Chapter 4, like chapter 3, is not about pie-in-the-sky theoretical suppositions or low-probability events. It identifies real problems, imminent dangers, and viable solutions to the gross mismanagement of America, Inc. by its elected or appointed leaders. The issues raised cannot be ignored any longer.

Chapters 5 and 6 provide an analysis of power and moneyed influence running amuck and show why America, Inc.'s power structure is dysfunctional and dangerous. The chapters delve into problems related to lobbying, influence peddling, a problematic "revolving door" between Congress and the special interests that guide and control lawmakers' decisions, and the resultant dangers of lobbyists' power, as well as problems associated with the degradation of science, the press, and similar abuses of power. Both chapters show how concerns with power, politics, and excessive self interest drive management decisions in the White House and Congress more than do concerns with the common good. In fact, they show the *development of a management oligarchy that is becoming dangerously powerful and disenfranchising many U.S. citizens in the political process.* They also detail why inaction, inappropriate decisions, and severe mismanagement abound in such key areas as oil dependency, global warming, environmental concerns, and control of information and the media. The real, negative costs and consequences of the abuse of power and the mismanagement associated with it are well documented, and they cry out for remedial action and change.

Chapter 7 defines what effective, good leadership looks like, and shows comparatively how the problems in America, Inc. are due to leadership of the most dysfunctional kind. It argues that the U. S. is in danger, not just from terrorism or other threats we hear about in the news, *but from the very people who have sworn to lead, manage, and protect it*, which constitutes mismanagement and leadership of the worst kind.

The chapter discusses the driving forces and motivations underlying the management approach of leaders in the White House and Congress. It defines "management by stealth" and details how it is used to quietly introduce earmarks and dysfunctional bills into the legislative process, as well as important rules and rule changes that alter government policy without public scrutiny and analysis. It shows how decisions in many areas, including environmental policy, oil dependency, taxation, and health, are supporting the economic and political agendas of the few, not the majority of citizens and other stakeholders in America, Inc. Coupled with "management by fear," management by stealth is increasing the power of U.S. leaders and quietly changing how the government operates at the highest levels. Additional tactics—e.g. gerrymandering—support a management style based on stealth and fear and further disenfranchise many citizens in the political process.

The chapter also talks about good "followership," the responsibilities of U. S. citizens and what they must do to get the leadership they deserve and need. Sound leadership isn't a one-way street; followers also have a responsibility to reverse or negate the mismanagement problems detailed in this and the preceding chapters, and a number of remedial steps toward this end are outlined.

Chapter 8 is a summary of the book, with a recap of what must be done to cure the ills laid out in previous chapters. Each of the chapters presents changes or remedial actions to address the problems being discussed, and Chapter 8 provides a summary and overview of some actions that U.S. leaders and citizens can pursue in the future to keep America strong.

> *This book will be controversial and it will be attacked by interests committed to the status quo. Nonetheless, its purpose is to focus on problems and dangers that must be confronted and solved, despite the resistance and expected attacks. Mismanagement at the highest levels in the White House and Congress is hurting the country and its citizens, and the prognosis is bleak if things don't change soon. The topics of the book are serious, and they must finally be taken seriously.*

1

Meet America, Inc.

Pick up any newspaper and you might read the following scenario: *A large glo-*
bal organization, formerly a giant in its industry, is having a rough time of it. Its
poor planning processes and intelligence capabilities are inadequate to help it deal
with today's uncertain, changing, and hostile competitive environment. Its man-
agement control processes are suspect and accountability is lacking. It's in dire
financial straits and has no idea how to pay off its debts. The creditors haven't
swarmed yet, but they are holding IOUs like the sword of Damocles over the orga-
nization. To make matters worse, the organization keeps borrowing, thereby per-
petuating the cycle.

This organization shouldn't be having these financial and other problems. It is
huge. With annual revenues of $3 trillion, it makes General Motors, IBM, and
Exxon-Mobil look like mom-and-pop operations. It is larger than the world's top
15 companies put together. It is also extremely diversified, operating in many dif-
ferent industries or sectors of the economy—defense, education, media, energy,
transportation, banking and finance, engineering, and the like. The organization's
size and diversification, however, haven't kept it from losing money annually and
accumulating $9 trillion in debt.

The customers of the organization are remarkably loyal, despite the fact that
relatively few of them benefit greatly from the organization's operations and lar-
gess. They regularly hand over their hard-earned money to fund this inefficient
behemoth in exchange for the services it provides. Though those services, truth be
told, have been less than consistent or up to their usual standards, customers
haven't boycotted the company or gone elsewhere to do business. Meanwhile, the
company managers live well, accepting high salaries and perks, regardless of the cost
to the organization or its customers.

Shockingly, many of this company's top executives are unqualified for their
jobs, lacking the skills and capabilities to manage the organization effectively. They
owe their positions instead to political connections, wealth, or blatant nepotism.
Most of these managers can't even get fired or be replaced easily, as they control the
very processes in place for hiring and firing personnel, including themselves.
Although the press has uncovered examples of corruption, deception, mismanage-
ment, and plain old poor judgment, these execs usually escape with a slap on the

wrist. In fact, their injurious behavior is often ignored, if not openly supported and rewarded.

What's the name of this huge, inefficient global organization? I'm sure you've guessed it by now. It's the United States of America—"America, Inc.," if you will.

Does it make sense to call it "America, Inc."? Is the U.S. government really like a corporation? In many ways it is. Some of the original colonies were char-tered as corporations. Many government bodies today—cities, town, bor-oughs—are often incorporated entities. Most importantly, however, America, Inc. looks and functions in many ways just like the large global corporation. It's time to consider this simple fact and its implications. Its time to cease explaining the poor performance of U.S. leaders by saying that "politics is different" or "this is how things are done in Washington." Consider the following.

America, Inc.

Like corporations, governments are human-created entities with perpetual life, limited liability, and legal rights.[1] Like large companies, our federal government sells securities and incurs debt. It holds patents and copyrights, advertises its products and services, and reaps handsome revenues in some of its businesses. The government engages in public relations activities and advertises what services it provides for its "customers." It communicates and justifies its strategies, includ-ing why it wages war and why it gives tax cuts to small portions of its customer base. The U.S. government has organization charts, defined roles and responsibil-ities, human-resource policies, graduated pay scales, and performance appraisal systems. Like the corporation, the government dirties and sullies the environ-ment. In the U.S., the top polluter is the military, an important "arm" or division of the U.S. government. Land deals, oil leases, and forestry permits granted by the government also have been shown to negatively affect the environment.

Like the large corporation, America, Inc. is effective, but not always for the majority of its shareholders or citizens. For example, since 1980, the incomes of families in the bottom 80% of the U.S. income distribution have grown by less than 1% per year, while they have literally skyrocketed for the top few percent of U.S. earners. Under President Bush, most of the benefits of reduced tax rates on earnings, dividends, and inheritances are earmarked for the top 5% of earners in the U.S. Certainly, the financial goals of this elite group are being met, but the same can't be said for the majority of Americans.

This inequity in U. S. income distribution certainly follows the lead of large corporations. In 1980, CEOs of the largest U.S corporations earned 42 times as much as the average worker. By 2000, they were earning over 500 times the average worker's salary. Clearly, large corporations are more effective for CEOs' goal attainment than that of the average worker.[2] Some aspects of corporate income distribution certainly are unfair, and America's seem just as inequitable and discriminatory.

Both big business and America, Inc. have P.R. problems. Recent polls show that the public believes that corporate executives are primarily bent on destroying the environment, cooking the books, and lining their own pockets.[3] In a Roper poll, 72% of respondents felt that wrongdoing is widespread and routine in industry, and only 2% felt that chief executives of large companies are trustworthy.[4] High energy costs, soaring oil company profits, major layoffs in the auto and other industries, excess profits and conflicts of interest in military contracting, etc. have only fueled the public's negativity.

Similarly, studies have shown that people increasingly don't trust politicians. In fact, a recent survey found that *only* politicians as a group rank as less trustworthy than corporate managers, despite the latter group's inflated pay and publicized unethical practices.[5] To some, the terms "crooked politician" and "crooked CEO" are redundant and "crooked" as a descriptive term is equally applicable in the private and public sectors. People don't trust corporate leaders, and they are just as skeptical and negative about their top elected officials, including the leaders of America, Inc. in Congress and the White House. The well-publicized activities of Jack Abramoff, Tom DeLay, "Duke" Cunningham, "Scooter" Libby, and others only support and add to these negative perceptions.

The distrust of corporate and political leaders certainly doesn't mean that all employees of corporations and America, Inc. are untrustworthy, evil, or incompetent. On the contrary, there are many qualified, competent people in America, Inc. and any large corporation. There are managers and workers who desperately want to change things for the better, and I have known many of them over the years. The problem often is that, while dedicated people try to improve management and organizational performance, *their efforts are thwarted, compromised, or negated by restrictive policies, rules, organizational structures, and poor management decisions that come from the top.*

In America, Inc., attempts at improving management are usually doomed to failure because of politics, poor management capabilities, and bad organizational design decisions by leaders in the Congress and White House. Good people are stifled in both the corporation and America, Inc., but this is creating especially serious problems in the latter case where horrendous mismanagement is leading to a host of major economic, political, and social ills, as well as roadblocks to change. U.S. leaders have been able to hide behind a protective shield of sorts that allows government waste, mismanagement, and even dangerous practices because America, Inc. is "different" and somehow immune to major pressures for change. But America, Inc. is really not as different as some might argue.

America, Inc. has many parts, "divisions," or operating units, just like the large global corporation. GE, GM, Wal-Mart, J & J, ABB, P&G, etc. have many far-flung divisions or businesses, but there is only one company or stock-market listing for each. J & J, for example, comprises about 200 different businesses, but one certainly can understand the concept and reality of the title, J & J, Inc. J & J is one large company, one legal entity. So, too, with the U.S. There are many parts or "businesses" within the federal bureaucracy of America, Inc., but one can still speak and think of it as one huge entity, managed by top-level people in the executive and legislative branches, but comprising many diverse elements or parts. The title, America, Inc., has the same logic and unifying force as the name of the multi-business, complex, and large J & J, Inc., GE, Inc., or GM Inc.

America, Inc. is first and foremost a political organization. The focus is on politics and maintenance of a strong power base to control scarce resources and important outcomes, including election success. But the large corporation is also a political entity. Power and politics mark corporate life, business dealings, and the quest to control scarce resources. One certainly cannot remove politics from the political arena. But removal of politics and the quest for influence over others in the corporate world is just as implausible. America, Inc. and the corporation are both political machines, and it's foolish or naïve to think that the U.S. holds a monopoly on political dealings and is somehow really different from its corporate cousins.

America, Inc. is certainly a global organization, just like the world's largest corporate enterprises. It competes and distributes resources around the globe. It engages in political activity and tries to effect changes in restrictive policies by other governments. It develops collaborate strategies with some governments to pursue common goals. It sells and uses influence and engages in planning and market intelligence activities. It outsources, subcontracts work, and forms alliances with other organizations, just like the large global corporation. *If it looks like a duck, walks like a duck, and quacks like a duck....*

To be sure, there are differences between large for-profit corporations and America, Inc. One certainly is the treatment of shareholders or owners. In Exxon-Mobil, Disney, Dow-Jones, and GE, shareholders have at least some power. They can affect company direction and policies. They occasionally oust CEOs and board members. They can sell their shares if they disagree with a company's projected strategic direction.

America, Inc. also tells its citizens that they are the owners and the government is there to follow their bidding. But this is rarely true. America spends its customers' money in any way it wishes. Even if customers don't like what the federal government does, they can't withhold financial support. They must pay taxes. There are elections, of course, so customers can occasionally exert some control. But given gerrymandering and other tactics of politicians and elected officials, this control is usually more illusory than real. America, Inc., including its executive and legislative branches and its main "subsidiary" divisions or units, have the real power. And unlike most other corporations, America, Inc.'s power includes the ability to invade virtually every aspect of peoples' lives, especially when its leaders say it is absolutely necessary, e.g. to fight a war against terrorism.

The biggest differences between America, Inc. and other global corporations can be seen when examining *performance*—efficiency or cost effectiveness of operations—and especially when considering the *decisional complexity* they face.

America, Inc. is not an efficient organization. It wastes money and other scarce resources. Its books are so badly managed and maintained that departments and other organizational entities routinely lose track of expensive equipment and millions (if not billions) of dollars. Lobbyists and special-interest groups raid America's coffers and skim a fortune off the top. Pork-laden bills waste billions on local, pet projects of senators and representatives, with no concern over squandered financial resources. U.S. budget deficits are increasing due to this waste and America's profligate spending. An efficient government could do much more with its resources, but America, Inc.'s top management doesn't care about efficiency. Without competent, accountable leadership, the trend toward increased inefficiency and larger deficits shows absolutely no signs of abatement.

Granted, not all large, for-profit corporations are models of efficiency, but for the most part, they put America, Inc. to shame. Despite the negative perceptions of high-level corporate management as a crooked group bent on wrongdoing and self-gratification, there clearly are good managers in corporate America who work hard to contribute to efficient and effective performance. There are technologies, decision processes, and ways of organizing and controlling work in corporations that lead to low-cost and high-quality performance. America, Inc.'s leaders can indeed learn something valuable by benchmarking certain corporate practices, processes, and organizational structures.

Another difference between America, Inc. and the large global corporation is in the area of decisional and operational complexity. As the environments within which organizations operate become more diverse, volatile, and uncertain, thereby increasing complexity—the number of factors that decision makers must consider when planning and executing plans—the job of management becomes tougher. *The U.S. faces increasing complexity, and its top management is increasingly exhibiting an inability to handle it effectively.* Let's consider this point further.

The Problem of Increasing Complexity

A big difference between America, Inc. and its large corporate cousins is the increasing complexity it faces. Corporations face a world full of complexity, to be sure. Competing in increasingly globalized markets against more and more capable competitors amidst massive technological changes certainly increases the complexity of decision making for company executives and strategic planners. Increasing complexity simply means that there are more data or variables—"more damn things to worry about," as one CEO expressed it—that must be analyzed before making major decisions. And the number of things that corporate leaders must worry about surely has been growing larger.

America, Inc., however, faces even bigger problems and greater complexity than any large corporation. The world in which it competes, economically and politically, is getting more difficult to manage. There is an ever increasing number of problematic events and conditions that its top management must worry about and handle to keep the country safe and secure. This growing complexity emanates from a number of important sources.

There are major *economic and competitive* forces that are challenging America. China, for example, is on a course to overtake the U.S. economically. Its annual growth rate of 8+% for the last quarter of a century overshadows America's rate of about 3% over the same period.[6] By some estimates, it has the world's second largest economy, just behind the U.S. with a GDP of about $6.5 trillion. China is currently the number 3 trader in the world, behind the U.S. and Germany, but already ahead of Japan. Its GDP is projected to beat that of the U.S. in the next 20 to 40 years, depending on rates of growth, currency evaluations, and levels of country debt. India, too, is showing strong growth numbers and also appears to be a competitive force that will affect America Inc.'s future economic planning and growth.

A major competitive arena that will surely heat up and intensify is that for important raw materials, especially oil. Imports of crude oil into China are already equal to those of the U.S. The prospects are that the competition for crude will surely increase, leading to a hotly-contested China-U.S. confrontation for oil in the Middle East, South America, and Africa. The U.S. has been the biggest bully on the oil block, but China is challenging this traditional position of power.

America, Inc. faces other economic challenges at home and in the world. A huge national deficit of $9 trillion shows no signs of decreasing. In fact, profligate spending promises to add to this suffocating burden. This debt, plus continued reckless spending and a lack of savings, surely increases the probability of economic stagnation in the U.S. The obligations of Social Security and Medicare alone will drive federal taxes up over 50% by the year 2040 unless something is done.[7] While America, Inc. probably can't go out of business literally, it certainly faces economic problems that will push it in that direction.

Military and arms issues often follow economic trends closely, adding danger to the increasing complexity facing management in America, Inc. With its growing economic resources, China has embarked on a process of strong military growth, and the EU's plans to lift the embargo on arms sales to China can only fuel and speed up this potential growth. China, indeed, may be able to develop a powerful global military with huge weapons caches, space-based assets, and expeditionary forces that will challenge those of the U.S.[8]

The growth of a *nuclear arms supermarket* only adds to America's problems and concerns. While the U.S. was focused on Saddam Hussein's nonexistent nuclear arsenal, the father of the Pakistani bomb admitted that he had been peddling bomb designs and hardware in a global "supermarket," a veritable nuclear Wal-Mart.[9] If a nation wants a uranium enrichment program to produce a bomb, the nuclear supermarket can no doubt aid in this effort. Exactly who has benefited thus far from this sale of bomb designs and uranium-enrichment technology is not yet known, but it certainly presents a scary and complicated picture for America, Inc.'s planners to deal with.

Any discussion of weapons, especially the nuclear variety, logically raises concerns about *terrorism*. Terrorists will try to attack the U.S. again—it's not a question of "if," but "when," we've been told time and time again. Are America's planning and intelligence capabilities up to the task in preventing and thwarting these inevitable terrorist moves? Not according to the 9/11 panel's report of December 2005 on the "scandalous" failure of the nation's antiterrorism efforts. America is still vulnerable, according to this blue-ribbon panel, and its leaders have not done enough to reduce the threat of catastrophic destruction. This, of course, presents a huge threat and complex set of needed plans and actions for the U.S. leadership to deal with effectively.

Will the country's leaders be able to marshal global support for its decisions on arms, terrorism, and military intervention in the future? The signs aren't good. Anti-Americanism has reached new heights. A recent Pew Research report says that "anti-Americanism is deeper and broader now than at any time in modern history."[10] A serious antipathy to things and actions American has even risen in Europe where many see Americans as selfish, indulgent, childish, and dangerously righteous and religious.[11] A German Marshall Fund survey of more than 13,000 adults primarily in Europe in June, 2006, revealed that the percentage of respondents who believe that the U.S. should take a strong leadership role in the world has fallen from 64% in 2000 to just 37%, and this number will likely drop further. Even our friends are turning against us and our leaders' policies, including those in the so-called war on terrorism.

A major BBC World Service Poll of almost 40,000 people worldwide completed between October, 2005 and January, 2006, asked respondents to rate countries' influence in the world on a scale from positive to negative.[12] The worst rating was for Iran for having the largest negative influence in the world—clearly, people have negative opinions about governments lying about their nuclear activities and intentions. *The U.S., however, was rated as the next worse.* The U.S. is seen as a mainly negative player in the world. People are suspicious of its motives, which bodes poorly for our leaders' ability to marshal support for future U.S. actions to control terrorism or oust unfriendly or dangerous governments.

Indeed, this distrust and suspicion have already surfaced. Many feel that Iran is lying about its nuclear intentions and desperately wants to build a bomb. Yet, the American hyping of a nuclear weapons threat in Iraq that never existed probably explains why the U.S. has taken a back seat to others in efforts to showdown or blunt Iran's nuclear programs.[13] The suggestion is that *one suspicious government can't really perform well in unmasking and controlling the activities of another suspicious government.* Better to leave the task to the European Union which, by the way, scored the most positive on the major BBC poll just mentioned.

The bottom line is that the cultural and political gaps between America and the rest of the world, including its allies, have grown wider. A task of top management is to create an effective intelligence network and form coalitions and strategic alliances with others so as to cooperate on the solution of complex problems, but U.S. leaders have not been up to the task. This obviously presents major challenges to U.S. leaders as they deal with increased globalization and its attendant political, economic, and military problems.

Another factor adding to the complexity of America, Inc. as a "going concern" is the *size* of the government bureaucracy, even at the highest levels. In any organization, there is a positive relationship between size and decisional complexity. As size increases, more and more work must be dedicated to knowledge sharing among a larger number of organizational units. Coordination becomes more and more a necessity, but it becomes increasingly difficult to achieve as organizations get larger with more differentiated parts. In fact, a critical boundary value with respect to size may be reached beyond which coordination and regulation become virtually impossible and decision responsibility and accountability become hopelessly blurred and problematical.

America, Inc.'s bureaucracy is huge, even at the very top, and it very likely is at or near the critical boundary value with respect to size beyond which efficient and effective performance are implausible. Attending to this huge bureaucracy and making it work is becoming an extremely complex task. Planning is increasingly difficult. Coordination across the large number of units responsible for U.S. intelligence activities, for example, is weak or nonexistent and turf and budget battles across the units only exacerbate the problem. This clearly presents major management issues and the possibility of dire consequences.

Members of Congress don't even read most of the bills they pass or legislation they create and vote on. There simply are too many bills and not enough time. Think about this: lawmakers who don't read the laws they create. It's a deplorable state of affairs. Size and complexity are out of hand, negatively affecting decision making at the highest levels of America, Inc.

There indeed are other forces facing America, Inc.'s managers that add to the list of problems and issues already noted. The U.S. is losing a scientific or technological race. Fewer engineers and scientists are being turned out compared to the numbers in countries like China, Japan, and India, and this bodes poorly for technological and economic progress. An oil crisis has never been handled adequately in the U.S., and the dependency on foreign oil is getting worse, not better. Natural disasters like 2005's hurricane Katrina, a host of global earthquakes, and the devastating Christmas 2004 tsunami, exposed the inability of the U.S. bureaucracy to respond effectively and use scarce resources efficiently. Global warming is increasingly being accepted as a valid and important threat, and even U. S. leaders will have to acknowledge and confront it soon. The money of large lobbies is seriously affecting decision making in America, Inc., in negative ways and distracting leaders' attention from other critical tasks. Etc. etc. This list of problems and challenges simply goes on and on.

The critical point is that the forces and problems just noted increase the complexity of decision making for America's leaders, and our leaders—the country's top man-

agement in the White House and Congress—cannot handle this complexity. They are not up to the task. America, Inc.'s management capabilities simply are not sufficient to handle the vast array of threats and problems facing the country. The handling of Katrina and its aftermath was and still is a management disaster. Management of the war in Iraq is constantly being attacked. Fiscal and financial mismanagement is leading inexorably to a severe economic shakeout. Ineffective management processes and an "unintelligent" organizational design in the intelligence community are creating huge problems, including turf battles, horrendous coordination, and conflicting responsibilities, putting the country at serious risk. Lobbyists rule Congress and bias legislation in favor of special interests, creating immense "pork" and waste, profligate spending, and even posing a threat to democracy in America. The attack on science and the press is another aspect of top-management action in the U.S. that is putting the country at an economic disadvantage and endangering the democratic process.

These are management and organizational issues that must soon be addressed. Something must be done soon to improve the management of America, Inc. at the highest levels before economic and social disaster strikes, and the present work is dedicated to this task.

A Not-So-Pretty Picture

Other similarities and differences between America, Inc. and the large, for-profit global corporation could be identified, but I don't want to belabor the issue. Here's what I want to emphasize presently to set the stage for later chapters:

- "America, Inc." is a concept and description with some validity. The U.S. is a huge global player with resources and power that dwarf those of even the largest worldwide corporate organizations, and it acts and looks in many ways like those corporations;

- America, Inc. faces an enormous amount of complexity and uncertainty due to (a) changing and challenging economic and political forces around the world, and (b) the size, design, and bungling nature of its own administrative bureaucracy; and

- The U.S. is being managed in ways that no large, for-profit company could tolerate if it hoped to survive and prosper. Even with its bad apples, the average global corporation's top management performs eminently better and more efficiently than America, Inc.'s top management team.

America, Inc. is an apt title and description. America, Inc. has perpetual life, limited liability, and legal rights like all corporations. It raises money from its customers. It sells securities and debt. It has global presence and power. It "sells" products and services worldwide, and it dominates many of the global markets in which it does business. America, Inc., however, is marked by incompetent top management and ineffective organizational structures. It is inefficient and terribly wasteful of scarce resources. It performs extremely well for a handful of its shareholders, but not for most of its citizen "owners" or stakeholders. Its fiscal and financial policies are terrible, and it's heading down a dangerous path toward insolvency. Budget deficits prevail and are growing dangerously larger. The overall environment within which the U.S. competes is becoming more complex and threatening, and its top management and their chosen organizational forms are incapable of handling this complexity.

America, Inc. is in trouble and faces potential disaster if this gross mismanagement continues. It's really this straightforward and basic.

For America, Inc. and the large global corporation, the following holds true:

Planning + Execution = Performance

America, Inc.'s top management is not planning and executing well, as subsequent chapters will show. Our leaders in the White House and Congress are making major mistakes that soon will hurt the country badly. There definitely are "bad" corporations and bad, even immoral leaders in them, and I certainly am not advocating that U.S. leaders copy or emulate bad corporate practices. I'm not asking that the U.S. become a profit-making entity. I'm simply arguing, based on years studying and researching the methods, performance, and viability of large corporations, that there are a few things about effective planning, execution, and organization that America, Inc.'s management can benchmark and learn from them. There simply are too many examples of gross mismanagement in America, Inc. to ignore them and their certain consequences any longer. Mismanagement problems must finally be addressed, and this book is dedicated to this necessary and vital task.

Let's begin by looking in the next chapter at major management and organizational problems at the very top of America, Inc., in the White House itself. We then in subsequent chapters can look at other top management shortcomings in planning and intelligence activities, leadership, financial matters, and the abuse of power and influence. Whenever possible, we'll attempt to offer solutions that address the management shortcomings noted. *The purpose here is not simply to identify and rail against management and organizational shortcomings, but to do something about them ..., finally.*

Again, let's look first at the venerable and traditional White House organization in the next chapter and see how many of the problems of America, Inc. actually flow down from the highest echelons of (mis)management.

CONCLUSIONS

America, Inc. faces enormous complexity and uncertainty that emanates from multiple sources—political, social, economic, and cultural. Sound management and organizational skills clearly are needed to cope with this situation. A focus on U.S. leaders in the White House, Cabinet, and Congress reveals that the managerial and organizational skills needed to cope with this complexity are sorely lacking.

"America, Inc." is a valid and useful concept. The U.S. functions much like the large global corporation, but it does so far less efficiently and effectively. The private-sector corporation has faults, of course, but it on average has management and organizational capabilities that America's leaders can benchmark and emulate fruitfully.

This book will show that *these skills are sorely lacking in the U.S.* The inability to deal with complexity and uncertainty is resulting in severe inefficiencies and wasted resources. More importantly, management deficiencies can lead to *dangerous* consequences. People need to know what's wrong with America, Inc.'s management and they must begin to get involved to correct a bad situation. This book is dedicated to that effort.

Endnotes

1. For an excellent discussion of governments as corporations, see "Can you name the largest corporation in the world?" in <u>Liberty For All Online Magazine</u>, Jan. 09, 2003.

2. Robert Frank, "The Income Gap Grows," <u>The Philadelphia Inquirer</u>, November 27, 2005, C1; also see Robert Frank and Philip Cook, "The Winner-Take-All Society.

3. Claudia Deutsch, "New Survey Shows that Big Business has a P.R. Problem," <u>New York Times</u>, December 9, 2005.

4. The Roper poll was conducted from July 28 to August 10, 2005, in a telephone survey of 1,001 individuals. See, too, the <u>New York Times</u>, Ibid.

5. Emma Blake, "Few Trust Corporate Managers, Survey Finds," in <u>The Wall Street Journal</u>, November 25, 2003. The survey was conducted during September and October 2003, by GFK Ad Hoc Research Worldwide, with nearly 22,000 respondents.

6. Charles Hutzler, "China May be on Course to Overtake U.S.," in <u>The Wall Street Journal</u>, January 24, 2005; see also, Mark Helphind, "Beyond the Rim," <u>The Wall Street Journal</u>, December 13, 2004, and Ian Garrick Mason,

7. Holman Jenkins, Jr., "Let's Make It Simple: Just Encourage Savings," in <u>The Wall Street Journal</u>, March 2, 2005, A17; "Next Challenge: Capitalist Competition," <u>The Philadelphia Inquirer</u>, July 18, 2004, C1.

8. "Beyond the Rim," op. cit.; see too, "Merci, y'all," <u>The Economist</u>, February 26, 2005, 9-10.

9. Trudy Rubin, "Nuclear Supermarket, Another Concern for the U.S.," <u>The Philadelphia Inquirer</u>, February 8, 2004, C3.

10. "Anti-Americanism: The View From Abroad," <u>The Economist</u>, February 19, 2005, 24-26.

11. Craig Smith, "Joking Aside, A Serious Antipathy to Things American Rises in Europe," <u>The New York Times</u>, February 14, 2003, A13; Andrew Higgins, "At Expense of U.S. Nations of Europe are Drawing Closer," <u>The Wall Street Journal</u>, December 23, 2004, A1.

12. For a full and complete discussion of this major BBC World Service poll, see the work of Globe Scan Incorporated, a public opinion and stakeholder research firm with offices in Toronto, London, and Washington, at <u>www.globescan.com/news_archives/bbcpoll06</u>.

13. This possibility, that the U.S.' previous mistakes hyping Iraq's non-existent nuclear arsenal has hurt its ability to create concern over Iran's nuclear intentions, was discussed in a number of articles and on a number of blogs I found. One such article is "Iran and the Bomb: A Credibility Gap that Cuts Two Ways," an editorial in *The Philadelphia Inquirer*, February 8, 2006.

14. For a good discussion of the size of the U.S. government bureaucracy, see Paul Light, "Fact Sheets on the New True Size of Government," The Brookings Institution, Center for Public Service, September 5, 2003.

2

Management And Organizational Problems At The Top: The Start of Something Bad

Strategic management decisions and major structural choices are usually made at or near the top of organizations. Analysis of top management's roles, responsibilities, and authority reveals much about who is accountable for critical strategic and short-term outcomes. Although it's only the tip of an organizational iceberg, management and structural decisions at the top affect much of what goes on at lower organizational levels, and a lack of management role definition and structural clarity in the highest echelons usually translates into lower-level problems.

America, Inc. lacks management and organizational clarity at the very top. This isn't the most critical problem or shortcoming identified in this book, but it's a logical place to begin an in-depth analysis of management problems and shortcomings. The White House and Cabinet represent a management quagmire that contributes to unclear accountability, poor performance, and even dangerous outcomes, including some of those introduced in later chapters of this book, so it certainly is an issue worth some analysis and comment. To explicate and clarify this point and the problems involved, let's briefly consider the role and impact of management and organizational structure on decision processes and results.

Organizational Structure and Management

In the large, global corporation, examining and understanding what's happening in the office of the CEO, the Executive Committee, a Corporate Planning Group, and the Board of Directors tells us a great deal about strategy and policy. Examining the elements of corporate structure—Corporate Center Groups, centralized functions, decentralized divisions, or strategic business units—tells us even more about strategy, while simultaneously giving insights into operations. The type of interdependence across corporate units or functions reveals a great deal about who works with whom, where coordination is necessary, and where different units share a common "turf."[1]

In-depth analysis of key management functions or units and the responsibilities within them provides additional information about how things are run and who's accountable for what. In the corporation, the Chief Executive Officer (CEO) usually is responsible for strategic direction or institutional strategy. The Chief Operating Officer (COO) typically deals with operational issues and coordination needs, e.g. across businesses or divisions. In Figure 2.1, the heads of the divisions report to a COO who helps make and support decisions about the operational needs of the businesses. The COO is also responsible for coordination across businesses. Assume, for example, that one of the centralized functional units shown in Figure 2.1 is Research and Development (R&D). By reporting to the COO, the implication is that emphasis is on "D," product or service development, not "R," pure research. "D" work is more short term and operations oriented, and the COO would be responsible for coordinating R&D work across businesses to ensure that product development goals and the needs of the divisions and their customers are being met adequately. If R&D reported to the CEO, the logical inference would be that emphasis is on "R," a longer-term research focus, not short-term needs. Structure, then, provides clues about operations and strategy and what are the critical issues management routinely must confront and deal with effectively.

Some companies are eliminating the COO role, opting to have critical centralized functions and businesses report directly to the CEO, who now necessarily assumes both a strategic and operating focus. This suggests that the CEO may desire to get closer to the pulse of operations, especially if he or she increasingly is being held accountable for company performance by the courts or by shareholders. Or it could simply suggest a perceived need to integrate strategic and operating objectives more closely and focus more directly on strategy execution. Whatever the underlying logic, the point again is that structure provides clues about what top management perceives to be the critical issues it must deal with routinely.

Figure 2.1

A Simple Top Management Organization

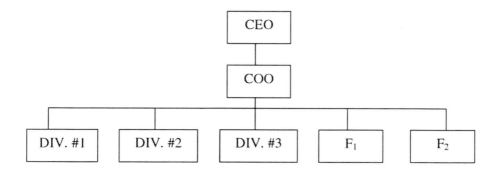

DIV. = Division   F = Corporate Function, e.g. R&D

Figure 2.2

A More Complex Organizational Structure

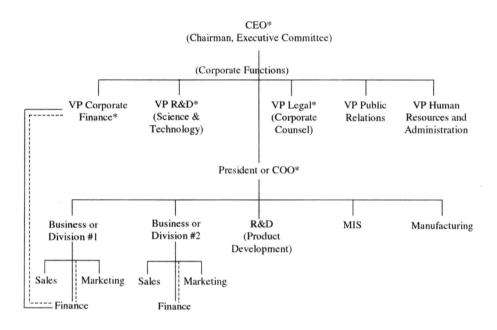

*   Member, Executive Committee

Most large corporations, of course, have more complex top-management structures than the simple one shown in Figure 2.1. Figure 2.2 presents one such hypothetical, slightly more complex case. The CEO in Figure 2.2 is still responsible for the strategic thrust or direction of the organization, but now an Executive Committee (EC) also is involved in strategic matters. The EC as a group discusses strategic issues and other matters related to the company's long-term success (e.g. mergers and acquisitions). The President or COO oversees the two operating companies or business units in Figure 2.2, as well as three functions whose work must be coordinated to service the businesses and support their competitive strategies (Product Development, MIS, Manufacturing). The President or COO is responsible for resolving conflicts across divisions about market overlaps or access to the common functions and, as a member of the EC, is also involved in planning or strategic matters, e.g. reviewing and approving the operating and strategic plans of the businesses. Whatever the actual roles and responsibilities of these top positions, they are usually spelled out clearly to avoid conflicts and costly redundancies.

The business or division leaders in Figure 2.2 have authority over sales and marketing, and this control enables the leaders to run these aspects of the business directly. Both divisions rely on common manufacturing, product development, and MIS services, and they share the functions' capabilities and expertise. The routines, rules, SOPs, or protocols for their coordination with business needs guide the interactions between the businesses and functions, interactions or dealings that are mediated by the President or COO.

The finance function in the two businesses shows either a solid- or dotted-line relationship. This function could (a) report solid-line to the V.P. of Finance and only "dotted-line" to the business head, designating a formal authority relationship and centralized control over a business' financial decisions; or (b) operate within the decentralized business unit, reporting directly to the business head and having only an informal, "dotted line" connection to the office of the V.P. of Finance. In both of these cases, role negotiations and job descriptions would define the responsibilities and accountabilities of the different finance personnel. The degree of delegation of authority and decision-making autonomy would also be handled routinely as part of these negotiations or discussions. It must be absolutely clear as to who's responsible for what, who has formal authority, and whose discretion prevails when differences or conflicting views in financial matters occur. The individual who ultimately has the final say and is accountable for a given financial decision must also be unambiguous. The structure and job definitions absolutely must provide this clarity of effort and purpose.

Another structural issue deals with the simple notion of effective span of control. As Figure 2.2 shows, the COO is responsible for the performance of two businesses or operating companies and three functions. Small spans allow more direct contact and control, and large spans make contact and control more difficult. Large spans can overwhelm a manager with too many direct reports and lead to poor or even no decisions being made. In the latter case, the companies would be "muddling through," with no clear strategic direction and operating focus, and this often is worse than poor decisions that can be evaluated and corrected. Type of company or operations also comes into play when determining an effective span of control. Span can be larger when companies under the COO in Figure 2.2 are alike (similar technologies, products, markets, distribution channels, customer demographics). The greater the number of *related* functional activities across business units (manufacturing, product development, and MIS needs), the larger the span of control can be. Span must be smaller when the companies are very dissimilar and the manager in charge must spend more time on many different problems and operating or strategic needs.

While very basic, this foray into organizational structure nonetheless has identified some key aspects of organization and management. *For planning and the execution of plans to succeed, top management must (a) create an organizational structure and define key jobs; (b) clarify authority, responsibility, and accountability; (c) focus on interdependence and coordination; (d) set up conflict-reducing mechanisms; and (e) ensure viable spans of control.* With these basic facts in mind, let's look at the top-management structure of America, Inc.—the White House organization, including the Cabinet—and benchmark it against these key aspects of management and organization.

The White House: A Lack of Management and Structural Clarity

An important place to begin an analysis of management and organizational structure is with the President and his Cabinet, as many important decisions flow from the top. As of this writing, the current Cabinet comprises 15 secretary positions, appointed by and presumably reporting to the President (Table 2.1), and at least 15 more Cabinet-level administrative offices, whose reporting relationships are varied and often ambiguous. Andrew Card was the White House Chief of Staff (COS) until March, 2006, when he was replaced by Joshua Bolten. Karl Rove is the Deputy Chief of Staff. (Rove resigned as this book was going to press. Leaving him in the discussion won't alter the present analysis). Normally, in a corporate-type structure, Rove would report to Bolten, a hierarchical higher-up. However, the history of the current White House reveals that Rove reports directly to the President and that other Cabinet level officials are subordinate to a powerful Deputy COS. The situation is clouded a bit more by the existence of a strong Vice President (VP). The VP in many ways can also be seen as sharing some of the duties and influence of the COS, and this is especially true when the VP's office is inhabited by a powerful person like Dick Cheney.

Table 2.1
Current U.S. Cabinet and Cabinet-Level Offices*

Cabinet

Office	Incumbent
Secretary of State	Condoleezza Rice
Secretary of the Treasury	Henry Paulson, Jr.
Secretary of Defense	Robert Gates
Attorney General	Alberto Gonzales
Secretary of the Interior	Gale Norton
Secretary of Agriculture	Mike Johanns
Secretary of Commerce	Carlos Gutierrez
Secretary of Labor	Elaine Chao
Secretary of Health and Human Services	Mike Leavitt
Secretary of Housing and Urban Development	Alphonso Jackson
Secretary of Transportation	Mary Peters
Secretary of Energy	Samuel W. Bodman
Secretary of Education	Margaret Spellings
Secretary of Veterans Affairs	James Nicholson
Secretary of Homeland Security	Michael Chertoff

Cabinet-Level Offices

Office	Incumbent
Vice President of the United States	Richard B. Cheney
White House Chief of Staff	Joshua Bolten (*Formerly Andrew H. Card Jr.*)
Deputy Chief of Staff	Karl Rove
Administrator of the Environmental Protection Agency	Stephen L. Johnson
Director of the Office of Management and Budget	Rob Portman
Director of the National Drug Control Policy	John P. Walters
U.S. Trade Representative	Susan Schwab
Director of the CIA	Michael Hayden (*Formerly Porter Goss and George Tenet*)
United States Ambassador to the United Nations	Zalmay Khalilzod
Under Secretary of Homeland Security for Emergency Preparedness, Response and Management	R. David Paulson
White House Counsel	Fred Fielding (*Formerly Harriet Miers*)
National Security Advisor	Stephen Hadley
Director of National Intelligence	J. Michael McConnell (*Formerly John Negroponte*)
Director of National Economic Council	Alan Hubbard
Director of Federal Bureau of Investigation	Robert Mueller

Total: 30 Cabinet-Level Positions

*This list was current at the time this chapter was being written. There indeed might be some changes since, but they don't affect the main thrusts of the points being made in this chapter.

The COS can be likened to the Chief Operating Officer (COO) in the previous corporate examples. Like the COO, he is involved in operations and execution of the top executive's strategy. He advises the President on political and policy matters and administers the White House organizational and administrative system. Gerald Ford said that the COS is a "filter" for the President, an executive who gets things done. Dick Cheney talked of the critical role of the COS in dealing with the Cabinet and the Congress and managing the press. Descriptions of the COS' role commonly include that of a central coordinating point in the White House.[2]

But what do terms like "dealing with" and "filtering" information for the President, Cabinet, and Congress mean? They don't mean having formal authority over the central functions of the Cabinet or the Congress to the same extent that the COO had in the previous corporate-based examples. Certainly, these terms imply influence, but not formal authority or even clearly defined responsibilities. These terms, especially "filtering," denote control over information that the President, Congress, and the press receive from the COS. This control clearly has implications for personal power, the ability to influence or bias the information that key people receive, and how critical strategic decisions are made. Having this influence without accountability for one's actions presents management and control problems in any organization, including the White House.

The situation regarding the COS and the job's attendant responsibilities becomes even murkier. A logical question about the COS' influence is "which COS and what influence?" Table 2.1 reveals the existence of different COSs in the White House, including the VP, with the implied structure looking something like this:

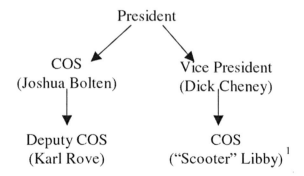

President

COS
(Joshua Bolten)

Vice President
(Dick Cheney)

Deputy COS
(Karl Rove)

COS
("Scooter" Libby)[1]

---

1.   Scooter Libby resigned his post because of the "Plamegate" affair, but I'll leave him in his position to further the discussion of roles, responsibilities, and accountability.

Who, then, is the COS who runs the White House and coordinates and deals with the Cabinet and Congress? Who is the "filter" of information who also gets things done? It looks as if it should be Bolten but, as mentioned previously, it's probably Rove. Or it could be Dick Cheney in some matters. The four COS types may get together, negotiate roles and responsibilities, and decide who does what, thus clarifying relative influence and accountability, but this probably is not how things work in the White House.

Obvious questions are raised by having more than one COS. Who's responsible for the actions of a "Scooter" Libby, who was recently sentenced to 2½ years in prison for his role in the "Plamegate" affair? (Shouldn't someone have direct authority over someone named "Scooter?"). Who defines the role and responsibilities of the various COSs and mediates "turf" conflicts when they occur? Does the President define the roles? Reagan supposedly treated his COS in a hierarchical way, putting him "in charge" of defined activities. Carter and Clinton were allegedly more active, working with their COSs and not delegating authority to them. But does a President affect what the Vice President's COS does? Does Bush control a Scooter Libby at all, or is that Cheney's job? Similarly, is Bolten responsible for Rove's actions and management responsibilities, or does the President deal directly with Rove and take responsibility for his actions? If Rove or someone else in this position screws up, who should take the heat?

This brings up another point about the role the V.P. plays and the management or organizational responsibilities that are central to this office. Is Joshua Bolten really equal to Dick Cheney, as the last figure might suggest? Is Rove formally more or less influential than Cheney? The V.P.—who takes over for the President if something dire befalls him—should be the real second-in-command, the real COO in a management sense who executes America, Inc.'s strategy, coordinates critical Cabinet functions, and deals with the Senate (the V.P. is President of the Senate). Cheney certainly is a powerful V.P. yet, historically, the role rarely has been this important or powerful. Someone like Cheney grabs power and wields it, but influence or authority certainly have not been normal accoutrements or defining characteristics of the V.P. role over the years.

The confusion and lack of clarity in organizational structure at the top of America, Inc. was driven home forcefully by the V.P.'s attempt in June, 2007, to "redefine" the branches of government. In addition to the Judicial, Legislative, and Executive branches, Cheney, in effect, proposed a separate "branch," arguing that the V.P. really is not part of the executive branch and thus need not comply with national security disclosure rules required of other executive-branch agencies. This amounts to a redefinition of organizational structure, with the V.P.

"branch" or "unit" as a separate entity, outside the rules, standard operating procedures, and demands for accountability that are imposed on other executive offices. The V.P. branch of government was positioned as separate and exempt from the controls and reporting requirements normally inherent in organizational structure. Even if this turns out to be a sad stunt, it highlights the lack of discipline in organizational roles and responsibilities at the very top of America, Inc.

The situation actually gets worse if one looks at span of control and responsibilities. The current cabinet plus cabinet-level administrative offices number at least 30 members. If the President's span of control is 1:30, this clearly is an untenable, unworkable structure because of sheer numbers and differences in work or job content across the cabinet-level jobs. A span of 1:30 is usually unworkable due to size of span alone, and differences across diverse cabinet functions make such a large span even more impossible to handle. Clearly, span must be reduced to allow for even a modicum of efficient and effective performance in the White House organization.

One way to reduce span of control is via changes in organizational structure. Again, use or creation of a COO position with direct formal responsibility for certain cabinet functions would reduce the President's span and make the structure more workable. This, however, has not been done, at least not formally. Some would argue that influence patterns and authority have been negotiated informally over the years, in other White Houses and Cabinets, and that the system is fluid and clear enough to work. This, however, is not at all apparent. Even if this informality worked in the past, the more complex and problematic political, economic, and social global environment that America, Inc. must deal with presently demands more accountability and logic in organizational structure and the design of management systems. Overlapping turf and unclear responsibilities make the situation ineffective and even potentially dangerous.

If organizational structure indeed provides clues as to operations and strategy execution in an organization, the top-management structure of America, Inc. says that the situation is a mess. Too many people and too many jobs or roles with no clear accountability for defined tasks only lead to mismanagement and poor decisions, especially if the key players have different or conflicting agendas. A large span of control exacerbates the structural confusion and lack of clarity and allows an almost renegade, subjective interpretation of how management and organizational processes work, the results of which are dysfunctional and even dangerous.

Dysfunctional Consequences of the White House Organization

Consider just one of America, Inc.'s stated top priorities: winning the war on terrorism and making the country safe. At the cabinet level, there are a number of individuals with responsibilities related to this goal or top priority. There is the Secretary of Homeland Security, presumably in charge of all security issues. But there is also a Director of National Intelligence who, presumably, as an intelligence "czar," coordinates and deals with all intelligence matters, including those affecting homeland security. And then there is the Director of the CIA who, traditionally, has run the show in intelligence matters. Add a Secretary of State, an Under Secretary of Homeland Security, a National Security Advisor, a few COSs jockeying for influence, a Pentagon intent on maintaining control over the intelligence budget, and you have the makings of management disorder, confusion, and conflict.

Adding a powerful V.P. to the mix makes things even more befuddled and dicey. Cheney, for example, has a national security staff that numbers 14 people, the largest VP staff in history, and they are actively involved in security matters.[3] "Alums" of Cheney's staff and his vassals in other government branches also wield influence. Add next the top people in the military with security or intelligence jobs, and responsibilities become even more clouded. Of all the people listed, who's really in charge of security and intelligence matters? Who's accountable for what, specifically? If a disastrous security breach occurs and a major terrorist attack occurs, where does the responsibility lie and what should be fixed?

Appointing a "czar" like Negroponte or McConnell does little or nothing to control the others involved with security, especially the military and the CIA and its independent operatives. The czar has no authority in a hierarchical sense. Indeed, Cheney was influential in ensuring that the National Intelligence Director could not interfere in the military chain of command, which severely limits the position's influence.[4] Having a czar may sound comforting to many citizens, but organizationally the position is weak, at best. Negroponte, McConnell, or anyone else in the czar role is not in charge of any of the other people responsible for aspects of intelligence and homeland security and, without formal authority, the role is that of a figurehead only.

Can the President control all of the Cabinet-level people having a role in keeping America, Inc. safe and achieve effective coordination and positive results? I doubt it. Organizationally, the different cabinet-level offices are independent, with separate budgets and a huge mass of bureaucrats within them. They have their own "turfs" and agendas which they will defend to the end. Appointments to key positions are often based on political factors and loyalty, not competence or capabilities. Cooperation sounds good in press releases, but the CIA or military, for example, is not about to bow to the wishes of the Director of National Intelligence, nor will others easily and voluntarily follow directives of the head of Homeland Security that might limit their own resources and power. *These are important management and organizational issues with potentially serious and dysfunctional consequences, and I return to them in much greater detail in the next chapter on planning and intelligence activities.*

What we have, then, is a White House organization that is a management quagmire. The sheer number of cabinet-level positions makes coordination and control difficult and boggs decisions down. Lines of formal authority are blurred. Informal influence rules, and such situations are often volatile, at best. Even in such critical areas as national security, roles and responsibilities aren't clearly defined and operational. Key players can resist the influence of others. Czars have no formal control over these players, and can only hope that they cooperate like "good corporate citizens." Turf and resources are protected at all costs, often with little consideration of superordinate goals, like keeping the country safe and secure.

In such an organization as the one I'm describing, people grasp power and influence. If something should go dreadfully wrong, however, *suddenly no one is to blame or accountable for the mishap.* Job definitions magically seem to preclude any responsibility for a negative performance outcome, and emphasis is on pointing the finger of blame toward someone else. Even when public opinion wants the person responsible for a major mistake to pay a price (e.g. former Secretary of Defense Rumsfeld with Abu Ghraib, Afghanistan, and Iraq), nothing happens, except maybe the President's giving the person a medal or recognition for work well done!

In addition to unclear authority and responsibility, multiple and overlapping positions, large size and complexity, and reliance on informal influence exclusively, there is one more problem in the White house organization that follows logically from the others and adds to the problem of accountability: namely, poor metrics or measures of performance. In the corporate world, performance metrics are usually fairly clear and typically agreed upon by key managers. Market share, profitability, customer satisfaction, shareholder value, stock price, etc., are generally recognized as valid and important measures of managerial and organizational performance.

In America, Inc., in contrast, top managers are rarely held accountable for such clear metrics or performance measures. Performance emphasis is on activities, not important outcomes or results. PR sessions and photo-ops focus on cabinet and other high-level meetings with many top people seemingly in deliberation and focused on getting things done, but rarely are the officials held accountable for solid, measurable outcomes. Mistakes are made, but the lack of accountability guarantees that learning doesn't occur. Small, "tactical" mistakes may occasionally be admitted to (e.g. "small" mistakes in Afghanistan or Iraq), but they surely will be repeated. The lack of accountability and learning allows top management to skate by and use its PR capabilities to advertise dubious "accomplishments" and progress. The true story of management's performance is clouded and controlled, as subsequent chapters will show in greater detail.

> *If, as argued above, organizational design—including structure, coordination mechanisms, and incentives—provides clues as to an organization's goals, operations, or methods of strategy execution, the White House-cabinet design and management system suggest an organization ill-suited for effective planning, control, and the successful implementation of strategy and goal attainment under conditions of complexity and uncertainty.*

This picture is not a very positive one. It suggests an organization and management team that are inefficient and ineffective, prone to making mistakes that can be costly, even dangerous, to America, Inc. These are serious issues. Wasting scarce resources and "muddling through" ineffectively are always problems. But in an increasingly complex environment marked by the economic, political, and social challenges laid out in the previous chapter, poor management and organization can eventually create major problems, including those soon to be discussed in subsequent chapters. A lack of organizational clarity at the top can translate into management and structural problems, including unclear responsibility and accountability, at lower organizational levels, which can breed yet additional roadblocks to efficient and effective performance. What happens at the top of an organization usually trickles downward, affecting operations, decisions, and organizational culture, while perpetuating and reinforcing the negative impact of mismanagement and inadequate organization that begins at the highest levels.

Changing the White House Organization

The organizational structure and management responsibilities in the Cabinet can be made clearer. Accountability and controls can be introduced, along with more formal management practices. Span of control can be managed better. The top-management team of America, Inc. can become more professional and effective.

There will be political resistance to any changes, to be sure. Politicians will argue that America, Inc. is "different," with its own specialized, even unique, needs. In my experience, however, managers *always* feel that their organizations are "different" or unique. Unique? No. "Different"? Perhaps in some ways, but the similarities in management practices across organizations and industries usually outweigh most differences by organization. America, Inc., can definitely benefit from sound management processes. Even if only small, incremental steps are taken, the management system and organizational structure at the highest level can become more rigorous, transparent, efficient, and effective.

Roles, responsibilities, and people. Figure 2.3 depicts a simple management process. Assume, for the sake of discussion, a new President and V.P. coming into office. The first set of tasks in Figure 2.3 focuses on roles, responsibilities, accountability, the authority of the various top Cabinet jobs, and the choice of qualified cabinet-level people to fill them. Emphasis here at once must be on organizational structure, peoples' capabilities, and the setting of priorities. The discussion of these critical issues can include important stakeholders outside of the White House, e.g. from the Senate and House, but this discussion is a first step that must take place.

Priorities must be discussed and determined in the early stages of Figure 2.3. It is true in all organizations that *when everything is important, then nothing is important.* Some tasks, like intelligence gathering or homeland security, currently may be more critical than other tasks, so priorities must be set and the responsibilities and authority of key roles determined. Just as the corporation defines key elements of organizational structure and related tasks (e.g. product or customer-based divisions, an R&D function, a strategic planning unit), so too the organizational structure of the White House must be determined with an eye to the critical strategic contingencies or competitive threats facing the country. The need is to identify the high-priority problems or opportunities America, Inc. faces, and then organize jobs and tasks so as to meet these challenges head on.

Part of the process of defining roles and responsibilities is simultaneously considering people to fill key top-management roles. Qualified Cabinet-level people with appropriate skills and experience are vital to the success of the management process outlined in Figure 2.3. *It is important that there be a "fit" or match among organizational needs, individual skills, and management capabilities.* A major problem occurs when people are chosen for critical top-level positions based on cronyism, loyalty, friendship, or family connections, resulting in unqualified people in the highest positions in the country. Recent problems with Iraq, pre 9/11 intelligence, Katrina, Homeland Security, etc. provide good examples of the results of management incompetence and insufficient forethought when creating a top-management team.

Choosing qualified people for high-level managerial positions in the Cabinet is critical, as is an unambiguous definition of responsibility, accountability, and authority. Structure must be clear. If the V.P. is to be "in charge" of certain Cabinet-level positions, his or her role must be defined and understood by all. If the President sets up an Executive Committee or a top-level "Team of Rivals," its duties and responsibilities must be clear. Direct reports and commensurate hierarchical authority also must be fixed and unambiguous. Emphasis must be on roles and responsibilities, not the choice of loyal cronies or supporters for key jobs who might be unqualified for the complex work at hand.

Identifying interdependence. The choice of cabinet-level officials and definition of duties and job responsibilities are not enough. How these people work together must also be defined. Having good people is necessary, but not sufficient. Clarifying who must work with whom, when, and why also is necessary. In essence, it is necessary to define *interdependence* and the *authority* supporting it, as Figure 2.3 suggests.

Interdependence can take various forms. If jobs or functions are independent, i.e. interdependence is low, little coordination is needed. If interdependence is high—if certain cabinet officials must work together closely to solve a problem, if each official is necessary, but not sufficient, for task completion—then coordination becomes important (e.g. between Homeland Security and the CIA). In these situations of high interdependence, informal methods of coordination are not enough. More formal methods are necessary, e.g. teams or units that are set up to achieve coordination across Cabinet positions. Key cabinet officials cannot remain independent and separate, "working alone together." They must interact purposefully, focusing on the integration of tasks and the achievement of common goals.

The clarification of authority is especially important when interdependence is high. Who makes the decisions and who has the final say when disagreements arise? Who ultimately has the authority and accountability for decisions and actions when interdependence is high? These are basic management questions but they must be answered, even in a White House organization. Use of "responsibility plotting," methods of job definition, and ways of generating agreement or consensus on goals can help the process immensely, ensuring that critical tasks get done and wasteful, overlapping, and conflicting activities are eliminated.[5]

Figure 2.3

A Management Process

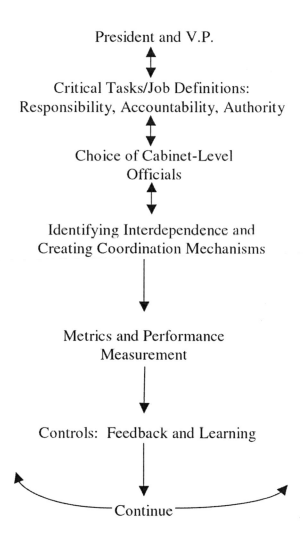

Performance metrics and measurement. Once all jobs, responsibilities, and interdependencies are determined, the top management group can concentrate on developing tactics and performance metrics consistent with the strategic and operating tasks that were previously defined. These metrics would be measurable, and there would be agreement as to the data or information defining or comprising them. Performance against measurable goals can then be assessed, resulting in organizational learning and a more effective management group at the helm of America, Inc.

The process is an iterative one. Planning and execution are not a one-way street; feedback about performance allows for learning, adaptation and change, and refinements to the management process, as Figure 2.3 indicates with its feedback loop. Controls, reviews of performance accountability, and learning are vital to change and adaptation, and the White House organization is no exception. Without them, the mistakes of the past are sure to be repeated, often with increasingly negative consequences.

The management process of Figure 2.3 is basically a version of a planning and strategy review process used by many companies around the globe, and one that could be applied to the White House organization. The planning and execution decisions and actions that are part of this process are needed to increase management and structural clarity in the White House organization. Current management disorder, including unclear responsibilities, accountabilities, and authority at the highest level, can only translate into even bigger problems throughout lower management levels of America, Inc., exacerbating problems of efficiency and effectiveness greatly. Time and tradition have worked over the years to create a White House organization that is inappropriate for the current level of decision complexity currently facing America, Inc. It's time for major change, regardless of how strenuous the resistance to change might be. The stakes are too high and the dangers too great to do otherwise.

To highlight these dangers, the next chapter builds logically on and extends the current arguments and considers the huge problems in the U.S. Intelligence Community. This community or loose federation of organizations is marked by serious organizational and management problems that reflect the lack of management and organizational clarity in the Cabinet. The importance of the intelligence community and its centrality in a hostile and complex world demand that additional analysis be devoted to these problems, including analysis and application of the key management and organizational design issues raised in the present chapter.

CONCLUSIONS

Organizational structure and management processes at the upper levels of large corporate organizations tell us volumes about strategy and the process of strategy implementation or execution. Structure and the design of management roles in these corporations usually are arrived at logically, with an eye to how to deal with complex competitive environments and achieve acceptable levels of efficiency and effective performance. Key specific concerns in the large global corporation include sound strategic analysis, careful job definition, clear responsibility and accountability, workable spans of control, clear performance metrics, and an ability to eliminate redundant and conflicting decision-making roles.

America, Inc.'s top organizational and management structure fails or comes up woefully inadequate on all of the above dimensions or critical issues. The White House organization is a jumble of sorts and hardly a model of efficiency or effectiveness. Unclear or overlapping responsibilities prevail, and accountability is nil. Effective coordination is nonexistent. Clear authority is lacking, except in the role of President. People are often chosen for important jobs for the wrong reasons. Bureaucracy rules and tie-breaking or conflict-reducing mechanisms are suspect. What's more, unless corrected or changed, this organizational and management structure can lead to even more serious problems, e.g. an inability to plan well, confront the serious problems facing America, Inc., and respond adequately to them.

Let's follow up on this last point and look at the problems and dangerous inadequacies in America, Inc.'s intelligence gathering capabilities. The discussion in this chapter indicated that planning and intelligence-related problems begin in the White House, and they certainly do. But the problems go much deeper and become more serious, as the next chapter will show.

Endnotes

1. For a good discussion of organizational structure, clarification of roles and responsibilities, and how coordination reflects task interdependence, see L. G. Hrebiniak, *Making Strategy Work: Leading Effective Execution and Change* (Wharton School Publishing, 2005), especially chapters 4 and 5.

2. These are some who define the COS as the second most powerful man in Washington, more important than the Vice President. The COS' job is generally described as overseeing the White House Staff and controlling access to the President, which makes him a central coordinating point in the White House. See, too, John Trattner, The 2000 Prune Book: How to Succeed in Washington's Top Jobs (Brookings Institution Press, 2000); Curt Lader, How to Prepare for the AP U.S. Government and Politics (Barron's Educational Series, 2002); Charles Walcott, Shirley Warshaw, and Stephen Wayne, "The Chief of Staff: Duties of the White House Chief of Staff," Presidential Studies Quarterly (Center For the Study of the Presidency, 2001); Dave Trulio, "White House Chief of Staff Describes Role, Principles, Concerns," The HARBUS Online, December 12, 2005; Martha Cottam, Beth Dietz-Uhler, Elena Mastors, and Thomas Preston, Introduction to Political Psychology (Lawrence Erlbaum Associates, 2004); and Shirley Warshaw, Powersharing: White-House Cabinet Relations in the Modern Presidency (State University of New York Press, 1996).

3. Daniel Benjamin, "President Cheney: His Office Really Does Run National Security," Slate, November 7, 2005.

4. Ibid. See, too, John Prados, "Intelligence: No Easy Fix," Bulletin of the Atomic Scientists, September-October, 2004, for additional discussion of the ideal and actual power of the National Intelligence Director.

5. For discussions of responsibility plotting and clarification and methods of generating agreement or consensus in organizations see Making Strategy Work, op. cit. Also, see Jay Galbraith, Designing Complex Organizations (Addison-Wesley, 1973) and L. G. Hrebiniak and W. F. Joyce, Implementing Strategy (Macmillan, 1984).

3

The Intelligence Community: Management Problems And A Clear Case of Unintelligent Design

Many problems have been noted in the world of U.S. intelligence since 9/11. By now everyone knows how the intelligence on Iraq's weapons of mass destruction was skewed toward a biased, predetermined outcome and how distortions of information were sold to the media and the public. It's clear now that U.S. intelligence agencies just weren't very good at penetrating the mysteries of terrorist networks and foreign societies. Dysfunctional, even bizarre, competition and a lack of cooperation across intelligence organizations have been detailed at length in the media. For example, a Pentagon unit—the Policy Counterterrorism Evaluation Group—competed with the CIA for the attention of senior officials in the White House and created its own intelligence data because Pentagon people weren't *pleased* by the information being generated by the CIA. The unit clearly didn't want the CIA's data to get in the way of its own opinions and leanings. There have been other turf battles over critical responsibilities and accountability, and even conflicts over more mundane, trifling issues, e.g., which agency—Homeland Security or the Justice Department—should raise the color-coded alert levels in the county's terrorism warning system, itself a costly debacle whose effectiveness has often been questioned or ridiculed.

There have been many publicized debates and resultant changes to improve U.S. intelligence capabilities in response to these problems, but progress hasn't been smooth or obvious. The resignation of Porter Goss as CIA Director in 2006 and the appointment of General Michael Hayden to take his place caused a bit of a stir. There was a good deal of argument, discussion, and hand wringing about leadership, Goss' effectiveness, Hayden's wiretapping activities while heading the

NSA, and the advisability of a military person heading the organization. Opinions ran rampant as to Hayden's or anyone's ability to turn the organization around and get it back on track with needed reforms and changes. Appointment of the first Director of National Intelligence or "Intelligence Czar" caused quite a stir and raised the hopes of better coordination in the intelligence community. Closer examination of the role, however, revealed the difficulties inherent in such a task and the huge obstacles to effective intelligence reform. Negroponte's resignation as intelligence czar raised questions about the viability of the job, whether real reform and progress were occurring in the intelligence community, and whether the changes were really more of a smoke-and-mirror phenomenon. The "tell-all" book by George Tenet, former CIA Director, about what really happened before the "slam dunk" invasion of Iraq basically added to the controversy, showing that years after 9/11, accusatory fingers are still being pointed and responsibilities are still muddled in the intelligence community. And so the discussion still goes on today, with promises of change and needed reform still appearing daily in the media.

The sad and frightening thing is that all of this talk and debate is absolutely useless. Major reform will not occur in the intelligence community. The actions being taken, including the appointment of a czar and the never-ending analyses by blue-ribbon panels, *won't make a bit of a difference.* No matter who is appointed as Head of the CIA or Intelligence Director or how much busy work is done by myriad "experts," the organizational structure and management shortcomings of the current intelligence community will ensure that effective reform cannot possibly take place.

> *To put it succinctly, the entire intelligence community is a huge mess. There are too many agencies marked by mismanagement, divisive politics, and a grossly unintelligent design. Unclear or competing responsibilities, a lack of accountability, ineffective coordination and knowledge sharing, and inappropriate organizational structures have stymied a once-strong ability in spying and effective intelligence. The intelligence community is close to being crippled, and there is little or no help on the way to reverse the paralysis or inertia that has been building. There's a great deal to worry about when it comes to intelligence, but nothing intelligent is being proposed to reform the intelligence community.*

This is a dangerous situation, to say the least. Let's look at the intelligence community and see what the huge problems are that are contributing to this sorry state of affairs. Let's then talk about the serious reforms that are needed to turn things around. A good way to begin is to consider briefly what good planning, intelligence gathering, and effective management and organization *should look like* and how, comparatively, the U.S. intelligence community is sorely deficient and suffering from a debilitating "Intelligence Deficit Disorder."[1]

Effective Planning, Intelligence, and Execution: The Key Capabilities

The performance of the large global corporation depends in no small part on sound planning and intelligence activities. The corporation exists in an ever-changing competitive arena that it must analyze and deal with effectively. It is no accident that the last two or three decades of business research and practice have focused heavily on critical competitive or industry forces and the strategic planning processes to deal with them.[2] Corporate and business planners have also been focusing on the internal resources and capabilities of organizations needed to implement their strategies effectively. Recent emphasis on planning and the execution of plans includes analysis of organizational structures, incentives, culture, information sharing, and coordination mechanisms as organizational factors that help make strategic and operating plans work and contribute to competitive advantage.[3]

Sound planning and implementation are also critical to the success of America, Inc. in a changing and increasingly competitive and hostile global environment. The structure and process of planning or intelligence gathering and the execution of intelligence-related plans, however, are severely flawed in the U.S. Major deficiencies in intelligence gathering and usage exist and they present a real danger to America, Inc. To validate this argument or assertion, let's consider a few characteristics or criteria of sound planning, organization, and execution. This treatment of necessity will be brief, but it is important to lay out at least a few criteria of effective management and organization against which intelligence agencies can be benchmarked and evaluated.

Objectivity. Good planning must be objective, employing sound data and reaching conclusions based on fact and data analysis, not predetermined conclusions or outcomes. The scientific method should be the driving force in planning or intelligence-gathering processes. Emphasis must be on a consistent, formal process of data collection and analysis, based on a reliable and valid measurement or representation of the phenomena being analyzed. The basic steps include the formation of hypotheses or expected results, collection of suitable data to measure the phenomena of interest, objective hypothesis testing, and conclusions based on the empirical findings. I've admittedly known managers "who never let facts get in the way of their opinions," but such an approach should never mark the planning or intelligence process.

Objectivity demands the use of performance objectives and metrics that are measurable. Intuition, feel, "tradecraft," or "art" certainly may come into play occasionally, but care must be taken to ensure that planning isn't too idiosyncratic or something driven solely by tradition, personal beliefs, and subjective analysis. Objectivity also demands that planners or intelligence gatherers are never under pressure to come up with the "right answers" or to massage data to ensure the validity of predetermined "facts."

Timely and valid data. Sound planning depends on good data, and good data must be *timely* and *valid*. Information about competitors, industry forces, or countries' nuclear arms programs obviously must be valid or correct. Basing plans or strategic moves on faulty data can be costly, even disastrous. Good data, however, also must be timely. Old, stale, or outdated information precludes good planning and the ability to predict and react effectively to external shocks.

Both timeliness and validity of information, then, are needed for effective intelligence and organizational adaptation. However, there is a catch here: *Timeliness and validity of information are negatively correlated.* A desire for validity and thoroughness in planning can actually hurt timeliness. In contrast, an overly strong emphasis on timeliness runs the risk of generating hasty and invalid information. Achieving the right balance between timely and valid information in the intelligence gathering process is a major challenge facing management, but it's one they must confront.

Use of multiple data sources. Planning or intelligence gathering always involves some degree of "uncertainty absorption." Organizations facing uncertainty usually try to eliminate or reduce it so they can act with some determinateness and certainty. Planning helps to reduce uncertainty and allow organizations to act.

Figure 3.1 shows a very simple model of uncertainty absorption. Managers responsible for planning analyze all sorts of external data, depending on the problem or issue at hand. The planners then test different hypotheses—e.g. the probable impact on GDP of interest-rate changes or oil price increases, the reaction of the U.S. dollar or other currencies to a Yuan revaluation, or the impact of an invasion of a Middle-East country on other states in the same region. Logical deductions or inferences are drawn from the hypothesis testing and related analyses as to the likely outcomes or results.

Figure 3.1

Uncertainty Absorption in the Planning process

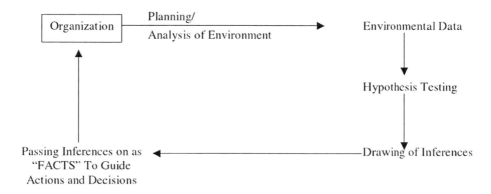

The derived inferences, however, are usually not disseminated as inferences, nor are the processes and tests by which the inferences were made always spelled out entirely to others. Rather, the inferences are usually passed on as "facts" or specific recommendation for action. A sales forecast is one such "fact," a number that guides many other decisions, but whose derivation or genesis is rarely fully explained to everyone using the forecast. Another "fact" is a recommendation to invade another country. In this case, most of the reasoning or the inferences behind the recommendation may need to be passed on because of the seriousness of the decision and possibly a lack of trust in those making it. What is actually spelled out under uncertainty absorption, then, depends on the issue at hand, but the usual case demands a high degree of confidence in the people doing the planning. The worst case scenario, of course, is when the data and analyses supporting the inferences are bogus, made up or massaged to create buy-in and support for a faulty premise or conclusion.

Given the potential danger of poor uncertainty absorption in critical planning areas, including extreme bias in the analysis of data and the existence of predetermined inferences, facts, or answers, it is prudent to rely on *multiple data sources* when gathering intelligence. Having different people or organizational units independently absorb uncertainty and arrive at important "facts" can provide a system of checks and balances and negate the impact of bias, chicanery, or fraud in planning.

The use of multiple data sources raises another potential need, however—namely, the need for coordination and conflict-reducing mechanisms. Multiple data sources and divergent facts derived from the planning process can lead to differences in opinion that must be confronted and handled. Processes for integrating information and generating agreement in the face of disagreement and conflict must be developed to make planning work, and these efforts demand time and other management resources.

Organizational structure. Organizational structure is vital to making strategy work.[4] Structure affects outcomes, including costs and the effectiveness of organizational plans and activities. It facilitates or inhibits the attainment of strategic and operating objectives, the development of scale economies, and the need for duplication of scarce resources. Structure facilitates or inhibits the focus on critical products, services, and geographical opportunities or threats, and thus is critical to effective execution.

Organizational structure also affects and reflects the degree or type of *interdependence* across important units or functions. Interdependence—the extent to which individuals or units must work together to achieve positive outcomes—in turn affects the need for *coordination* or *integration* across these same units. The greater the interdependence built into the structure, the greater is the importance of coordination for goal attainment.

Structure comprises two aspects or elements: (1) the design of the organization in terms of "boxes and lines," which indicates the location of scarce resources (e.g. centralization vs. decentralization) and levels of authority, responsibility, and accountability; and (2) the mechanisms employed to achieve effective coordination or integration, including the requisite sharing of knowledge or information across interdependent units or people. Structure plays a big role in organizational performance. It has a major impact on how efficiently and effectively organizations perform. It is not a "passive" element in how organizations operate. Rather, it is central to the success of those operations, including, as we'll see, within the intelligence community.

Clear responsibility and accountability. These issues are part of organizational structure, but they deserve a separate mention because of their importance. People must know who's responsible for what, when, and why for effective performance to occur. Coordination is impossible if the various task responsibilities that must be integrated are unclear or unknown. Overlapping or redundant responsibilities cloud the picture further: when *everyone* is responsible for something, *no one* is responsible or accountable, and important decisions fall into the cracks. Add a lack of authority to the mix of unclear responsibilities and absolutely nothing gets done. Decisions aren't made, turf battles run rampant, and titles and figureheads abound with no legitimate power or authority.

In these situations, people usually turn inward, worried about their own unit's piece of the resource and influence pie. Budget battles become sacred, not performance outcomes. Cooperation suffers as each competing unit asks "what's in it for me," even when presented with important superordinate goals. Unless corrected, such a situation of unclear responsibility, accountability, and authority leads to poor, even disastrous performance. And when the poor performance inevitably occurs, time and effort are usually spent *blaming others* for the mishap and absolving oneself of all responsibility for failure, *not* on finding solutions to the problems at hand. This is mismanagement at its very worst.

Open-mindedness and the right culture. Planning or intelligence-gathering requires a culture based on open-mindedness, integrity, and a quest for the right answers. Managers cannot be afraid to challenge colleagues or superiors on the data employed in planning, the inferences and facts derived from them, or the decision processes by which the facts are determined. "Taboos," rules, or norms that impede confrontation, negatively affect trust and mutual respect, or prohibit the challenging of official positions cannot be tolerated, as they negatively affect intelligence gathering and, ultimately, performance results.

Managing culture is important, as it affects behavior and performance. Studies clearly show the negative impact of cultures of concealment, arrogance, intimidation, or fear of challenging or changing "official" positions on how managers and their organizations perform,[5] and such cultural aberrations must be dealt with. Similarly, the existence of incentives that thwart cooperation or motivate destructive competition cannot be tolerated because of their negative impact on culture and performance. The execution of plans will fail if people don't have skin in the game. Likewise, performance will suffer if individuals are rewarded for doing the wrong things. Incentives fuel managers' motivations, guide behavior, and affect culture, a critical fact in all organizations, including America, Inc.

Let's now turn to the U.S. Intelligence Community and analyze its structure, processes, incentives, and culture and compare the findings to the general points just made.

The Intelligence Community:
Unintelligent Design, Poor Management, And An
"Intelligence Deficit Disorder"

The past performance of the U.S. intelligence community—the CIA, FBI, NSA, and other agencies that provide strategic and tactical intelligence—can, at best, be rated as poor or marginal. The Bay of Pigs fiasco and failure to see or predict the implosion of the Soviet Union certainly began the erosion of confidence in our intelligence agencies, and much has happened since to raise additional red flags about the continued decline of the agencies and their inability to get things right. The 9/11 Commission's final report and a host of other publications have raised levels of dissatisfaction with U.S. Intelligence. Missed signals before the attacks, the inability to penetrate al Qaeda, important data that weren't acted on, and poor cooperation among intelligence agencies all contributed to the success of the 9/11 attacks, which some see as the worst intelligence-management failure in our country's history.

Iraq has highlighted further the failures or shortcomings in U.S. intelligence capabilities. The information about Saddam Hussein's weapons of mass destruction was not only dead wrong, it's been argued that the information was made up, massaged, and exaggerated to justify an invasion that already had been decided upon. The claim that Hussein was building a hidden network of mobile labs capable of brewing all sorts of biological weapons was based on the reports of a single Iraqi defector, codenamed "Curveball." Colin Powell's presentation to the U.N. Security Council in 2003, critics say, was premised almost exclusively on this single, shaky pillar of evidence.[6] Powell himself doubted the evidence of this and other sources on Iraq, it was learned later, but he went along with the party line in his U.N. appearance and presentation of the evidence against Saddam Hussein.

Documents that supposedly substantiated claims that Iraq was trying to buy uranium from Africa proved to be fake. Prewar assumptions about resistance in Iraq were totally inaccurate. At Abu Ghraib, soldiers supposedly faced enormous pressures to produce, even make up intelligence, lots of it. No exit strategy was ever discussed or developed as an integral part of an overall intelligence design and war plan. Even tactical planning proved faulty, as a host of complaints emerged from troops in Iraq about inadequate supplies and aging vehicles that lacked armor protection against roadside bombs and attacks.

Many other examples could easily be provided, but most by now are well known and documented. For present purposes, suffice it to say that recent U.S.

planning and intelligence activities have been poorly managed. An abundance of data suggest, among other things, that:

a. planning has not always been objective, but driven by predetermined facts, massaged data, and means-justifying-ends arguments;

b. multiple data sources weren't always employed, and even when they were, efforts to "connect all the dots" to arrive at logical conclusions were weak;

c. pressure existed for people to come up with the "right answers," and this could be seen at all levels of intelligence gathering, from the troops on the ground to U.S. Cabinet members;

d. intelligence data often were not valid, but were acted on anyway;

e. uncertainty absorption was biased and manipulated by a relatively few people responsible for planning and intelligence activities in order to create buy-in and support; and

f. incentives and the intelligence culture did not support open-mindedness, integrity, and a quest for the "right things" in the intelligence process.

These issues are important in and of themselves, but they mask much deeper problems with America, Inc.'s intelligence community. There are other problems receiving far less attention that are at the *causal core* of the aforementioned issues. There are shortcomings in management and organization that drive, create, and affect many of the more obvious planning and intelligence failures, and they deserve a great deal of attention. There are (a) core problems and (b) symptoms of the core issues, and the former deserve our undivided attention even more than the latter.

These underlying core problems are the *structure* of the U.S. Intelligence community and the management woes related to it, including poor *coordination* or *integration* of intelligence activities. A related core problem is a *culture* that motivates the wrong behavior and output in the intelligence community.

Organizational Structure: The Intelligence Community

It was argued in the previous chapter that organizational structure reveals a great deal about how organizations are managed and how they operate. It also was argued that structure affects important outcomes and organizational performance, and that the logic and clarity of organizational design tell us a great deal about management capabilities.

> *Against these criteria, the U.S. intelligence community is an organizational and management nightmare. It not only is not solving intelligence problems, it's actually working hard to create them.*

Before proceeding further, it would be useful to define what agencies or organizations comprise the intelligence community. This should be simple enough, but even here one encounters prophetic difficulties. Articles and political commentators often refer to the 15 or 16 "main" intelligence agencies. Most people are familiar with some of the names—the CIA, FBI, NSA—but not with others. With even 15 or 16 agencies, one can begin to question whether they all are necessary. The problem gets much worse, however.

There indeed are many other agencies or organizations beyond the core 15 or 16 that are responsible for intelligence activities. Table 3.1 shows one listing of U.S. intelligence and security agencies that boggles the mind, that of the Federation of American Scientists. The FAS Intelligence Resource Program's count reveals 64 different agencies, sub-agencies, or subordinate units that are responsible for intelligence and security. In addition to the 15 or 16 agencies that provide strategic foreign intelligence, their list includes selected military intelligence and security organizations, as well as agencies responsible for security responses to transnational threats, including terrorism, cyber warfare, computer security, and covert employment of weapons of mass destruction.[7] And the FAS notes that the list is probably not complete! Sixty four or more organizations—intelligence gathering is obviously a huge business.

Table 3.1

FAS Intelligence Resource Program:
U.S. Intelligence and Security Agencies*

"Official" Organizations

National

United States Intelligence Community
National Intelligence Council (NIC)
Counterintelligence Center (CIC)
DCI Center for Security Evaluation (CSE)
DCI Crime and Narcotics Center (CNC)
DCI Counterterrorist Center (CTC)
DCI National Virtual Translation Center (NVTC)
DCI Weapons Intelligence, Nonproliferation, and Arms Control Center (WINPAC)
DCI Special Security Center
National Counterintelligence Executive (NCIX)
Terrorist Threat Integration Center (TTIC)

Central Intelligence Agency

National Security Agency

National Geospatial-Intelligence Agency (formerly NIMA)

Defense Intelligence Agency

Federal Bureau of Investigation

Other Defense Department

Assistant to the Secretary for Intelligence Oversight

Under Secretary of Defense for Intelligence
Under Secretary of Defense for Policy

Assistant Secretary of Defense for Networks and Information Integration

Defense Information Systems Agency

Defense Advanced Research Projects Agency

Defense Protective Service
Defense Security Service

U.S. Special Operations Command

Army
Army Deputy Chief of Staff for Intelligence
Intelligence and Security Command

Navy
Office of Naval Intelligence
Naval Security Group Command
Naval Criminal Investigative Service

Marine Corps

Air Force
Air Force Technical Applications Center
Air Intelligence Agency

Other Federal Agencies

National Security Council
President's Foreign Intelligence Advisory Board
Office of National Drug Control Policy

Department of Homeland Security
Information Analysis and Infrastructure Protection

Energy Department
Office of Intelligence

Justice Department
Justice Intelligence Coordinating Council
OIG—Office of the Inspector General
OIPR—Office of Intelligence Policy and Review
DEA—Drug Enforcement Administration
NDIC—National Drug Intelligence Center
USNCB—U.S. National Central Bureau
AFT—Bureau of Alcohol, Tobacco, Firearms and Explosives

State Department
INR—Bureau of Intelligence & Research
INL—Bureau of International Narcotics and Law Enforcement Affairs

CT—Counterterrorism Office
DS—Bureau of Diplomatic Security

Treasury Department
Office of Intelligence Support
Office of the Under Secretary (Enforcement)
FINCEN—Financial Crimes Enforcement
FLETC—Federal Law Enforcement Training Center

National Archives and Records Administration
Information Security Oversight Office

*See http://www.fas.org/irp/official.html

Intelligence gathering is not only a huge business, it's also a very expensive business. The latest estimates of what it takes to run the intelligence community is about $40-50 billion a year, *or more than $100 million a day.* This is a big and costly business, to be sure.

The size of the intelligence community in the range of 15-64 agencies or more immediately raises red flags that should worry anyone with management concerns. Large numbers often suggest redundancies and overlaps in effort. Large size is often associated with the waste of financial and managerial resources, as well as the poor use of expertise. Large size usually implies bureaucracy and a host of coordination problems that detract heavily from the benefit one might expect from a $100 million-a-day-plus expenditure.

Pinpointing clear responsibility and accountability with so many like organizations is virtually impossible. The typical case with large numbers is that a host of agencies are responsible for intelligence, but no one is clearly accountable for major intelligence mistakes. Usually, no one organization will readily admit accountability for failures, as it's much easier to point the finger of blame at many others who are also responsible for planning or intelligence tasks. Some might argue that large numbers do not constitute a major problem, contending that organizational structure can position all of the organizations, hierarchically and laterally, so as to control for size and form a coherent, integrated intelligence effort. The argument usually has merit, but it doesn't hold water in the intelligence community. In fact, *the structure of the intelligence community only exacerbates the problems due to size alone.*

Figure 3.2 shows an attempt by Carroll Publishing in 2005 to draw an organization chart of the intelligence community.[8] The only change I made to their excellent effort is a modification of the relationship between the Director of National Intelligence and the CIA, adding a "dotted" or "dashed" line relationship to indicate a lack of formal authority. What can be inferred from the chart about the state and effectiveness of the U.S. intelligence community?

First, the organizational structure in no way reduces the complexity due to the large number of intelligence agencies or organizations. Independent units, redundancy, and overlapping responsibility rule the day and the structure does little or nothing to position all of the intelligence units, hierarchically or laterally, to suggest a coherent, logical, integrated effort.

Second, the absence of solid lines and the prevalence of dashed or "dotted" lines reveal that formal authority and accountability are weak or nonexistent. Across intelligence agencies or organizations, there is informal influence and "tasking authority," which is not formal authority. The only formal authority is seen within agencies or organizations. No one, not even the Director of National Intelligence, has formal control over the myriad units shown in Figure 3.2.

Third, having just mentioned the Director of National Intelligence, a related problem can be identified. Given the bureaucracy and ineffectiveness of the intelligence community and the recommendations of the 9/11 Commission and others, people clearly desired a cure for intelligence ills. The appointment of a Director of National Intelligence, under the Intelligence Reform and Terrorism Prevention Act of 2004, however, doesn't provide the wanted cure. In fact, it only adds additional bureaucracy to the organizational mess shown in Figure 3.2. The new director has no authority to match his presumed responsibility (which to many observers is still unclear). He supposedly is in charge of everything related to intelligence, but his lack of authority indicates he's in charge of nothing. His attempts at leadership will likely be rejected by heads of the other intelligence agencies and actually lead to additional, intense inter-agency wrangling. The response to perceived problems in the intelligence community by the White House and Congress was one that added a figurehead, additional bureaucracy, and unclear authority and responsibility to an already unclear and sprawling bureaucracy, hardly a sound management action.

The 2004 act also created a National Counterterrorism Center (NCTC), despite the existence of a counterterrorism capability in the CIA, adding to a duplication of resources. The NCTC added to the hierarchy in the intelligence community and created more bureaucracy, according to some critics. The center can only work if it can effectively integrate data from the disparate computer systems of the other intelligence agencies, but so far it has not been successful in doing this. In addition to added bureaucracy, then, the NCTC introduced new problems, new technology needs, and kinks in its operations that negatively affect its performance capabilities.

Fourth, formal mechanisms for coordination, integration, or knowledge transfer across intelligence organizations are virtually nonexistent. Informal mechanisms surely must exist, but Figure 3.2 shows nothing to suggest that the intelligence community is a well-oiled, integrated machine that easily transmits vital information to the units or people most qualified to deal with it. On the contrary, the organization chart suggests a bunch of independent agencies with separate budgets and charters that are not at all concerned with coordinated effort, a suggestion often validated in the media and within the halls of Congress.

The organization of the intelligence community, then, only accentuates the concerns noted upon seeing the large number of agencies responsible for intelligence gathering and security in America, Inc. One can easily conclude that:

> *The structure of the intelligence community is a nightmare of inefficiency and ineffectiveness. Too many agencies "work alone together." Coordination or integration is weak or nonexistent. Authority and clear accountability are lacking in a structure with redundant, overlapping responsibility. The complexity and size of the intelligence community suggest management problems and an inability to deal with a complex, changing, and increasingly hostile global environment.*

This is not a pretty picture I'm painting. Terrorist organizations are most certainly planning incursions against the U.S. on a continuing basis. Foreign governments are shopping in a nuclear arms supermarket. Countries are planning military invasions or other methods of regime control. Sound planning and intelligence gathering are vital to U.S. security, but Figure 3.2 and implications of the discussion thus far suggest that this security is by no means assured. America, Inc.'s intelligence system is sorely lacking compared to those in large, global corporations, and this deficiency spells potential disaster. Large size, an unwieldy number of intelligence agencies, unclear authority, responsibility, and accountability, and poor coordination suggest an intelligence community beset with so many problems that it can't possibly do the job that's required, regardless of how much is being spent.

There are even more problems, however. Besides the size, complexity, cost, and redundancy of agencies in the intelligence community and the lack of coordination across them, there are additional major problems among the intelligence organizations shown in Figure 3.2 that make the situation even less effective and more prone to major mistakes.

Figure 3.2
The Intelligence Community

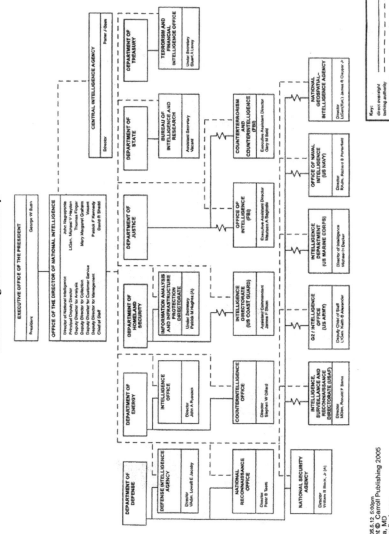

version 2005.5.12 5:00pm
Copyright © Carroll Publishing 2005
Bethesda, MD
www.carrollpub.com
info@carrollpub.com
(301) 263-9800

Lack of timely and valid information. The intelligence community needs better, more timely information. "America needs more spies," as one publication put it.[9] A lack of penetration into terrorist organizations has hurt, and presently is hurting, intelligence efforts. The first critical task or sine qua non in any system of planning and intelligence gathering is the collection of timely and useful information. Without this basic step, all that follows is tainted or useless.

Using the information obtained. Even when intelligence agencies receive good information, they simply don't have sufficient skilled operatives who are capable of analyzing the data, drawing inferences, and passing their conclusions on for further action, according to some analysts.[10] They don't have the people who are skilled in "connecting the dots" and drawing valid inferences. Prior to the 9/11 attacks, for example, U.S. intelligence agencies didn't have a single competent speaker of Pushto (the language of the Taliban) in active service.[11] Having good information is not sufficient if no one can understand and use it.

Relatedly, information is often collected and never passed on to the right people. I myself have seen this problem in corporate and government organizations: data are collected and "stored" because the people who can interpret and act on them simply aren't known. Or there is little incentive to share important information. Knowledge sharing problems exist and are even magnified in the intelligence community, which clearly detracts from performance.

Power and dependency. Knowledge sharing depends heavily on a culture that values cooperation and performance against superordinate goals. An excessively competitive culture fosters the hoarding of information, not the sharing of data for the common good. As a former CIA official once put it: "you don't go to work everyday in the intelligence community with the idea, 'what can I share.' It's 'what can I protect.'"[12]

This suggests the existence of power differences and power struggles. In an organizational structure like that in Figure 3.2, with unclear authority, responsibility, and accountability, power differences, politicking, and attempts at influence reign. Power is the obverse or reverse of dependency.[13] Making others dependent on one increases one's power or influence. Developing critical data that others don't have but desperately need, and then doling out the important information in bits and pieces, but at a high price and with the right "strings" attached, maintains one's power. Or holding on to the information, not sharing it, and using it oneself fosters one's standing and bolsters one's power or influence, which can get in the way of knowledge sharing and overall performance of the entire intelligence community.

Additional Intra-Organizational Problems

Things actually get even worse. A recent exhaustive and well-designed study of the decision processes and analytic culture within the U.S. intelligence community documents additional management and organizational problems with potentially negative consequences.[14] Some of the findings are particularly striking and frightening.

First, the study shows that analysts who collate and summarize information and pass it on to superiors are not rewarded for the *quality* of their work, but for the *quantity* of work. Emphasis is on volume, writing for the "daily briefs," not coming up with fewer, but particularly insightful, intelligence reports. Promotion and advancement are based on production, not getting things right.

Second, the scientific method is ignored and emphasis is on "tradecraft," the "art" of intelligence gathering and analysis. Tradecraft suggests a "mysterious process" learned only through indoctrination and elaborate rituals. Tradecraft implies, "that the methods and techniques of analysis are informal, idiosyncratic, unverifiable, and perhaps even unexplainable."[15] It implies that there is no formal system for measuring the validity or reliability of the analytic methods commonly being used and relied upon. Emphasis, then, is not on scientific inquiry, hypothesis testing, and objective refutation or confirmation of the hypotheses. Rather, analysis is subjective, focusing on the analyst's art and idiosyncratic tradecraft, not an objective approach to planning and intelligence gathering and testing.

Third, and perhaps most striking of all, the study reports that there is a search for the *acceptable* in intelligence work, not for identification and support of less popular, divergent opinions. An emphasis on a consistent "corporate judgment" fosters a tendency toward groupthink and a selective bias for the official company position. Indeed, the corporate judgment becomes the accepted norm and changing it is highly unlikely.

> "Once any intelligence agency has given its official opinion to policymakers, there exists a taboo about reversing or significantly changing the official or corporate position to avoid the loss of status, trust, or respect."[16]

This means that official positions become sacred, and analysts with divergent ideas and opinions are silenced or shunned. Rejection or alterations of official positions run the risk of analysts' losing influence and standing. Differences in thought and creativity are driven out of the organization. A management culture develops that threatens deviants with the loss of position, influence, and prestige.

A related conclusion is that it is extremely difficult for an intelligence agency to change its official position, once it has made one known. Such flip-flopping would be perceived as incompetence or poor judgment and performance, a perception that threatens a loss of status, funding, and access to important policymakers.[17] *It's better to be decisive and stick to one's story, even if it's wrong!*

Such a management approach and organizational climate clearly suggest a detrimental effect on the capabilities of intelligence agencies and their ability to get work done effectively. Add these issues to those previously discussed and the inescapable conclusion is that the intelligence community currently is not an asset, but a liability in a complex and increasingly hostile world. It is an intelligence community *not* marked by the use of valid data, open mindedness and objectivity in the data collection process, or clear responsibility and accountability. Its culture works against effective cooperation, intelligence sharing, and discovery of the real facts. This is dangerously ineffective, and steps must be taken before the situation gets worse.

A NEEDED REORGANIZATION

The problems of the intelligence community demand a total rethinking and reorganization. Nothing less will suffice.

Since World War II, there have been scores of studies, commissions, blue-ribbon panels, etc. on needed changes and reforms in the intelligence community. Recommendations have focused on a host of areas, including technology, data analysis, culture, organization, and even management. But what's changed as a result of this work? Very little, especially in the area of organization and management. The normal output of the studies includes a huge number of recommended activities, with nary an impact on observable outcomes, real results, or changes in agency behavior. Complex, busy charts and presentations showing countless activities and interactions add confusion rather than clarity, and critical underlying issues of authority and accountability are never confronted adequately. The problems of the intelligence community certainly demand much more than this.

Adding more bureaucracy to the existing bureaucratic quagmire will not help. Creating figureheads or czars to make people feel safer or better is not an effective option if the czars have no authority and limited influence over independent agencies. Building in more impotence and avoiding clear authority, responsibility, and accountability are foolish and dangerous courses of action. It's time to commit to a real change in management and organizational structure. It's time to eschew silly cosmetic and purely politically-based restructuring games, commit to a major fix, and focus finally on:

1. A New, Logical Organizational Structure

2. Clear Authority, Responsibility, and Accountability at the Agency/Top Management level

3. Effective Coordination/Integration Mechanisms, and

4. Building a New Intelligence Culture

A New Organizational Structure

Drastic changes in structure are needed, as there simply are too many agencies or organizations currently responsible for intelligence activities. A new structure should be created using a logical process that focuses on strategic and operating issues, including measures of efficiency and effectiveness, *not* purely political issues. Attention should also be directed to the elimination of unnecessary or redundant agencies, despite their political standing or traditional status in the intelligence community.

In the corporation, organizational structure plays a central role in the implementation of strategy. Strategy fuels the choice of structure which, in turn, enables management to focus on and achieve key strategic and operating outcomes. The creation or modification of structure can be envisioned as a *decision process that focuses, step by step, on key strategic and operating factors in the choice of organizational design units or elements.*[18]

Large global corporations, for example, are designed around critical strategic thrusts or areas needing attention, e.g. by customer (Consumer Products Group and Government Products Group), product (P.C. Division, Mainframe Division, Cadillac Division), or geography (North American Division, Asian Division, Western European Division). These divisions, groups, or structural subsets represent a way to reduce large problems to smaller, more manageable pieces. They also allow managers to focus, strategically and operationally, on the needs or requirements of important customers, products, or geographical areas. Emphasis clearly is on effectiveness, or "doing the right things" in such a structure,[19] as the placement of structural boundaries around a critical focus like a product line ensures that sufficient attention and resources are devoted to it. A division or organizational unit focusing on the needs of a product line globally virtually guarantees an adequate concern with the performance of the line against competitors worldwide. There are few diversions; managers and others can devote time and attention to product-line-related tasks.

Three intelligence units. Consider now a proposed organizational structure for the intelligence community (Figure 3.3). In this structure, reporting to the President of the U.S. through a Director of Intelligence Services are the Heads of three new intelligence groups or units: *Foreign Intelligence, Domestic Intelligence, and Military Intelligence.*

Strategically and operationally, these groups and their foci make sense; they capture the essence of the content of major U.S. intelligence activities. The three structural units combine all of the existing agencies into parsimonious groups that look at intelligence activities in a practical, logical, and empirically-justified way. They focus on the right strategic areas and integrate the foci and activities of a large number of agencies into three logical thrusts.

As in the design of the large global corporation, the structure of Figure 3.3 shows an important emphasis on effectiveness—focusing on the right things. Critical strategic and operating groups logically center on foreign, domestic, and military intelligence requirements and efforts in the same way the global corporation centers attention on customers, products, or geographical regions. The division of resources and labor in Figure 3.3 focuses on critical tasks or areas of concern, in two cases on geography and special intelligence needs (foreign and domestic intelligence), and in one case on major military units and their needs, the assumption being that each of the three intelligence groups is important and deserves dedicated management attention. Consistent with an emphasis on effectiveness, the focus of the new structure is immediately on just three agencies and three heads, not the 15-64 separate independent units currently in the intelligence community, and this clearly reduces size and complexity at the highest levels. The dedication of people, money, and other resources, coupled with the focus and "market" orientation associated with each of the dedicated intelligence groups, aids and abets an emphasis on effective performance.

The Head of each new group obviously is critical and powerful. In the area of Foreign Intelligence, for example, the Head has *authority* and *budgetary control* over all agencies in this area. He is no figurehead, but is truly a manager and czar of sorts, in charge of all foreign intelligence operations and responsible indirectly to the U.S. President and directly to the Director of National Intelligence. This is an important and necessary change and a major departure from the hodgepodge of the current structure of the intelligence community and its lack of clear authority and accountability. This change alone can do much to transform a loosely-coupled, ineffective system into a more robust decision-making entity.

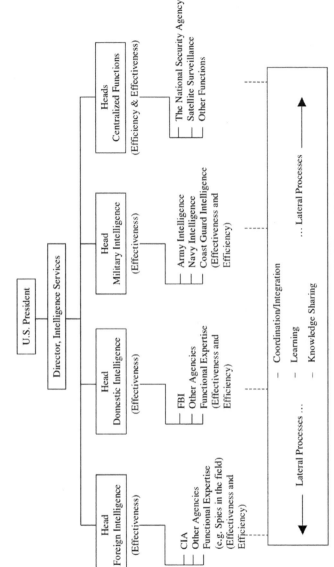

Figure 3.3
Proposed Organizational Structure:
The Intelligence Community

The Head's job can be made more feasible by reducing his or her span of control and eliminating or combining some of the agencies or organizations currently responsible for foreign intelligence. Figure 3.3 names only the CIA under Foreign Intelligence for illustrative purposes. Careful analysis of tasks and redundancies would determine what additional agencies should remain or be melded together under the umbrella of Foreign Intelligence, keeping in mind that fewer is better than too many, but that more than one is needed to provide the multiple sources of data needed for effective planning and intelligence.

So, too, the Head of Military Intelligence oversees and makes decisions with the Director of Intelligence Services about the different military branches' intelligence units and efforts. Probably the most critical issue here deals with redundancy or duplication of effort. Does each branch of the military service (Army, Navy, Air Force, and Coast Guard) need its own intelligence capability? Can some resources or capabilities be combined to reduce redundancy and costs, without sacrificing the intelligence needed for military purposes? Can the Military Intelligence group be designed to ensure that the right information is collected to service all branches of the military while, simultaneously, increasing efficiency with less duplication of resources? Each branch's having its own intelligence capability most certainly is strongly based in tradition, but the possibility of reorganization and elimination of unnecessary duplication of effort still must be considered carefully. *Less duplication always means lower costs, but it doesn't have to denote lowered intelligence effectiveness.*

The same analysis can be done under Domestic Intelligence, where the Head is in charge of the FBI and some small number of combined agencies. Again, the emphasis is on culling the large number of agencies involved in domestic intelligence to reduce span of control and eliminate excessive redundancy of resources and efforts, while simultaneously fostering effective performance. Mention of the FBI, however, raises a side debate and perhaps another organizational design consideration.

A Debate: Intelligence vs. Law Enforcement

Figure 3.3 shows three primary intelligence units: Foreign, Domestic, and Military. Domestic intelligence includes the FBI, but some have argued that the FBI is *not* an intelligence agency but, rather, a law enforcement agency.[20] Others disagree, arguing that the FBI is indeed a major force in intelligence operations and should remain a key player in the intelligence community.[21] Only the experts in this area can debate the merits of issues such as these but, for present purposes, it must be stressed that the outcome of such a debate would necessarily affect organizational design decisions. Let's pursue this point to show how structure would follow function, task, or strategy in the intelligence community, based on the assumed role of the FBI.

As mentioned, some analysts suggest that the FBI might lack the skills, incentives, capabilities, culture, and training programs to produce a crack intelligence organization, or even the patience to be one. Prevention of terrorist activity requires a slow, thorough process of collecting data and drawing inferences over time. It demands following up on a multitude of weak, ambiguous clues and somehow "connecting the dots" to flesh out a picture of possible terrorist activity. In contrast, law enforcement focuses on getting convictions and, often, doing so quickly. Collecting evidence, interviewing witnesses, etc. soon after a crime or a bust is necessary before the trail goes cold, so emphasis is on speed and tightly focused investigations.

The FBI, according to the latter position, is a law-enforcement machine. This is why, the argument goes, the training of agents focuses on areas not directly applicable to intelligence mustering and analysis but on skills or activities more in line with an enforcement role, e.g. firearms training, self-defense, and arrest protocols. Including it under Domestic Intelligence may be a suboptimal organizational design decision. It might be better to differentiate the FBI from the intelligence side of the business and let it focus on its core competence—law enforcement. Prevention is an *ex ante*, anticipatory activity, whereas enforcement is *ex post,* an activity after the fact that requires different skills and capabilities. The Domestic Intelligence unit shouldn't be hampered or constrained by law enforcement or police matters and, without these constraints, can better focus on intelligence, along the lines of Britain's MI5 and other countries' domestic units.

On the other hand, the contrasting point of view is that the FBI is truly an important intelligence provider as well as a law enforcement agency, and the two are inextricably related. Certainly, the argument goes, part of this organization has been involved over the years with discussions and identification of terrorist threats. There surely are analysts within the FBI trained in intelligence gathering, data analysis, and connecting the dots logically to thwart terrorism, and these intelligence capabilities must not be discarded. They can logically be retained and used to achieve intelligence-related goals and feed information to the law enforcement side of the organization. If, then, the FBI is truly an important intelligence provider, it should remain under the Domestic Intelligence group shown in Figure 3.3. A structural separation of the FBI from Domestic Intelligence or a structural differentiation of intelligence and law-enforcement activities would make little sense.

Whatever the outcome of such a debate about the role of the FBI, *it's important to understand that the debate is healthy and indeed must occur* This is precisely the kind of analysis needed in an overhaul of the intelligence community to increase its effectiveness and eliminate the sorry state of affairs that currently exists. Organizational structure must follow strategic or operational purpose and a thorough analysis must logically precede a choice of structure and the development of requisite skills and capabilities that are needed to achieve the purpose.

There, of course, are other options for the restructuring of the intelligence community besides the three-pronged one discussed here. The critical issue to understand presently is that the current situation of many competing, independent, unfocused agencies within the intelligence community is too complex, unwieldy, and dysfunctional, and drastic, not cosmetic, change is needed. *Reorganization with an emphasis on structure, capabilities, authority, and accountability must occur to make the intelligence process more efficient and effective.* This is the primary message here and it cannot be avoided much longer.

Let's continue the discussion of the structure of the intelligence community, building on Figure 3.3, and consider the role of centralized units that support the three intelligence groups.

Centralized functions. Figure 3.3 shows concern with efficient performance and expertise, as well as effective performance. Reporting to the Intelligence Director are the heads of various centralized functions or units, e.g. Satellite Surveillance and the National Security Agency (NSA). The NSA exists presently and is one of the largest components of the intelligence community. The other example of a possible centralized function—satellite surveillance—has been made up by me to explain the contributions of a centralized organizational structure to performance and how to choose between centralized and decentralized capabilities.

The emphasis now, looking at the centralized units, is partly on efficiency, as well as an effective performance. The logic is one of developing and sharing expertise and avoidance of costly, redundant resources and processes. If one could argue, for example, that satellite surveillance is basically the same process or function and relies on the same technology or methods for both Foreign and Military Intelligence, duplication of this capability in each area would be costly and unnecessary. Developing a centralized "critical mass" of experts and sophisticated surveillance capabilities would enhance performance, while also offering the prospects of knowledge sharing and increased efficiency while servicing the two intelligence heads. If, on the other hand, a Head of one of the two new intelligence groups could show why a dedicated surveillance resource is absolutely necessary to his organization, then the capability would remain decentralized, housed in both the Foreign and Military Intelligence groups.

The point is that there must be adequate discussion and justification for the location and use of scarce resources. Issues related to centralization vs. decentralization must be debated as they usually are in the large corporation, to ensure both efficient and effective performance. The Heads of the three intelligence units will naturally demand that all resources for decision making be under their control, but this is not always the optimal case for efficiency. Similarly, centralization of resources always reduces the costly duplication of resources, but, again, it's not always the optimal case for effective performance. The costs and benefits of alternative structures must be analyzed and debated.

The National Security Agency provides a good example of the value of a centralized agency or function.[22] The NSA, long labeled the "No Such Agency" by Washington insiders because of the secrecy surrounding it, had come into the limelight in 2006 because of its domestic wiretapping and the raging arguments about the President's right to conduct secret surveillance of Americans without getting permission from the Foreign Intelligence Surveillance Court. (I'll not touch upon whether the wiretapping is or is not in violation of federal law. I'll stick to a managerial and organizational argument, consistent with the book's main thrust). The NSA is the chief cryptographic (code making and breaking) and signals intelligence agency in the U.S. intelligence community. Its mission is to collect foreign communications and analyze them for the entire intelligence community. It also provides secure communications capabilities for the military and officials in the U.S. government. It is a huge organization, supposedly employing 35,000 or so workers, and is one of the largest units in the intelligence community.

The mission and performance goals of the NSA make it a natural candidate for a centralized function reporting to the Director of Intelligence Services, shown in Figure 3.3. It serves the entire intelligence community. It has valuable expertise and a critical mass of qualified people capable of a clear focus on cryptography, analysis of messages, and safe communications. It should perform as a centralized "corporate center," core competence group, or functional resource servicing multiple organizations, as then both efficiency and effective performance are reasonable goals. The NSA could have people assigned to the three intelligence units, or it could move people across the units in an attempt to share knowledge and avoid "reinventing the wheel" over and over again.

Allowing each of the three intelligence areas to develop its own NSA-type capabilities would be duplicative and costly, and probably injurious to performance. Each couldn't develop the needed expertise or critical mass to perform effectively, despite the cries and pleas of the intelligence heads to control all of their own resources. Centralization makes sense because of the "relatedness" of cryptographic and communication work, skills, and technologies across the three main intelligence units. Tasks or technologies that are the same or highly similar across separate structural units are usually candidates for centralization.

<u>Structure within intelligence units</u>. A similar structural logic can be applied *within* each of the three intelligence groups to determine whether functions service all of the agencies operating under each structural group, or whether functions or capabilities exist across agencies within the three groups.

Under Foreign Intelligence in Figure 3.3, for example, decentralized, covert operations ("spies in the field") must be employed by the CIA and other agencies. Moles work to penetrate terrorist organizations all over the globe. The task of these players is to generate useful and timely data from the field so that the various agencies know what's going on and can focus on doing the right things. It would have to be determined whether the CIA and all of the other agencies under Foreign Intelligence would have their own dedicated spies, or whether all agencies would employ the same spy resources and their collected information. One set of resources for all agencies under Foreign Intelligence would denote centralization *within* this unit and a quest for efficiency and commonly-used expertise to ensure sound performance. Each agency in the Foreign Intelligence unit having its own spies would denote decentralization and each agency's quest for its *own special needs* and effective performance. Again, discussion would occur among the Director of Intelligence Services, the Head of Foreign Intelligence, and the agencies within this intelligence unit to determine the best allocation and use of scarce, valuable resources.

The emphasis on effectiveness and efficiency in organizational structure within the three main units is certainly consistent with those same thrusts in the large global corporation. For a particular product line worldwide, for example, a corporation may emphasize efficiency or a low-cost strategy to allow the product line to be competitive and profitable. Structure would focus on a functional organization or process specialization (centralization) to achieve high volume, standardization, repetition, and economies of scale for the particular product line. This is the same emphasis just discussed when describing the quest for efficiency without sacrificing effective performance within the main intelligence agencies in Figure 3.3. The three main intelligence units guarantee a needed "market" focus and an emphasis on effective performance. Centralization across or within the three major units indicates a concern with efficiency, the sharing of knowledge, and the repetition needed for development of strong expertise. Both effectiveness and efficiency are important and both must be taken into account when designing organizations, including those in the intelligence community.

The structure I've proposed is far from perfect, nor is it the only option possible. The intention presently is *not* to force or argue for only one solution, but *to signal the fact that drastic changes are needed in the structure of the intelligence community. The present structure is unmanageable and can only continue to generate intelligence errors and dangerous outcomes. It's time for major changes.*

Clear Authority, Responsibility, and Accountability

A related benefit of the structure in Figure 3.3 is an improved focus on clear authority, responsibility, and accountability. With fewer Heads, their duties and responsibilities can be spelled out with the Director of Intelligence Services. The authority of the top person in each of the intelligence groups over the agencies below him can be formalized and clarified so as to define accountability for "what" and "when" in a clear and succinct fashion. Similarly, the Head can help define the responsibilities of those who report to him or her. Metrics can also be developed for the key personnel in the centralized functions to measure their contributions to the different intelligence areas. In the world of corporate management, clarification of authority, responsibility, and performance requirements is a vital aspect of organizational structure, and the same holds true for the U.S. intelligence community.

Figure 3.3 also shows a Director of Intelligence Services with real authority and clout. This position reports directly to the president. It has solid-line authority over the Heads of the three intelligence groups and the centralized functions. This person has budgetary control and the Heads of the three intelligence units must work closely with him to coordinate activities and share important centralized expertise. This is a *real* Director of Intelligence, not a figurehead, speaking puppet, or additional bureaucratic overlay.

Turf battles and related problems of responsibility and authority are bound to arise in the early stages of consideration or implementation of any new structure, including the one shown in Figure 3.3. Opinions as to why changes won't work in political organizations that are somehow "different" and immune to sound organizational analysis and management scrutiny certainly will proliferate and be abundant, but the political and turf issues are weak and divisive and represent the very issues that have created the existing mess in the intelligence community, so they must be confronted. Methods of clarifying roles and responsibilities and eliminating conflicts between or among line and staff managers in the different intelligence groups or functional areas of Figure 3.3 can be fruitfully employed, and processes can be used to confront disagreement and arrive at consensus about key areas of accountability and needed authority.[23] These tasks won't be easy, given inertia and the usual resistance to structural and other change, but they are necessary to improve the performance of the U.S. intelligence community. The leadership of America, Inc. must finally bite the bullet and confront the issue of real reorganization.

Coordination, Integration, and Knowledge Sharing

In the post 9/11 world, analysis of intelligence errors has constantly mentioned the poor coordination across intelligence agencies. The work of the Director of Intelligence Services and the centralized functions just discussed does much to ensure discussion and coordination *laterally*, across intelligence groups or areas. This is not sufficient, however, given the complexity and uncertainty of intelligence work.

Figure 3.3 suggests the need for *additional lateral coordination and knowledge sharing across intelligence groups*, beyond that attained through the sharing of functional expertise. Specifically, additional lateral coordination and knowledge sharing can be accomplished by various means, including formal structure, intergroup task forces, and other ad-hoc methods in the intelligence community that focus on the interdependencies across groups or agencies and how to handle them.

Consider the case of high interdependence—when different units across the intelligence groups and the centralized functions absolutely must interact and work together simultaneously to solve a problem, e.g. a hypothetical code-breaking problem that cuts across and affects each of the three main intelligence units. All units in this case must participate in problem solution, as no one unit alone is sufficient to get the job done. There is high interdependence and a strong need for cooperation to accomplish a complex task.

In these cases, an ad-hoc or project team with members from the different intelligence units and the NSA can be charged with the responsibility of problem solving, lateral coordination, and knowledge sharing. Teamwork is vital to solving a problem that each unit or function cannot solve alone. All bear the responsibility and all must be involved at once. A centralized function or area of competence (the NSA) would work with members of the three intelligence units to tailor and share critical information dealing with the hypothetical code-breaking problem. Performance metrics also would be developed for the joint task and all members would be accountable for the team's decisions and actions since all are responsible and necessary for successful task completion. Teams can work, if the critical aspects of responsibility, clarity of goals or performance metrics, and incentives to cooperate are handled appropriately.

Additional modifications of the operating structure and routines within the organizational design of Figure 3.3 can be implemented to improve coordination or integration and knowledge sharing. For example, a matrix-type structure can be employed to share expertise and coordinate activities laterally (Figure 3.4). In this organization, analysts from the NSA would be co-located, reporting both to superiors in the NSA, their home organization, and to personnel within the intelligence groups responsible for cryptographic code-breaking and other analyses of the content of foreign communications. These reporting relationships can be "solid" or "dotted" line, but they represent dual responsibility and multiple lines of communication. The co-located NSA expert is responsible for knowledge sharing and integration between the NSA and the intelligence units in the "matrix diamond" shown in Figure 3.4. The Director of Intelligence Services or one of his subordinates would be responsible for tie-breaking in the case of conflicts or disagreements that occur during these lateral coordination activities. [24]

Figure 3.4

A Matrix Organization: The NSA and the Three Intelligence Units

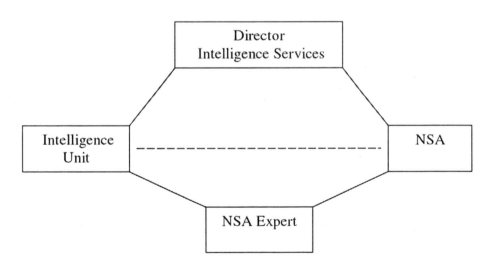

The matrix structure and other approaches to lateral coordination and knowledge sharing can work effectively, if leaders in the intelligence community focus more on joint decision making and problem solving and less on turf battles and hiding important information from each other. Emphasis must be on lateral coordination, communication, and information sharing, not hoarding or protecting vital data, and on "connecting the dots" to achieve important intelligence-related outcomes. The necessary focus is on learning and sharing the knowledge derived from it. Much like the large, global consulting firm, methods must be developed to share the knowledge created in one part of the intelligence community with people in other parts of the organization. The consulting firm is routinely involved in knowledge creation and knowledge sharing, with an eye on using the shared knowledge to service clients and increase revenues. It doesn't want to have different people in different parts of its worldwide structure constantly rediscovering the wheel; new information and processes representing a breakthrough anywhere must be disseminated throughout the organization so others can learn the new ideas and methods as quickly and effectively as possible. So, too, in the intelligence community where processes of information gathering by military intelligence may be useful to domestic or foreign intelligence efforts as well, and, thus, should be shared and coordinated as efficiently as possible.

Coordination, integration, and knowledge sharing via the methods just discussed can occur at any level of the intelligence community. The important issue is *to recognize the need for lateral communication and commit to setting up the methods to achieve it.* Corporations cannot survive with only vertical "silos" and little or no lateral coordination. America, Inc.'s intelligence community is no exception to this rule.

Building a New Intelligence Culture

Managing culture is important to strategy execution and organizational performance. As suggested above, the culture of the intelligence community is affected by "taboos," norms, goals, and behaviors that are actually detrimental to intelligence efforts. How, then, does one change culture? How does one eliminate cultural problems due to mismanagement and improve the climate and performance of the intelligence community?

One might start logically by examining closely the culture and operations of a successful intelligence agency. On Iraq and illicit weapons, for example, only one agency was close to being right—the Bureau of Intelligence and Research in the State Department.[25] It's a *small* agency, so it's probably not mired in bureaucracy and red tape that slow things down. Its approach is purely *analytical*, so it probably adheres closely to the *scientific method* discussed above. Its analysts tend to be *experienced, older*, (most in their 40's and 50's), and they tend to come from *academic backgrounds*, which likely adds to their *expertise, independence*, and ability to *challenge* accepted analyses, taboos, or the *corporate* point of view. Their emphasis at work is on *intense analysis* and *quality* of work, not the quantity and daily quotas usually imposed on intelligence analysts. They clearly are *qualified* and know how to collect data and then "*connect the dots*" effectively.

Virtually all of the emphasized characteristics go contrary to the taboos, processes, and performance constraints, noted above, that negatively affect the culture of the intelligence community and its ability to get the job done. Studying a successful agency doesn't guarantee success elsewhere, but it certainly is a good start. Even if intense analysis of an agency's success shows that its performance was due to luck, probability, or some statistical or other aberration, the comparative effort would not have been wasted. Learning would occur, and this is important in planning and intelligence efforts. Internal analysis and benchmarking can pay big dividends, even in the intelligence community.

Other steps to improve the management of culture have already been suggested. Changing structure, for example, including redefining roles, responsibilities, and integration mechanisms, can effect culture change. *Not only does culture affect behavior, but behavior also affects culture.*[26] Changing structure, then, can bring about culture change. Defining jobs and accountabilities clearly and then reinforcing desired behaviors and outcomes can actually create a performance-related climate and a culture of pride emanating from effective intelligence-related performance. Similarly, changing span of control along with a redefinition of responsibilities can change behavior, and behavioral change over time will lead to culture change.

Changing people, too, can affect culture change. Putting leaders in charge of the three new intelligence groups or units of Figure 3.3 who demand excellence and who hold subordinates accountable against clear, measurable performance metrics can do a great deal to create a desirable and productive management and organizational climate. Giving the heads formal authority supports the climate of accountability further and ensures that things get done. Clear responsibility and authority also can reduce politics and "influence games," although they can never be eliminated fully.

Using the right incentives is at the core of effective culture change. Finding the right people, defining their jobs and responsibilities clearly, and then providing strong incentives to perform against agreed-upon goals will certainly coalesce to affect culture positively and create a performance-based management climate.

To effectively change culture in the intelligence community, then, it is important *not* to focus on it directly, but to affect it indirectly and powerfully by focusing on:

1. *Changing structure*, including roles, responsibilities, authority, and spans of control;

2. *Changing people*, adding managers or leaders who don't eschew accountability, who relish good performance, and who have a high-achievement orientation; and

3. *Changing incentives and controls* to reward the right things and hold people accountable for their performance.

By changing structure, people, incentives, and controls, managers can slowly but surely eliminate dysfunctional taboos and norms and positively create a culture within the intelligence community to deal with the complexity and uncertainty that characterizes the global environment facing America, Inc. It's time to bite the bullet and tackle these important tasks.

A Quest for Intelligent Design

Rome wasn't designed and built in a day, nor will critical changes occur overnight and effortlessly in the intelligence community. The present system and methods of intelligence gathering and information dissemination, however, are severely flawed and change must soon begin. The structure, processes, and organizational culture of the existing intelligence community outlined in this chapter suggest a strong case of "unintelligent design" or an "intelligence deficit disorder" that needs a strong and focused corrective response by leaders in the White House and Congress. Nothing less than a total reconsideration and reorganization of the country's intelligence capabilities will suffice.

It's time for action and leadership in this important area. It's time to confront the normal, lame excuses and the major obstacles to effective planning and do what's right to restore the luster and effectiveness of U.S. intelligence activities. *There are too many dedicated and qualified people in the intelligence service who are hampered by a defective organizational design and mismanagement at the highest levels of the intelligence community. It's time to help them do their work by instituting changes such as those suggested in this chapter.*

CONCLUSIONS

The conclusions derived from this analysis are strong and critical to the successful redesign and redeployment of the intelligence community in America, Inc. Failure to act soon on these issues will continue to put the U.S. in a dangerous position in a hostile global environment.

First, the U.S. intelligence community is a management and organizational mess, marked by too many units, unclear responsibility and accountability, little formal authority, and poor coordination or integration across intelligence agencies.

Second, the poor—read ineffective and inefficient—structure and management capabilities are dangerous to U.S. security. More than money and wasted or misused expertise is the issue here. At stake is the future safely of the U.S. in a world growing extremely hostile to it.

Third, a complete reorganization of the intelligence community is in order ..., finally. The days of unclear accountability, excessively redundant responsibilities, endless bureaucracy, and purely political approaches to intelligence gathering and information use must finally end. Continuation of the "same old, same old" can only lead to disaster.

Fourth, the culture of the intelligence community must be revitalized and changed. The current culture is dysfunctional and only exacerbates the many management- and organization-related problems identified.

The present chapter presents one possible reorganization. It's far from perfect and it's not the only possible solution, but something is needed to move the intelligence community away from its present dysfunctional inertial state to a more viable and realistic one. It's time for change, a time for concerted, effective action, and, hopefully, the present chapter can jumpstart the needed conversation.

Endnotes

1. R.M. Gerecht, "Intelligence Deficit Disorder," The Wall Street Journal, May 9, 2006.

2. One of the biggest contributors in this area is Michael Porter's *Competitive Strategy* (New York: Free Press), 1980.

3. Discussions here range from simple human resource issues to in-depth considerations of core capabilities or core competence in organizations. See, for example, C. K. Prahalad and Gary Hamel, "The Core Competence of the Corporation," Harvard Business Review (May-June, 1990), 79-91; P. Selzrick, Leaders in Administration: A Sociological Interpretation (New York: Harper and Row, 1957); and for a good review of resources and capabilities, see Robert Grant, Contemporary Strategy Analysis (Blackwell Publishers, 2002), esp. Chapter 5. For a good analysis of strategy execution, see L. G. Hrebiniak, Making Strategy Work: Leading Effective Execution and Change (Wharton School Publishing), 2005.

4. A good discussion of the role of structure in strategy execution can be found in Making Strategy Work, Ibid, Chapters 4 and 5.

5. See, for example, Jim Collins, Good to Great (Harper Business, 2001); "More Problems for Mitsubishi as Six are Arrested," The Philadelphia Inquirer, June 11, 2004; "Enron's Watkins Describes 'Arrogant' Culture," The Wall Street Journal, February 15, 2002; "When Desperate Firms Merge, Cultures Often Collide," The Wall Street Journal, February 14, 1997; "The Case Against Mergers," Business Week, October 30, 1995; "AMD Says Intel Intimidates Clients," The Wall Street Journal, September 24, 2003; "Ed Zander Faces Go-Slow Culture at Motorola," The Wall Street Journal, December 17, 2003; and L. G. Hrebiniak, Making Strategy Work, op. cit.

6. David Barstow, "Doubts on Source for Key Piece of Data Were Suppressed," The New York Times, April1, 2005.

7. To see the FAS (Federal of American Scientists) Intelligence Resource Program's list of U.S. Intelligence and Security Agencies, go to www.fas.org/irp/official.html

8. Carroll Publishing, Bethesda, MD, 2005; go to www.carrollpub.com or email at info@carrollpub.com

9. "America needs More Spies," The Economist, July 12, 2003, 30-31.

10. "Where Does U.S. Intelligence Go From here—and Were They Really to Blame? Intelligence Digest, September 27, 2001.

11. Ibid.

12. "Panel: U.S. Intel Structure Still Needs Work," Fox News Channel, June 6, 2005; see, too, www.foxnews.com/printer_friendly_story/0,3566,158758, 00.html

13. L. G. Hrebiniak, Making Strategy Work, op. cit., Chapter 9.

14. Rob Johnston, Analytical Culture in the U.S. Intelligence Community (Washington, D.C.: Center for the Study of Intelligence, The CIA), 2005.

15. Rob Johnston, Analytical Culture, op. cit., p. 18.

16. Ibid., p.23

17. Ibid., p.23

18. L. G. Hrebiniak, Making Strategy Work, op. cit.

19. Many authors have discussed "doing the right things" and "doing things right" when explaining effectiveness and efficiency, respectively, but I believe that one of the first was Chester Barnard in The Functions of the Executive (Harvard University Press, 1938).

20. Richard Posner, Uncertain Shield: The U.S. Intelligence System in the Throes of Reform (Rowman and Littlefield, 2006; see too, "Time to Rethink the FBI," The Wall Street Journal, March 19, 2007.

21. John Mudd, "In Domestic Intelligence, the FBI is Definitely on the Case," The Wall Street Journal, Letters to the Editors, March 21, 2007.

22. The NSA has been garnering a lot of press because of its wiretapping of U.S. citizens, so this discussion reflects many articles I read and even television/ radio broadcasts I saw or listened to intently. One really good source is Tish

Wells compilation of facts, "The NSA: What's Known or Not," <u>The Philadelphia Inquirer</u>, January 26, 2006.

23. For discussions of responsibility and accountability plotting and the process of role negotiation, see L. G. Hrebiniak and W. F. Joyce, <u>Implementing Strategy</u> (Macmillan, 1984); Jay Galbraith, <u>Designing Complex Organizations</u> (Addison-Wesley, 1973); and L. G. Hrebiniak, <u>Making Strategy Work</u>, op. cit.

24. For a good discussion of the matrix structure and the matrix diamond see Jay Galbraith, <u>Designing Complex Organizations</u>, op. cit., and S. Davis and Paul Lawrence, <u>Matrix</u>, Addison-Wesley, 1978.

25. Douglas Jehl, "Tiny Agency's Iraq Analysis is Better than Big Rivals'," <u>The New York Times</u>, July 19, 2004.

26. L. G. Hrebiniak, <u>Making Strategy Work</u>, op. cit.

4

Fiscal And Financial Irresponsibility And a Looming Crisis

America, Inc. is not a profit seeking or a profit-making entity, but it still must concern itself with revenues and costs. It must worry about debt and try to balance spending with revenue streams. It needs to remain solvent to provide services to its "customers," citizens who rely on the government for their security, Medicare, and retirement incomes, and its "investors," the same citizens who fund and invest in government operations with their tax and savings dollars. A sound financial status is also vital to the conduct of international finance so as not to jeopardize the credit rating of the country and the trillions of dollars it borrows from abroad to buy cars and TVs and fight wars. America, Inc. must service its stakeholders and be financially and fiscally responsible just like the large global corporation.

> *The problem is that U.S. leaders are <u>not</u> acting responsibly. They are hurting the U.S. and its citizens. . The fiscal and financial policies of U.S. leaders indicate a refusal to face long-term realities, and their short-term, myopic thinking is setting the stage for very serious financial problems. Fiscal and financial mismanagement is leading the country down a dangerous path toward a certain economic crisis. This irresponsible behavior and mismanagement simply must cease before it's too late.*

No one likes doom-and-gloom reports. A colleague in marketing once told me that bad news doesn't sell. The general public shuns bad news and would rather hide behind the uplifting outcomes of TV reality programs, feel-good stories, and game shows that make millionaires out of ordinary people. It's far easier to muddle through, day-by-day, and avoid the hard, scary facts that might demand remedial action or hardship. Even if my marketing colleague is correct, there still is a festering issue that must be confronted: when the leaders of a country also shun reality, ignore the economic warning signs, and continue muddling through, with no agenda for change and seemingly oblivious to the problems and dangers that are surely becoming more real, then everyone need worry. Sad to say, this is the case when one considers the financial and fiscal health of America, Inc.

Muddling Through: Situation Normal and Getting Worse

There are mixed messages on the U.S. economic front in the last quarter of 2007, but with the negative data definitely gaining momentum.[1] On the positive side, there are still projections for modest growth in the economy. Some economists are still projecting sustained growth in 2008 and beyond of approximately 2.5% or so a year, certainly not a doom-and-gloom projection by any means. Stocks have had a decent run up. Federal Reserve Chairman Ben Bernanke offered upbeat assessments of the economy on a number of occasions, pointing to inflation that is under control and suggesting that low interest rates would be stable for a while, a message received warmly by Wall Street and the global markets. Foreign governments remain somewhat bullish on the U.S., still providing $billions in loans and investments and signaling a continued faith in the U.S. as an economic haven.

Still, there definitely is a dark side to the economic trends. The U.S. trade deficit in 2006 was a record, for the fifth year in a row, and 2007 is looking no better. The bursting of the real estate bubble, driven by huge problems in the subprime segment, wreaked havoc on financial markets and portends continuing troubles in this important sector of the economy and others as well. Global economic volatility and the huge moves by central banks to combat it certainly validate the impact the collapse of the sub-prime market is engendering. Productivity growth is slowing, a troubling development that suggests increasing inflation. Former Federal Reserve Chairman Alan Greenspan mentioned the "R" word (recession) in a speech, saying that there is a good probability of a U.S. recession, a negative prognostication that directly contradicted Bernanke's optimistic assessment of the economy. Greenspan flip-flopped on the value of the Bush administration's tax cuts, an action he previously backed, raising serious questions about fiscal responsibility and political influences on financial decisions. Even Bernanke himself seemed to flip-flop a bit: in January, he had raised the prospects of a "debt spiral" in the U.S. leading to a fiscal crisis, a message that clearly went against the grain of his later positive assessments of the economy. Relatedly, articles have also warned about increasing personal debt, the costs of Social Security, wage levels, a fiscal gap, the price of oil, etc.

So, where do we stand in the fiscal and financial realm? Are U.S. leaders managing the problems and aberrations well and taking care of business effectively, or do we need to heed a warning made by *The Economist* that there is a "danger time for America" ahead, a time to reevaluate carefully the fiscal and financial state of the country? Should we take the title of Greenspan's book literally—*The Age of Turbulence*—or slough it off as a catchy marketing ploy?

> *The fact is we shouldn't be too sanguine or optimistic about America, Inc.'s economic situation. There definitely is trouble brewing. Storm clouds are forming, and they are being seeded heavily but quietly by the financial and fiscal mismanagement of U.S. leaders in the White House and Congress. The lack of strategic thinking and overly strong emphasis on short term fixes by U.S. leaders are blinding us to the dangers that surely lie ahead.*

Is there really the possibility of economic turbulence ahead due to gross mismanagement by U.S. leaders? You judge for yourself. I'll present the data and you decide if they have merit.

DEFICITS AND DEBT: A HEAVY AND DANGEROUS BURDEN

The outstanding public debt of the U.S. in the fall of 2007 is over $9 trillion. This debt has been growing at the rate of around $2 billion per day, or about $200,000 per second. With the increases in spending being projected, this figure could easily soon reach *a quarter of a $milliom of new debt per second*. In mid-March, 2006, the House and Senate voted to increase the statutory ceiling on U.S. debt to $9 trillion, and additional increases are sure to come. Before long the total public debt will be over $30,000 for every man, woman, and child in the U.S.

This is a huge amount of debt and it should make U.S. citizens very nervous, but people are so used to hearing daily about $billions and $trillions that this massive debt never makes a powerful and lasting impression. People are desensitized to the vast amount of money being spent and wasted, so let's put things in perspective with a simple example or two. Consider the following:[2]

- A *million* dollars in tightly bound $1,000 bills would result in a stack *four inches* high;

- A *billion* dollars would produce a stack over *three hundred feet* high; and

- A *trillion* dollars in tightly wrapped $1,000 bills would result in a stack over *sixty miles* high. Sixty-plus miles! (How high would $9 trillion rise?)

Or consider the fact that a person with a million dollars can spend $1,000 a day for about three years, assuming no interest income. A person with a billion dollars can spend $1,000 a day for *three thousand* years. And someone with a $trillion can spend $1,000 a day for *three million* years!

These are significant numbers, but we often lose sight of how huge and important they are. We're so accustomed to hearing about government spending that we virtually forget what these numbers actually mean and how they affect everyone in the US. Let's delve further into spending, deficits, and debt in the U.S. and see how these large debt numbers can actually affect our lives in very significant ways.

Cicero's Advice and Ben Franklin's Warning

"The budget should be balanced; the treasury should be refilled; public debt should be reduced; and the arrogance of public officials should be controlled." (Cicero, 106-43 B.C.).

"He that goes a-borrowing goes a-sorrowing." (Ben Franklin, 1706-1790).

The leaders of America, Inc. have grown deaf to Cicero's and Franklin's admonitions over the years. Like the large global corporation, America, Inc. must worry about revenues, costs, and the accumulation of debt. It must balance revenues and spending and avoid excessive deficits.[1] The history of managing deficits and total debt in the U.S. however, presents a picture that Cicero and Franklin would protest and abhor.

Figure 4.1 shows the actual U.S. national debt from 1940 through 2006, as depicted on the U.S. National Debt Clock.[3] The trend is remarkable and undeniable. Even accounting for inflation—e.g. by converting all of the debt numbers to year 2000 dollars, as the debt clock does—the shape and trends in debt accumulation are clear and significant. Debt is increasing at an alarming rate, especially

---

1. Occasional deficit spending or Keynesian injections in moderate, controlled amounts to inject cash and life into a flat economy are useful, as long as total debt remains manageable. The emphasis here is on excessive deficit and debt creation, which the remaining discussion considers.

in the last two decades, and there is every reason to believe that this trend will continue.

Figure 4.1

National Debt from 1940 to Present

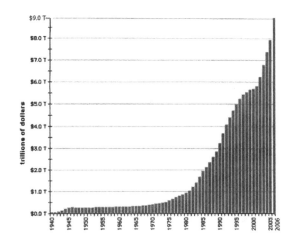

Source: U.S. National Debt Clock
http://www.brillig.com

The U.S. is the largest debtor nation in the world, and the debt has been amassing significantly and quickly. Figure 4.1 shows that the national debt took over six years to rise from $5 trillion to $6 trillion, but less than two years to surpass the $7 trillion mark. On October 18, 2005, the debt rose to over $8 trillion, pushing the enacted legal U.S. debt ceiling closer to maximum, causing Congress to increase the debt-ceiling to $9 trillion in 2006. There is little doubt that actual debt will soon begin to approach the $10 trillion mark.

Figure 4.1 is a stark reminder of how our leaders in Washington are plunging America, Inc. further and further into debilitating debt. It suggests, too, that the simple passage of time exacerbates the debt position. In the last few fiscal years, over $300 billion per year was paid out in interest on the national debt (a stack of $1,000 bills, how many feet high?). Such an interest burden represents a significant percentage of the total U.S. budget receipts, almost 20% of every income tax dollar paid, and this amount is taken off the top before other programs and needs are funded. The interest cost in recent budgets, for example, is greater than the monics set aside for education, housing, transportation, science, and technology combined. It takes ALL of the taxes paid by ALL of the taxpayers west of the Mississippi River just to pay the interest on the National Debt each year.[4] It's like burning hard-earned tax dollars in the fireplace, a huge waste that will continue to increase with the size of the total U.S. debt surpassing $9 trillion. Coupled with inaction or, worse yet, additional ill-planned actions by our leaders, financial management like this can lead us into increasingly dangerous economic territory.

As bad as this debt picture looks, it gets even worse if one considers the total U.S. *fiscal gap*, which measures the present-value difference between the country's projected future expenditures and tax receipts. The fiscal gap has been estimated to be *$63 trillion*, which clearly overshadows the $9 trillion debt figure I've been disparaging.[5] This figure is not the figment of someone's liberal imagination; it comes from a highly respected source—the U.S. Treasury. The figure is derived by looking at projected receipts and expenditures, including outlays for Social Security, Medicare, Medicaid, prescription drug benefits for the elderly, etc., and calculating the present value of these future cash flows. The result is a $63 trillion shortfall, which will drive the country into fiscal and financial ruin. Economic collapse is inevitable unless U.S. leaders assume a long-term view, start managing differently, and take the action steps to address this deplorable and dangerous situation.

Despite the size and growth of our total debt, America's top politicians in the White House and Congress assiduously avoid discussions of it and its negative consequences, soon to be enumerated. They do talk occasionally about *deficits*, but they ignore the total debt and fiscal gap issue. A deficit is the amount of overspending our leaders do in one year. If receipts from taxation do not cover spending at home, the U.S. sells debt to make up the difference. It creates deficits and then pays for them by printing more money. Relatedly, the current account trade deficit refers to the debt the U.S. assumes by buying more foreign goods than it sells to foreigners, thereby resulting in a net negative balance.

All deficits cause problems. They force the U.S. to borrow money to cover the shortcomings in revenue. Domestic deficits increase the issuance of debt to fund government programs. Trade deficits force the sale of IOUs to foreigners, thereby having them finance our government's deficit. The interest on these IOUs increases the deficit for any given year, as well as the accumulation of the total debt shown on Figure 4.1. Deficits are important, as the sum of all yearly deficits is added to the total debt owed by America, Inc.

Politicians in the White House and Congress focus occasionally on funding and reducing deficits, which on the surface seems laudatory. However, they usually move funds around in such a way that the deficits are stabilized or reduced in "smoke and mirror" fashion, by cutting parts of the yearly budget and moving funds from one budget category to another. More significantly, they often move funds under the pretext of deficit reduction to garner more money for themselves and their favorite programs, which actually increases the size of the deficit. Let's look at how top U.S. lawmakers fiddle with the deficit.

"Fiddling with Deficits" While America, Inc. Burns

Politicians often tinker with deficits to make a bad financial situation look better. For example, they raid Social Security funds and use them to reduce the deficit. The Social Security Trust has been running a large surplus for years, and the federal government has treated the surpluses as assets, funds to reduce the yearly deficit.

If, hypothetically, Social Security takes in $150 billion more than it pays out in any given year, the excess supposedly goes into the Trust Fund, the famous "lockbox" or safe haven for accumulated surpluses. In fact, there is no lockbox. The money is used to reduce the deficit. If the projected deficit is, say, $450 billion, that figure is "reduced" to $300 billion by using Social Security surplus to fund government needs. If the deficit had been $100 billion, the politicians could brag about a government *surplus* of $50 billion and pat themselves on the back.

What happens to the $150 billion that never makes it as cash into Trust Fund? The federal government simply deposits IOUs into the fund (bonds to be paid later) and actually counts the IOUs as an *asset*. Amazing. The funds are spent on current federal programs to reduce the deficit, and yet are still included as assets on the fed's balance sheet. The truth is that the deficit is still there, total U.S. debt increases, and the value of the "assets" will actually lead to additional deficits in the future when they are redeemed and paid off. I would call this a case of "creative" accounting, clear and blatant deception, and gross mismanagement, while the politicians call it sound bookkeeping for deficit reduction. They've done this for years, and the total outstanding debt of the U.S. keeps getting larger, which hardly suggests sound management of taxpayer dollars.

The driving force behind this deception is short-term thinking. Managers in large corporations must balance short- and long-term needs and concerns. Care must be taken that short-term pressures (e.g. Wall Street analysts' demands for current earnings) don't lead to decisions that jeopardize or bankrupt a company's strategy and long-term prospects. Some corporate managers violate this need and make bad choices, of course, but for the most part, managers aren't driven solely by short-term decisions. Shareholders and company boards usually play a part in ensuring that a long-term, strategic view isn't ignored by top management.

Short-term decisions in America, Inc. also shouldn't sacrifice long-term prosperity or place huge financial burdens on future generations of people who had nothing to do with the accumulation of the vast amounts of debt in the first place. America, Inc.'s leaders, however, are managing poorly: they are playing with short-term fixes (e.g. stealing from Social Security) and mortgaging the future by adding to and then ignoring a huge national debt that is growing dangerously. They are acting irresponsibly and myopically, ignoring looming financial woes and thinking more of their own political needs than the country's long-term financial well-being. This may not be illegal, but it certainly is not sound fiscal or financial management either.

"Guns vs. Butter." Another example of fiddling around with the budget is the classic "guns vs. butter" trade-off. In this trade-off, with its related "dances" and "chants," emphasis is placed on budget cuts and re-appropriations of funds, seemingly to reduce or control the budget deficit. Again, however, lawmakers and politicians do few things that reduce or eliminate a habitual and omnipresent yearly shortfall. And what they do usually detracts from social, educational, and other programs ("butter") while consistently funding ever increasing military budgets ("guns") and increasing the deficit significantly.

In February, 2006, the House approved $39 billion in budget savings that would be realized over a five-year period. This sounded good, on the surface. But with an expected budget deficit at the time of $300+ billion, these spending cuts did little or nothing to reduce the financial shortcoming, much less the overall accumulated debt. Furthermore, the spending cuts were overshadowed by a proposed bill for $70 billion in tax cuts over the same five-year period. The deficit would actually worsen, not get better, as a result of the two bills. While spending cuts were being touted in a supposed deficit-reduction campaign, a separate bill was being proposed with little fanfare that would worsen the debt picture. The cynical among us might even believe that the separation of the spending and tax change bills was being done purposely, hoping that people didn't put 2 and 2 together and see that the touted deficit-reduction effort was really a farce, given the overall net impact of tax changes that would increase the deficit.[6]

In addition, the spending reductions in the 2006 budget included cuts to Medicaid, student loans, food stamps, child support, police hiring grants, Amtrak, community development, home-heating assistance, and other programs that hurt low- and middle-income Americans. In contrast, there were increases in the Defense budget, resulting in a figure of about $450 billion for defense and homeland security. The net outcome, astoundingly, was that *U.S. military spending in 2006 equaled the rest of the world's total combined military expenditures.* The 2007 budget followed basically the same pattern, with some cuts in social and educational programs and increases for the military because of Iraq and Afghanistan. For FY 2008, the Pentagon will spend about $460 billion plus cost add-ons of approximately $150 billion for Iraq and Afghanistan. Putting things into perspective, defense spending will have doubled since the mid-1990s, while other programs have taken a hit and seen their budgets reduced disproportionately. "Guns" clearly seem to be the winner in the battle for funds and for the dubious distinction of being the major contribution to U.S. debt.

Another way of looking at the "guns-and-butter" data is to consider spending as a percentage of income tax dollars paid into U.S. coffers. In 2006, direct military spending took 27 cents of every income tax dollar. Coupled with the amount still being spent to pay for past wars and military build-ups and other benefits paid to veterans, total military spending rose close to 40 cents or 40% of every tax dollar received. In contrast, investments in renewable energy and conservation received significantly *less than a penny* of the income tax dollar, while affordable housing and nutrition combined claimed about *a nickel.*[7] The opportunity costs of a ballooning military budget include doing without adequate health care for many, affordable housing, more head-start programs, better schools, more teachers, etc., as the latter receive a smaller and smaller proportion of available tax receipts. Combined with the interest payment on the national debt, military spending and the interest burden account for nearly 60% of tax receipts, a taxing burden indeed. With the projected shortfalls in Social Security and Medicare and Medicaid, and with the growing healthcare problems in the country, clearly a continued emphasis on the same-old forms of military spending and increases in a huge national debt make little economic sense and only further the woes of financial mismanagement.

A disastrous event on August 1, 2007 brought the "guns-vs.-butter" issue into even bolder relief. The Interstate 35W Bridge in Minnesota collapsed and plummeted into the Mississippi River, killing or injuring scores of victims. The bridge was considered structurally deficient since 1990, but only patchwork repairs were done primarily because of the cost involved. The disaster clearly raises a red flag: in the U.S., 74,000 bridges or more are rated as structurally deficient and the total cost of repair is estimated at about $190 billion. Repairs have been delayed because of this cost, as the states can't proceed with work on all problem bridges without federal aid.

The bottom line is that the situation cannot be confronted adequately without substantial federal support. But will the necessary support materialize? Support in the past has not been adequate, obviously, given the backlog of work and the potential dangers that have accumulated over the years. Given the tight federal budget and the massive amounts being spent on the military and repayment of interest on the national debt, an adequate level of future support seems problematical. But given a world-leadership position in military spending of $600 billion plus per year, even a 10 percent cut in the generals' weapons wish-list would fund the needed repairs in just a few years. A bigger cut, of course, would accelerate the needed repairs and probably save many lives. But, again, is adequate help to the states forthcoming?

The past penchant for spending on "guns" over most socially beneficial projects suggests that the required levels of support won't materialize very rapidly. The additional fact that the majority of funds earmarked for federal highway spending since 1970 has not gone into alleviating highway congestion or fixing deteriorating roads but, rather, *has funded thousands of congressmen's pet home projects or rewarded lobbyists*, also suggests a bleak prognosis for the country's bridge-related ills. Add next the certain future demands for the repairs of other elements of infrastructure nationwide, especially in large urban areas, and the prognosis becomes even more pessimistic.[8] The total cost for needed improvements to the country's roads, airports, water systems, dams, and bridges has been estimated at $1.6 trillion, a formidable amount indeed. Yet, much can be done *if* our leaders in Washington would only show some resolve.

Surely, the military budget or the total sum dedicated to "guns" can be pared significantly. Of the roughly $600 billion in the military budget for 2008, how much is being allocated to earmarks or pet projects, and how much represents waste and excesses that have not been scrutinized or challenged by Congress? Is it still absolutely necessary for the Pentagon to fund and run hundreds of bases worldwide? Couldn't U.S. military leaders be forced to examine these huge holdings more critically and perhaps save taxpayers $billions? Adding in other costs—e.g. for the inefficient and ineffective Department of Homeland Security, nuclear weapons costs, Selective Service requirements, defense stockpiles, etc.,—drives up the military take of available funding. It also, however, increases the probability that substantial savings could be found and redeployed for currently under-funded programs and infrastructure repairs if a reasonable effort was made to examine these costs carefully.

The military budget should be trimmed actually, given a new military mission of confronting terrorists, engaging guerrillas in insurgencies around the world, and reducing the focus on traditional methods of waging war.[9] More money should logically be spent on CIA operatives and spies in the field rather than on grossly expensive, powerful weapons systems, aircraft carriers, fighter jets, and submarines in the new war against organized bands of terrorists and rag-tag groups of "Islamofascists." Yet, it is the high-priced items that are the favorites of the Pentagon, and they are dominating government spending, reducing the funds available for social, educational, infrastructure improvement, and other programs. Cutting some of these big-ticket items from the budget would certainly provide funds for these other uses and needs. It takes guts, however, to stand up to a massive military machine and the military-industrial complex, and U.S. leaders haven't yet shown the needed resolve.

Another source of funding for infrastructure repairs would logically be an increase in the federal tax on gasoline, a levy which hasn't risen since 1993. An added benefit of raising this tax significantly would be a drastic drop in gasoline consumption and a reduction in the horrific oil dependency facing the nation (see Chapter 5). Adding the gasoline tax receipts to those of a reduced military budget would help immensely with infrastructure projects and other programs.

Certainly there are other options available for active deficit reductions and for funding of needed projects, but it's clear from their behavior that: (a) U.S. leaders really aren't interested in reducing deficits and the national debt; (b) they're more interested in earmarks and getting their "share" of budget resources, regardless of the impact on debt; and (c) in a battle of "guns vs. butter," the management of America, Inc. has typically emphasized the former over the latter, which fuels the debt burden of the U.S. and leads to other social ills.

> *U.S. debt is huge and is growing larger by the day. The profligate spending of our leaders and lawmakers is the norm, with a focus on short-term "fixes" and manipulations of the budget, not sound programs to reduce debt and focus on the critical needs facing the nation. Certain costs are legitimately increasing (e.g. health care), but politicians' spending habits, re-election concerns, dysfunctional deference to the military, and fear of "biting the bullet" and taking the necessary steps to confront the debt picture are also fueling the growth of red ink. Financial mismanagement is certainly alive and well in America, Inc.*

Ineffective management and waste. The huge U.S. debt is being fueled further by greedy management and waste. The prime motivation of many lawmakers seems to be "I'll get mine" or "what's in it for me," not managing effectively. Much more of a fuss needs to be made over "pork-barrel" legislation and government waste.

The huge interest payments on the national debt represent a measure of waste and huge opportunity costs. So do pork projects.[10] In the summer of 2005, Congress approved $223 million to build a bridge between Ketchikan, and Gravina Island, Alaska, with the expected real cost estimated at over $315 million or more than $23,000 for each citizen of Ketchikan. The "bridge to nowhere," as many have come to call it, replaces the need for a five-minute ferry ride between the two points, apparently a monumental hardship for the handful of people who use the ferry! Why even consider such a silly bridge? Because someone else is paying for it. Because U.S. lawmakers feel that they're all entitled to feed equally at the pork trough. Because members of Congress won't balk at wasteful spending by their colleagues and jeopardize their own selfish pork projects.

Other pork projects have included $50 million to create a rainforest in the state of Iowa, a real necessity, of course; $250,000 to two universities for research to cut asparagus-industry labor costs; $519 million in farm subsidies to a co-op, the largest miller and marketer of rice, representing more money than that received by farmers in 12 other states combined; $26 million to operate draft boards, even though there's been no selective service draft since 1973; $2 million to construct a parking lot at a Catholic institution in Texas where it really wasn't needed; $ millions paid to farmers not to farm; and $2.5 trillion a year, or about *$7 billion a day*, supposedly spent on disaster preparedness, which apparently was still not enough to allow the federal government to reinforce New Orleans' dikes or efficiently evacuate the city during the hurricane Katrina disaster. $7 billion a day is spent to fund FEMA, an organization whose management and organization are terrible and totally beyond repair, according to a government committee report in April, 2006, putting this spending in the same wasteful category as pork-barrel spending.

Add the waste due to extensive lobbying efforts and the costs go up even more. Lobbyists have power and they use it (see Chapter 5). Just look at the corporate tax bill passed in Congress in October, 2004. Every lobbyist in Washington, D.C., even bad ones, got something from this bill. *The Economist*, quoting John McCain, stated that this bill, a real disgrace, could easily be named the "No Lobbyist Left Behind Act."[11] It supposedly focused on job creation in manufacturing, but "manufacturing" included tobacco farmers, bow-and-arrow makers, timber producers, Hollywood studios, architects, native Alaskan whaling captains, and race-track owners. Chinese ceiling-fan companies saw $44 million in tariffs eliminated. Why? Because someone in a high place pleaded for help for the company that sells about one-half of the ceiling fans sold in the U.S., clearly a case of hardship and dire need!

Another pork-stuffed bill that Congress rushed to passage, with many law-makers not reading it, is also a disgrace, a lobbying and pork creation at its worst. It provided money for a museum in Punxsutawney in honor of Punxsutawney Phil, the Groundhog Day celebrity. And why not add money to fund mariachi music in Nevada, a Rock and Roll Hall of Fame in Cleveland, wild hog control in Missouri, and protection of sunflowers in North Dakota? In total, $15.8 billion of the bill was dedicated for such pet projects or congressional "earmarks." This clearly is a cost of congressional caprice, once again born by taxpayers. $15.8 billion is a lot of money and a lot of waste, and it just adds to the U.S. debt.

Attaching earmarks to bills is a favorite pastime of Congress. "Bad" earmarks favoring a few special interests are added to "good" bills to sneak them through the legislative process, without public scrutiny. Earmarks are added by some members of Congress to help other members, e.g. their colleagues who may be facing a tough re-election test. Some earmarks actually aid the passage of unpopular or contested bills, e.g. the provisions added to the 2007 $100 billion war appropriations bill for the Iraq war for spinach farmers in California ($25m), peanut storage costs ($74m), salmon fisheries ($60m), and asbestos mitigation at one plant ($50m). The number of earmarks, predictably, has grown in popularity. From small numbers just a couple of decades ago, the number of earmarks in fiscal 2005 approached 16,000 that were added to federal spending bills, and the number in 2006 added significantly to the problem.

It's just not Congress, by the way. Even Presidents and First Ladies love pork and earmarks. Laura Bush has her 21st Century Librarian Program, which last year provided $25 million in grants to train people in her favorite occupation. President Bush pushed for over $200 million to teach sexual abstinence in high school, a program thus far with no positive results. (This program was being funded, by the way, while the Education Department's overall budget was being cut.) Some earmarks sound good—e.g. Bush's $100 million for a Teacher Incentive Fund or $5-plus billion for the Army Corps of Engineers for wetlands projects—but they nonetheless are a kind of pork, not necessarily reflecting an outcome of public debate or achieving the positive result suggested by the title of the projects. Rank does have its privileges, including in the area of White House earmarks and favorite pork projects.

Even "good," positive-sounding projects are not immune from pork, lobbying, and wasteful spending. For example, as mentioned above, despite the $700 billion or so budgeted for federal highway spending since 1970, only a very small percentage has been added to our road system. The huge majority of the money allocated hasn't gone to alleviating highway congestion or fixing deteriorating roads. Rather, these huge grab-bag spending bills target congressional home districts and reward lobbyists, and they are not usually debated by lawmakers. Federal highway spending clearly can be seen as a "pork highway," not a public-good program.

Other examples of waste can easily be provided, but the point is already painfully clear: pork and expensive favors are just part of doing business in America, Inc., with the guy in the street footing the bill. Lobbyists affect spending far beyond pork-barrel legislation and how government leaders squander citizens' hard-earned money, and I'll delve more deeply into this issue in Chapter 5. The point being stressed presently is that many of America, Inc.'s leaders seem to be a greedy and/or wasteful bunch, and it's costing all of us a lot of money and adding to an already huge federal deficit.

So, what's the big deal? There are some who would argue that pork and waste only account for a "small" portion of the total federal budget, and thus present no threat. They usually add that "this is the way business in done in the government," and we just have to accept it as a cost of doing business in America, Inc. This is the way things work.

This is pure nonsense. Even two percent of the federal budget still represents $50-60 billion or so in waste, and this isn't insignificant—it represents a fairly high stack of tightly-bound $1000 bills. The Congressional Research Service put a $64 billion cost on earmarks or pork-barrel legislation for the 2006 fiscal year, and it estimated that there were almost 16,000 earmarks in fiscal 2005 appropriations alone. The huge military budget is very likely full of earmarks and pet projects that fall easily into the category of wasteful spending. This suggests that the *actual* total waste in government is most certainly higher than the estimates that are occasionally published, and that the real cost is even greater and more debilitating. To paraphrase the late Senator Everett Dirksen of Texas, a billion wasted here, a billion wasted there, and before you know it, you have lots of money being wasted.

But pork and waste suggest other important implications for America, Inc. Our leaders or mangers in the White House and Congress supposedly are role models. If waste, pork, and favors purchased via lobbying and greasing palms represent the norm—the modus operandi in America, Inc.—the wrong message is being sent. Politicians, it suggests, routinely are allowed to benefit from pork-barrel bills, waste, and "creative" accounting that at times seem akin to immoral, if not strictly illegal, activity. If they can do it, why can't others? Why can't we all feed at the trough? Is it possible that the routine behavior of U.S. lawmakers and lobbyists actually has fueled even more despicable behavior in the boardrooms of some large public corporations? Is it possible that individuals and companies actually cheat on their tax preparations to make sure that "they get theirs"?

Our leaders in the White House and Congress must be effective and principled managers, but their actions often belie the point. They certainly seem to avoid the moral high ground when it comes to pork and waste, and even seem to get away with outlandish behavior that would result occasionally in criminal indictment for the rest of us. This is not sound management with the good of America, Inc. in mind. Profligate spending and waste are hurting most citizens, while also setting up the country for serious financial repercussions.

Consumer Debt and Lack of Savings

Before considering the downside consequences of the gross financial mismanagement and potential cures in America, Inc., one more ingredient must be added to the economic caldron that is coming to a dangerous boil: namely, the huge and increasing amount of consumer debt and the lack of savings in the U.S.[12] Consumer debt reached an all-time high of over $2.2 trillion in early 2006, and by the beginning of January, 2007, had risen to a whopping new record of over $2.4 trillion. Home mortgage debt growth increased 13.8 percent in 2005 and only 8.9 percent in 2006 due to the slump in the housing market but, adding home mortgage debt to consumer debt, Americans owe over $9 trillion, a sum equal to the present total U.S. debt. In fact, Americans have never been more leveraged: loan-to-value ratios—the loan amount as a percentage of property value—have never been higher, growing to 86.5% in 2006 compared to 78% in 2000.[13] Equity is being replaced by more and more debt, which is a dangerous trend that would only exacerbate the problems of an economic crisis.

Looking within the real estate market reveals an even darker, more ominous picture. The performance of the sub-prime market—real estate loans to people with lower-than-average credit ratings—is extremely worrisome, with nearly 1.2 million foreclosure filings in 2006, a huge 42% increase over 2005. Troubled loans—90 or more days past due—rose to $14.2 billion in the second quarter of 2007 compared to $9.5 billion in the same quarter in 2006.[14] With experts predicting a tidal wave of new defaults and foreclosures, the economic well-being of the country could be negatively affected in a major way. These numbers and trends cannot be dismissed or taken lightly, as the huge volatility in financial markets in 2007 due to troubles in the sub-prime market would attest.

"In debt we trust" is increasingly the motto of the U.S. consumer. Credit and debt rule U.S. households. Consumer debt and credit have consistently exceeded disposable personal income over the last half-decade or so, which is extremely troublesome: *people are consistently spending more than they make.* The average household spends about $2000 a year on finance charges, which leads to even more consumer debt. Pressure on consumers to increase credit card debt may force more people to make minimum payments on their balances which, in the case of a $12,000 card balance, can mean close to $18,000 paid in interest before wiping out the debt. These are big and horrendous numbers. In his book, *Credit Card Nation*, Robert Manning called credit cards "yuppie food stamps," a kind of perceived "social class entitlement" that more and more people are relying on to pay their bills.[15] If, as argued previously, U.S. leaders in the Congress are spending like drunken sailors, many of their constituents are hopping from pub to pub with them. Our leaders have shown the way to financial irresponsibility, and many people are apparently following their example.

In light of these debt figures, it's not at all surprising that Americans' personal savings are at an all-time low. In 2005, savings fell into negative territory at minus 0.5 percent, compared to +6 to 9% in Europe and Asia. At the end of 2006, the Commerce Department reported that the country's personal savings rate had fallen even further, to a minus 1 percent, the lowest level since the great depression. Americans are spending what they earn, then some. The savings rate stood at 10.8 percent of after-tax incomes in 1984, and obviously has been declining ever since to its current negative figure. It may be that Americans have the feeling that its "wimpish to save" or not necessary to do so, but the truth very likely is that they cannot save because of their debt.[16] Government leaders should clearly be thinking of ways to *encourage savings,* but they certainly haven't been doing so.

Consequences of Fiscal and Financial Mismanagement

The consequences of debt for consumers in the U.S. are real and frightening. Personal bankruptcies hit an all-time high in 2005 and 2006 because of rising interest rates and increasing debt-maintenance costs. America, Inc.'s citizens are up to their eyeballs in debt and it will limit their future spending options. But the huge personal debt and the lack of personal savings also hurt the country. Savings equals and fuels investment in the flow of funds in the economy. Without positive savings, the country is denied an important source of investment capital, causing the U.S. to look elsewhere and incur additional debt. This is why the sum of funds borrowed from foreign countries is so high. This explains why China's holdings of foreign currencies and securities, including dollars and dollar-denominated securities, is making Beijing a giant in the financial world and a potential problem for the U.S.

There indeed are serious problems that are already affecting the U.S. as a result of mismanagement. There are yet other threats that could easily become sad financial realities in the not-too-distant future. Some of these problems and dangers have been implied above, but it's important to summarize them to show the severity of the situation facing the country.[17] Our leaders in the White House and Congress must finally acknowledge the seriousness of these problems and do something about them, before the country and many of its citizens are hurt financially.

Debt increases the cost of government. The national debt is ballooning, and so are the interest payments on it. A significant portion of every tax dollar—approximately 19%–20%—goes to pay this interest. This is a real cost and a high opportunity cost, as the U.S. must forego other programs and the satisfaction of other needs as a result of the high interest charges. Consider, again, the huge fiscal gap of $63 trillion discussed previously. As spending on programs like Social Security and Medicare increase, more money will be borrowed to cover those cash outlays. The interest on the increased debt needed to close the fiscal gap will become an onerous burden that eventually will consume a greater and greater portion of available cash, destroying or limiting a host of other programs and benefits. The impact of huge government expenditures and the onerous national debt will severely affect the U.S. economy is a negative way.

Debt crowds out private borrowing. Debt can cripple business and economic growth. When the federal government borrows to cover the deficit between what is spent and what is brought in as tax revenues, it absorbs some of the saving done by families and firms, saving that otherwise would have remained available to finance investment in new technologies, plants, and other innovations.[18] There is a finite amount of capital available at any time to finance economic growth and expansion, including business innovations. If the government sucks up a good percentage of the available capital, there is less left for the private sector. This can hobble economic growth and the number of jobs available to individuals.

Debt sucks up and wastes potential investment monies. Given the additional fact that consumer savings have recently turned negative, there are even fewer sources of investment funds, which exacerbate the negative impact of government debt even more. The trajectory of increasing debt and negative savings suggests that sources of investment and needed innovation are being depleted and serious consequences like economic stagnation are fast becoming likely.

Debt burdens us and future generations. The huge national debt someday will have to be reduced, as it cannot continue to rise unabated. Who will pay for this debt reduction? We will, as well as our kids and grandchildren, that's who.

When the Social Security bond "assets" come due, we and our kids and grand-kids will have to ante up. When foreign governments want to cash in on the $ billions in IOUs the U.S. has been giving them, people who aren't responsible for the debt will have to make good on it. In 2003, the Treasury paid off the last of the 30-year bonds that financed the Vietnam War; today's taxpayers finally have finished paying for the mistakes of Lyndon Johnson, Richard Nixon, and others. Tomorrow's taxpayers will have to pay off Social Security "lockbox" assets and the cost of the Iraq debacle.

Is this the right or moral thing to do? Many feel it isn't, starting with Jefferson who felt that those who incur debt are morally bound to pay it off themselves, not pass it on to others who had nothing to do with incurring the debt.[19] Law-makers have routinely been adding to a mounting U.S. debt. The implicit moti-vation is that it's not "our" problem—it will be someone else's when the debt becomes due. There definitely are questions of morality and equity here. Law-makers are not held accountable for the debt that will burden others, which makes it easy to ignore Jefferson, increase debt, and pass it on.

It's time that our leaders exhibit the same fervor and commitment to reducing the debt as they've shown in creating it before the burden becomes unbearable. It's the right thing to do.

Trade imbalances can take on a negative political flavor. The U.S. spends about $800 billion more abroad than it rakes in annually, so it needs funds to support this deficit. It needs foreigners to cover the debt and invest in the U.S. This has been occurring and foreigners are holding America, Inc.'s debt in record amounts. If they should sell or demand payment on the bulk of the dollar-denominated IOUs from the U.S. and opt instead for Euro-denominated invest-ments, the U.S. dollar, inflation, and economy would take a major hit.

Will China and others suddenly lose their appetite for U.S. investments? Hopefully, not. But if the U.S. debt keeps climbing, and monetary woes lessen the value of the investments, this appetite could change for the worse. If the value of the dollar keeps falling, it could spark a new wave of inflation and cause spend-ing cuts and unemployment increases, leading to recessionary pressures. Interest rates would rise, stock prices would very likely suffer, few Americans could buy houses, and personal bankruptcies and mortgage foreclosures would increase because of higher variable interest rates.

There are also potential problems on the political front. For example, if the U.S. should side with Taiwan in a China-Taiwan standoff, political trouble could lead to economic woes for the U.S. Certainly China or other countries don't want to do something dumb to hurt the value of their investments, but political problems and national gesturing may override strictly economic concerns. Politics can lead to "non-rational" decisions, and China has financial and political clout in the world to get its way. Its holdings of foreign currencies and securities are over $1 trillion, a sum greater than the economic output of all but nine countries.[20] China's economic clout certainly can translate into political clout and actions that potentially override strict economic considerations. This certainly has happened before in the world, and it very likely will happen again.

If one considers which countries are holding the bulk of the U.S. debt in addition to China—Saudi Arabia, Russia, Venezuela, and Iran—the political threat, as well as an economic one, becomes even clearer. Could politics drive these countries to reduce or eliminate their holdings, driving down the value of the dollar, causing interest and home mortgage rates in the U.S. to go up, while also hurting the political clout of the country in the eyes of the world? Could political factors outweigh economic rationality and drive countries to act in such a way as to hurt U.S. interests and standing abroad? These are not totally unlikely events; they could materialize and cause problems, so sound management demands consideration of these contingencies in future planning.

American consumers may tighten their belts. For the past few years, U.S. growth has been funded heavily by consumers borrowing heavily against the value of their homes. Savings, it is recalled, are now negative and consumers are spending more than their disposable incomes. But if consumer debt continues to increase, leading to more personal bankruptcies and mortgage foreclosures, things will really turn sour for the U.S. Consumer spending on foreign goods will drop. China and other countries will turn to Europe and other parts of Asia looking for continued growth. They'll become less interested in financing America, Inc.'s spending and trade deficits. Investment funds into the U.S. will slow dramatically. As demand drops, the U.S. will be forced to promise higher returns to sell more IOUs and win back foreign investment. Interest rates will increase, leading to yet larger federal deficits and interest charges. Rates on mortgages and credit card debt will also increase, causing consumers to buy less, etc. and the cycle would continue full circle, adding to America's woes.

There is no way out of this mess, except doing the right thing: shrink the deficits and reduce the total amount of U.S. debt. *The financial management of America, Inc. has been deplorable. Increasing debt looms as an ever-growing economic and political threat to the standing of the U.S. in a volatile world. It's finally time to get on firmer economic ground.* What can be done to manage the situation better?

There really are only two possibilities to confront these economic woes: (a) cut spending drastically and (b) focus on a fiscal fix by raising revenues. The second option includes revamping the tax code to increase its efficiency and effectiveness on the revenue side of the equation. Let's focus first on reduced spending.

CONFRONTING DEFICITS AND DEBT

There are a number of steps U.S. leaders can take to confront and finally manage the problems of high deficits and debt.[21] Cures won't come easy, but it's time for America, Inc.'s leaders to take action.

Take Action ..., Finally

The first step is for U.S. leaders and lawmakers to follow Cicero's and Franklin's advice: *every effort should be made to cut government spending and borrowing.*

President Bush and many of his predecessors obviously rarely met a spending bill they didn't like. Bush's history especially has been to spend, spend, and then spend a bit more and, until very recently, Congressional leaders have supported the president's spendthrift ways. In the last half decade or so, federal spending by the "conservatives" in power has increased about 30%. They have approved "budget extensions" like additional money for Iraq and Afghanistan, despite an already huge defense budget. Members of Congress have been financially "arrogant in the last couple of decades," again referring to Cicero, opting to "get theirs" by supporting pork-laden bills and not worrying at all about higher-level goals and needs. Some have compared recent Congressional spending to that of drunken sailors, but as John McCain counters, such a comparison is unfair and even insulting to relatively responsible and conservative drunken sailors.

There literally must be a score of programs ripe for the budget ax starting with the military budget, but U.S. leaders haven't had the courage to tackle them head on. It's about time that they act as responsible managers and make a concerted effort to curtail their wasteful ways. This won't be easy, as pork and waste are everywhere, spending habits die slowly, and resistance to budget cuts will be massive, but spending must be cut before more serious consequences prevail. A solid and symbolic step would be the *passage of a strong balanced-budget Constitutional amendment.*

The Gramm-Rudman Act was passed in 1987 to instill fiscal and financial rationality by legislating the elimination of federal deficits. The Budget Enforcement Act of 1990 and other attempts at controlling spending were added to the arsenal of weapons to control spending. Sadly, however, this type of "control" experiment hasn't worked. Lawmakers and the President have found ways around the law.

Using Social Security funds to reduce the deficit and then using creative accounting to turn the deficit into "assets," as described above, has been a pervasive ploy to avoid confronting the reality of the debt picture. Another ploy has been the shifting of more and more spending "off budget." Much of the funding of the wars or actions in Iraq and Afghanistan, for example, has not been included in the defense budget, where it belongs. It has been moved "off budget," and separate spending requests have been granted by Congress to conduct these military campaigns. The official budget is not affected, despite the obvious increase in spending and debt accumulation.

Passing a new, stricter Constitutional amendment to prohibit deficits and demand balanced budgets would help solve the problem. The time has come for drastic action, and this certainly fits into this category. Will America, Inc.'s leaders take such a strong management-related action? I hope so before the spending/ debt crunch hurts us badly.

Another step that can be taken to reduce debt is to *eliminate all earmarks, many of which constitute "pork" and frivolous projects.* If funding requests can't stand alone and withstand public scrutiny of their supposed benefits, they should not be allowed to be attached to other spending bills and become enacted without passing muster. The fact that about 16,000 earmarks sneak through Congress each year suggests that they have questionable benefit for the country and could be eliminated. (The ethics reform bill of 2007 does little or nothing to reduce the number of earmarks; it may actually motivate *increased* numbers, as Chapter 5 points out). The benefit of eliminating earmarks would be a reduction in spending, hence decreased debt, and a symbolic move that the White House and Congress are taking leadership and providing a role model of sorts in a war on spending, debt accrual, and unbalanced budgets. Such a bold move would definitely be applauded by the majority of Americans.

Another plausible and effective step is to focus on the fiscal side and increase revenues, either by increasing taxes or revamping the U.S. tax code.

Fiscal Responsibility: Cures for Taxing Problems

Clearly, reducing budget deficits and U.S. debt via spending cuts is the preferred option. Revamping or refocusing the tax code, however, is a viable choice because of inherent problems and inequities in the existing tax laws, corrections to which can lead to increased revenues. Coupled with spending cuts, this two-pronged attack can finally begin to attack the debt problem.

Is tax reform necessary? Consider the following. The tax code, for starters, is hopelessly complex. President Bush promised to restrain government spending and make the tax code simpler and fairer. He's done neither. His tax cuts have dramatically complicated the tax system in the U.S., with the *tax code growing by 10,000 pages* in his first term alone.[22] Imagine the difficulties inherent in navigating a complex tax code of mammoth size. Imagine the loopholes that dedicated lawyers can uncover in a huge, rambling tax code. Consider the appalling fact that taxpayers spend over $100 billion annually on tax preparation and filing fees. *Effective management for the common good is impossible under such conditions of complexity and waste.*

Complexity of this sort also surely leads to all kinds of inequity and problems of fair treatment under the code. Corporate tax revenues, never very high, have fallen from 4% of GDP in 1965 to about 1% at present.[23] In the latest version of the proposed federal budget, individual income taxes are providing roughly 50% of total revenue receipts, while corporate income taxes are providing only 7.5%, down from a high of 40% during World War II. In 2000, American companies paid an average of only $14.75 in taxes for every $1,000 in gross revenue, a figure reported by the government's General Accounting Office, and this is significantly lower than the proportion of gross revenue paid by individual taxpayers.[24]

More than 60% of U.S. corporations owed no federal taxes in the period of 1996-2000, when the economy was booming and corporate profits skyrocketed, and America's largest 275 corporations paid less in corporate taxes in the years 2001-2003, despite increased profits.[25] Because of write-offs, deductions, and tax loopholes, the companies reported *less than half* of their actual profits to the I.R.S. In contrast, ordinary wage earners have to report every penny of their earnings. The corporate "haves" certainly seem to have more influence in America, Inc. than the average man in the street.

On May 1, 2006, Senate lawmakers dropped a tax provision that would have generated additional billions of tax dollars from the oil companies, which reported record profits during the latest oil-price crisis. Simply put, inventories bought at lower prices by the oil companies could be costed out or written off at the much higher cost levels of more recent inventory purchases, thereby reducing their profit liability on paper for tax purposes and allowing them to escape a fortune in tax liabilities and reap billions in additional profits. This LIFO treatment of inventories favoring the large oil companies never made big news, but it helped the companies immensely, if quietly and stealthily. And clearly there are no such favors for the majority of individual tax payers who must ante up and provide the major portion of tax revenues in the U.S. Our leaders in the Senate clearly seem to be allies of the big companies when it comes to tax policy, not the average individual U.S. taxpayer.

The lack of balance in all of these numbers is appalling: corporations seem to be escaping the tax collector, while individuals relatively are footing more of the burden. However, the tax code doesn't only discriminate between corporate and individual taxpayers, it also discriminates among individuals as to their tax burden. In effect, the rich are indeed getting richer and the poor, poorer, a cliché or truism, to be sure, but one that accurately describes the result of U.S. tax policies.

Even as wealthy Americans increase their portion of the country's wealth, they're paying a *smaller share* of the income tax burden. In 1973, the wealthiest 20% earned 44% of U.S. income, by 2002 this had increased to 50%, and all indications are that this share is still growing. Since Bush's tax cuts in 2001 (most of which have been extended or made permanent), the top 20% of taxpayers are paying 1 percent less of the overall share of tax liabilities, while middle-income wage earners are paying 2 percent more of the total tax burden.[26] The gap between "haves" and "those who have less" is definitely widening. Adding in the "have nots," and it is clear that *there is a growing financial apartheid in the U.S.*

The politicians argue, of course, that the tax cuts favoring the few have actually sparked the economy and raised money for the U.S. This is pure nonsense and a "smokescreen," at best. A former Republican economic advisor, N. Gregory Mankiw, argues that activity generated by the capital gains tax cuts made up about one-half of the lost revenue. The rest? It's called a deficit. Similarly, the President's Office of Management and Budget points out that tax cuts don't pay for themselves: over the past three years, with tax cuts in effect, federal revenue was $316 billion less than the OMB had predicted it would be without the tax cuts. From 2001 to 2005, federal revenue fell at the average rate of 0.6 percent, adjusted for inflation and population growth. The shortfall? Again, call it a deficit and a major contribution to the mounting U. S. debt.[27]

The point is that the tax cuts are not paying for themselves. The wealthy are benefiting, but the country and the average man on the street are being hurt. Politicians espouse and argue for the benefits of tax cuts, but their beliefs either are based on "faith" or a "company line," or they simply reflect slick politics. They certainly aren't based on solid empirical evidence. This is financial mismanagement, again, and it's hurting people and putting the country deeper into debt.

Management by stealth.[2] A good example of fiscal problems and a process of management stealth can be seen in the Alternative Minimum Tax (AMT). The

---

2.   Management-by-stealth as a leadership style is treated in greater depth in Chapter 7. As is emphasized then, the negative consequences of this management or leadership style go far beyond the AMT's silent impact, and include a host of other outcomes and activities that injure the public good.

AMT began in 1969 to close the loopholes that really wealthy families used to avoid paying any federal income tax. It was originally aimed at the rich—the "fat cats" with legal and financial advice who could totally escape the tax collector. What's happening now is that the AMT is hammering the middle class and the government is quietly allowing the carnage to continue, while simultaneously lowering the tax burden of the wealthiest Americans. This represents a type of "management by stealth"—knowing full well what's happening, knowing how the original purpose of the AMT has been undermined, and yet letting the tax quietly continue to wreak havoc on the overtaxed middle class. Consider the following numbers.

The first levy of the AMT touched few taxpayers, the "fat cats" just mentioned. More and more people have joined the taxed "elite" over the years, however. In 2001, about 1.8 million people paid the tax. In 2003, the number jumped to 2.3 million. But now, the number is increasing exponentially, as more Americans face the possibility of a huge tax bite. From the 3 million people or so who paid the tax in 2004 and the estimated 4+ million in 2005, the number is expected to jump to near 30 million people by 2008 and 35 million by 2010. A recent change in the tax law will provide relief to a couple of million taxpayers, but the number who will fall prey to its provisions by 2010 is still huge.

Why has the government allowed this quiet, creeping taxation on the middle class, while enacting and extending tax cuts to wealthier Americans? *Because elimination of the AMT would add another $600 billion or more to the projected 10-year deficit.*[28] It's better, the administration's and Congress' reasoning seems to be, to keep the AMT and penalize a huge number of taxpayers, while simultaneously giving a nice kickback to a few Americans, hopefully in a quiet, stealthy way.

This type of fiscal management is contradictory. While it openly flaunts the benefits of tax cuts, it's also raising taxes and collecting huge amounts of money, *in effect, admitting that its tax cuts alone would have devastating consequences for deficits, not the touted benefits at all.* It's also sneaky quiet in that 2006 budget deliberations omitted an exception Congress had passed to give relief to many negatively affected by the AMT. The status quo was maintained without fanfare or publicity, behind a thinly-veiled promise to consider tax reform someday.

(Cynical observers might also say it's also sneaky or stealthy in that the bulk of taxpayers getting hit by the AMT are in the more affluent "blue" states. This is an added quiet benefit of the AMT, so to speak—being able to quietly and raise tax revenues, while also ensuring that the "right" Americans are getting clobbered—in this case, obviously *not* the political right).

Tax reform is desperately needed. In a poll conducted by *The Economist* magazine of 100 economics professors, U.S. tax policies won low marks.[29] These experts are extremely critical of the tax cuts that are a central component of recent economic policy. More than 70 percent of them are concerned about America, Inc.'s fiscal health and its ability to weather the upcoming budget crisis when baby-boomers demand more from U.S. coffers. A huge majority of these experts feel that deficits are a major problem, and a significant number feels that deficits and debt represent a true upcoming crisis. Tax cuts are a large part of this problem, but the data also suggest that the entire tax code is a major contributor to present and projected economic woes.

The present tax system is also unfair. Under the present system, the policeman who makes $70,000 in annual wages very likely pays a higher percentage of his salary to the federal government than an executive who makes five times that amount in capital gains. This has prompted some to suggest that today's tax code has become anti-worker, not just anti-middle class.[30] Such policies, coupled with the negative and devastating impact of the AMT, demand that something be done soon in the name of equity, sound fiscal policy, and effective management of resources.

Finally, saving needs to be encouraged. At minimum, even if the present tax structure is retained despite its complexity and inequity, changes in the tax code should motivate positive savings, e.g. by having a greater proportion of all savings reduce the tax burden of individuals and families. An incentive to save is needed to reverse the negative effects of overspending and massive debt on taxpayers and the country.

<u>Biting the tax bullet</u>. The fiscal gap referenced above is huge, and at a net present value of a negative $63 trillion, it can push the country to economic ruin. Wishing and hoping won't make it go away. What has to happen is our leaders must increase taxes in some areas and reduce spending in others. This to some is heretical and radical, but I'm afraid our leaders must bite the bullet and start planning and acting now before it's too late.

As already stated, federal discretionary spending must decrease dramatically. Waste must be curtailed and earmarks eliminated. Budget items—including sacred military expenditures—must be pared significantly. The future commitments of Social Security and Medicare benefits must be restructured, as the present realities of entitlement growth spell disaster. The present course of action simply cannot continue.

One huge problem is that members of Congress aren't motivated to bite the fiscal and financial bullet. America, Inc.'s leaders won't take needed actions that might jeopardize their popularity or chances for re-election. It's better to ignore the issues and foist them off on future leaders. Members of Congress don't pay sufficient attention to the problems of Social Security. Why? *Because they're not included under the Social Security program.* They have their own separate and lucrative retirement plan independent of Social Security. You can bet that the woes of Social Security would have been confronted by now if our leaders relied on it as much as most Americans do.

The same is true of health care. Members of Congress have their own health coverage, with no deductibles, no co-pays, and with no restrictions on the number of physician visits, and this wonderful treatment plan costs each of them about $35 a month.[31] Thirty five dollars! If this wasn't the case, don't you think that our leaders would have confronted the huge and mounting health-care problems in the country by now? The present system simply offers lawmakers no real motivation to attack and correct the Social Security and health-care woes facing most of the citizens of America.

Re-election concerns of lawmakers and hiding the truth from the public must finally take a back seat to an open discussion of and debate on these fiscal and financial matters. No one will embrace or like these words, but the time has finally come to confront debilitating economic problems and avoid a certain crisis in the not-too-distant future. Economic collapse isn't inevitable. It can be avoided if the leaders of America, Inc. make some difficult decisions, and the sooner the better.[32]

Tax-reform options. It's also a good time to revamp and simplify the tax code and consider fairer tax policies. I'll mention just one option of tax reform (there certainly are others) that would go a long way to achieving this equity: the flat tax. The typical taxpayer spends more than 30-40 hours sifting through tax receipts and records. Total expenditures for tax preparation are more than $100 billion annually. Numerous hours are spent trying to comprehend tax publications and avoid making costly mistakes.

A flat tax would simplify things immensely.[33] A two-page 1040 form would likely suffice. There only would be two or three tax brackets. Eliminated would be the complex maze of rules, exceptions, loopholes, and other debilitating aspects of a tax code with over 10,000 sections of law. The AMT can be eliminated, ending the inequities and problems associated with this poorly devised and implemented program. A flat tax would be easier to manage. Gone would be the myriad analysts, consultants, lawyers, and government watchdogs who currently manage the present tax code so poorly. Of course, having so many people with a vested interest in keeping the same old inefficient and ineffective system represents a huge reason why Congress' passage of tax reforms like the flat tax won't happen easily. It explains why many who read this proposal will be up in arms, suggesting the gross naiveté and foolishness of a flat-tax proposal and attacking the sanity and credentials of anyone daring to offer such a solution to a complex and debilitating tax code. Still, one can hope that effective leadership, sound management, and especially *strong public opinion* will soon prevail, forcing lawmakers to finally handle America, Inc.'s taxation inequities.

It's definitely time for all concerned citizens to let Congressional leaders know about a mounting dissatisfaction with their spending habits and the present imbalanced and unfair tax system. It's time for a popular rebellion of sorts and increased involvement of the citizenry in forcing fiscal and financial reform before the "reality show" of gross mismanagement is allowed to play out. It's time to hold U.S. leaders accountable for mismanagement, profligate spending, waste, and a biased tax code. Simply put, it's time for needed changes on the financial and fiscal front before serious economic woes befall the country.

These changes won't come easy. The existing power structure in America, Inc., fueled by lobbyists' money and special interests, will certainly stand in the way or increase the complexity of change, as the next chapter suggests.

CONCLUSIONS

"You load 16 tons, and what do you get, another day older and deeper in debt." (Song by Tennessee Ernie Ford, Circa 1955).

Everyday, America, Inc. and its citizens go deeper in debt. The U.S. is a debtor nation, a surprising and unsustainable fact for a world power. The debt is huge and is increasing at the rate of almost *a quarter of million dollars a second*!! This simply cannot continue.

An economic storm is approaching and U.S. leaders and lawmakers are seeding the clouds with financial and fiscal misdeeds and poor management capabilities. These leaders are managing the U.S., slowly but surely, into economic turmoil. The consequences of this financial and fiscal mismanagement include no or negative economic growth, debt burdens on generations yet to come, severe currency devaluation, inflationary woes, heavy emphasis on "guns" over "butter," and even a loss of political and economic power in the global community. The tax burdens on individuals will become increasingly burdensome, and the gap between the well-off and those barely making it will grow into chasm proportions. The $30,000 in debt for every man, woman, and child in the U.S. is a real figure, one that has to be repaid. This debt cannot be ignored.

Something must be done soon. Spending must be cut and deficits reduced. The tax code must be revamped and simplified significantly in favor of a more equitable tax solution. Stricter laws must regulate spending, including repulsive pork-barrel projects and Congressional "earmarks" that primarily help members of Congress and special interest groups.

If Congress and the Executive mansion aren't run by "knaves and fools,"[34] we can expect that changes will occur and sounder financial and fiscal management policies will prevail. If, indeed, "knaves and fools" continue with their destructive ways, America, Inc. will be facing some major problems and their debilitating consequences in the very near future.

What can the rest of us do? We can save and reduce personal indebtedness. We can tell our leaders in Congress to act and cut spending. We can tell them to consider tax reform. We can demand that they think and act with the good of the country and its "shareholders" in mind, rather than continue to act in a selfish, detached sort of way. We can vote to get rid of knaves and fools.

We as American citizens must act and use our collective influence to begin to reverse the effects of the financial mismanagement of America, Inc., and our lawmakers and leaders must finally respond to this collective influence. A failure to do so will lead us surely to financial disaster.

Endnotes

1. Numerous sources were considered when trying to evaluate and prognosticate U.S. economic trends. The differences in opinion among experts and the volatility of the financial markets and consumer opinion lead naturally to a conclusion that mixed economic messages were the norm, not the exception, over the first nine months of 2007. The case going forward is clearly more negative, as this chapter tries to show.

2. A number of sources provide data such as these. See, for example, Larry Burkett, *The Coming Economic Earthquake* (Chicago: Moody Press, 1991).

3. Ed Hall, *U.S. National Debt Clock FAQ*, October 28, 2005. See edhall@ brillig.com or http://brillig.com/debt_clock/faq.html.

4. Debt figures vary in their estimates including the percent of GDP or the federal budget receipts accounted for by interest on the national debt. For present purposes, the total receipts in 2006 of approximately $2.2 trillion were taken from a number of sources, including the Mid-Session Review, Budget of the U.S. Government, Fiscal year 2007, and the interest on the national debt was taken from The Debt-UWSA National Debt Clock. The fact about all taxes west of the Mississippi paying the interest on the national debt can be found on: www.geocities.com/cmcofer/intesest.

5. Lawrence Katlikoff and Scott Burns, *The Coming Generational Storm* (MIT Press, 2004); see also Lawrence Katlikof, "Drifting to Future Bankruptcy," *The Philadelphia Inquirer*, October 22, 2006, and N. Ferguson and Lawrence Katlikoff, "Going Critical: American Power and the Consequences of Fiscal Overstretch," *The National Interest*, Fall, 2003.

6. See, for example, J. Kuhnherr, "House Approves $39 billion in Cuts," *The Philadelphia Inquirer*, February 2, 2006; J.D. McKinnon and J. Calmes, "A 'Lean Budget' From Bush Cuts Mainly at Home," *The Wall Street Journal*, December 8, 2005; J. Irons, "The Budget Battle," *The Philadelphia Inquirer*, November 27, 2005; G. Jaffe and J. Karp, "Bush's Defense Budget Puts Off Cuts to Weapons," *The Wall Street Journal*, February 7, 2006.

7. For more information on these spending priorities and how the federal government spends our tax money, see the National Priorities Project and its findings, e.g. in the *Conspiracy Planet*, April 16, 2007 (www.

conspiracyplanet.com); see, too, Robert Dreyfuss, "Financing the Imperial Armed Forces: A Trillion Dollars and Nowhere to Go but Up." Tomdispatch.com, June 6, 2007, and in the CommonDreams.org News Center, July 16, 2007.

8. See "Pork Highway," *The Wall Street Journal*, Editorial, March 30, 2004, for an analysis of infrastructure needs and problems and federal highway spending; see "Aging Infrastructure: How Bad Is It?" *The Wall Street Journal*, Hot Topic, August 4-5, 2007.

9. See "House Approves $39 Billion in Cuts," "A Lean Budget," and "The Budget Battle," Ibid. See also G. Jaffe, "Rumsfeld Details Big Military Shift in New Document," *The Wall Street Journal*, March 11, 2005; and J. Calmes, "As Bush Vows to Halve Deficit, Targets Already Feel Squeezed," *The Wall Street Journal*, December 21, 2004; see, too, "Financing the Imperial Armed Forced." Ibid. and John Nichols, "An Overwhelming Cote for Waste, Earmarks, and Corruption," *The Nation*, August 5, 2007.

10. There have been many good "pork" examples in the popular press. See, for example, "Roll Out the Pork Barrel," *The Economist*, August 2, 2003; "Fiscal Outrages in America: Veto One for the Gipper," *The Economist*, June 19, 2004; D. Wallechinsky, "Are Your Tax Dollars Being Wasted?" *The Philadelphia Inquirer Parade Section*, November 6, 2005. This last article has many good examples of waste, arguing that such ridiculous expenditures should not be tolerated.

11. See "Lobbyist's Delight," *The Economist*, October 16, 2004; "The Cost of Congressional Caprice," *The New York Times*, Editorial, December 3, 2004; E. Andrews, "How Tax Bill Gave Business More and More," *The New York Times*, October 13, 2004; "Fresh Pork for Punxsutawney Phil," *The Philadelphia Inquirer*, 2005.

12. "How Much Debt Can We Afford?" *Des Moines Business Record*, December 4, 2005; J. Wasik, "U.S. Consumers Reeling from Higher Debt Burdens," *Bloomberg News*, January 17, 2006; J. Laurier, "U.S. Consumer Debt Reaches Record Levels," World Socialist web site, January 15, 2004; W. Branigan, "U.S. Consumers Debt Grows at Alarming Rate," *Washington Post*, January 12, 2004; "Consumer Credit," *Federal Reserve Statistical Release*, February 7, 2006; "Consumer Credit," *Federal Reserve Sta-*

tistical Release, March 7, 2007; "U.S. Households New Worth Climbs to Record High," *Associated Press*, March 9, 2007.

13. "The Subprime Market's Rough Road," *The Wall Street Journal*, Hot Topic, February 17-18, 2007.

14. Ibid. See, too, Alan Zibel, "Thrifts Hurt by Mortgage Problems, Report Says," from the Associated Press, reported in *The Philadelphia Inquirer*, August 22, 2007.

15. R. Manning, *Credit Card Nation: The Consequences of America's Addiction to Debt* (Basic Books, 2001).

16. M. Crutsinger, "American's Personal Savings: Minus 0.5 PCT," *The Philadelphia Inquirer*, January 31, 2006; "Personal Savings drop to a 73-year low," *Associated Press*, February 1, 2007.

17. The following discussions borrows from: Bill Winter, "How to Solve the United States' $6,736,489,356,420.66" Problem, "*Marc Brands Liberty*, September 21, 2003; P. Peterson, *Running on Empty* (Farrar, Strauss & Giroux, 2004); M. Crutsinger, "Fed Chief Warns of Dangers of Deficits," *The Philadelphia Inquirer*, December 3, 2005; A. Cassel, "When Priorities Just Don't Add Up," *The Philadelphia Inquirer*, December 17, 2004; J. Aversa, "Deficits Called the Biggest Problem," *The Philadelphia Inquirer*, March 11, 2005; J. Aversa, "Greenspan Says Big Trade Deficits Cannot Continue," *The Philadelphia Inquirer*, November 15, 2005; "Record Deficit: At $60.3 Billion, the Trade Gap for Nov. Topped Expectations," *The Wall Street Journal*, January 13, 2005; S. Murray, "Fiscal Restraint Shifts Spotlight to Deficit," *The Wall Street Journal*, February 8, 2005; F. Harrop, "Why U.S. is Really in His Debt," *The Philadelphia Inquirer*, February 2, 2006; "Scares Ahead," *The Economist*, October 2, 2004; G. Ip, "Fed Member Cites Risks to Economy," *The Wall Street Journal*, January 14, 2005; "Storm Clouds Ahead," *The Economist*, January 29, 2005.

18. Winter's *Marc Brands Liberty*, article op. cit, and others, Ibid, make this point in a forceful and clear way.

19. D. Wessel, "How the U.S. Deficit is a Moral Issue," *The Wall Street Journal*, November 4, 2004.

20. Andrew Browne, "China's Reserves Near Milestone, Underscoring Its Financial Clout," *The Wall Street Journal,* October 17, 2006.

21. Most of the references indicated in notes 15, 16, 17, and 18, op. cit., touch on or discuss many of the actions that are needed to manage the problems of high deficits and debt.

22. "A Boundless Vision, Alas," *The Economist,* September 11, 2004.

23. "Corporate Tax: Time to Hiss," *The Economist,* January 31, 2004.

24. "Corporate Tax Holidays," *The New York Times,* Editorial, April 13, 2004.

25. J. McKinnon, "Many Companies Avoided Taxes Even as Profits Soared in Boom," *The Wall Street Journal,* April 6, 2004.

26. "Income Inequality: A Gap that Saps Trust," *The Philadelphia Inquirer,* August 22, 2004.

27. Many of the facts noted in this paragraph have been expanded and summarized in the following excellent editorial: "Bad Math, Slick Politics: We'll Pay Eventually." *The Philadelphia Inquirer,* May 30, 2006; see also Chris Satullo, "A Bracing Heresy: Tax Cuts Don't Pay for Themselves," *The Philadelphia Inquirer,* June 17, 2007.

28. "A Boundless Vision," *The Economist,* op. cit.; D. Leonhardt, "Case of Vanishing Deductions: Alternative Tax Called Culprit," *The New York Times,* February 21, 2005.

29. "The Economy and the Election: The Dismal Science Bites Back," *The Economist,* October 9, 2004.

30. R. Wyden and A. R. Emanuel, "Simple Tax, Fair Tax," *The Wall Street Journal,* January 17, 2006.

31. See Don Sloan, M.D., *Practicing Medicine without a License,* Caveat Press, 2006, for more information about this and other health-care issues and problems.

32. *The Coming Generational Storm,* op. cit; "Drifting to Future Bankruptcy," op. cit.

33. "Simple Tax, Fair Tax," op cit.

34. A Cassel, "Another Week, Deeper in Debt," *The Philadelphia Inquirer*, March 19, 2006.

5

Power And Influence Gone Wrong: The Lobbyist Scourge and Costly Mismanagement

Differences in power and influence exist in all organizations. The large for-profit corporation is marked by power differences, as is America, Inc. Power and politics are not the domain of only "political" entities but, rather, are omnipresent and inevitable in all organizations, in both the private and public sectors.

Power is important, first, because it affects organizational performance. If those in power are supporting the right things, the probability of successfully executing desired strategies and operating plans is increased. If those in power are doing and supporting the *wrong* things—the wrong strategy, financial goals, or global mission—the negative impact on performance is inevitable. The job of top management in any organization is to understand and manage the power structure to ensure that it supports desired goals and benefits all or most of the organization's stakeholders.

Power is important, secondly, because it defines an organization's governance structure, including who makes critical strategic decisions and who is represented in the decision making process. A management oligarchy that is limited or biased in terms of stakeholder representation can overwhelm the decision process and eliminate the critical checks and balances that ensure the right strategic direction for an organization. A powerful management oligarchy can deprive constituents of their rights to due process and participation in organizational affairs.

Finally, power is important because it affects an organization's ability and proclivity for change and renewal. Excessive power in the hands of a few can create inertia, resistance to change, and an inability to adapt to new and demanding economic, social, and political realities.

On all of these counts, the power or influence structure in America, Inc. is dysfunctional. It's supporting the wrong things and inhibiting change. Leaders in the White House and Congress are being influenced and controlled by powerful lobbyists and narrow interests, and the exercise of statutory and executive power is often contrary to the critical social and economic needs of the country. A powerful management oligarchy has developed and it's severely curtailing the rights and participation of many stakeholders in key decision processes. In America, Inc., abuses of power, influence, and control are increasing, with serious negative consequences.

This abuse of power at the highest levels of America, Inc. is mismanagement at its very worst. It is leading inexorably to many serious problems above and beyond those already identified in previous chapters, and is costing the country and its citizens dearly. The influence of powerful lobbyists has become a scourge, a cause of serious affliction or trouble for the country. Let's examine these assertions by briefly considering, first, how power differences come about and are perpetuated. We'll then examine the influence of lobbyists and the special interest groups they represent, explain their power base, and see how a mismanagement of power is actually hurting the country. In the next chapter, additional abuses and mismanagement of power are noted, including attacks on science and the press.

Power and Dependency

Power is social influence in action. It always implies or denotes a relationship. Power indicates the ability of an actor in the relationship (a person, organization, or country) to get others to perform in certain ways or change their behavior to suit the influential actor. Power defines the probability that one person, organization, or country can carry out its own agenda, despite resistance from another person, organization, or country.

There are different sources and explanations of power in organizations. My research and the work of others suggest that a fruitful and useful definition or conception of power is in terms of dependency.[1] In a relationship between two people, organizations, or countries, A & B, this view holds that:

Power is the obverse or the opposite of dependency. A's power over B varies as a function of B's dependency on A.

This definition suggests two critical conditions that give rise to power differences between A & B.[2]

1. *A has power over B in direct proportion to A's having something B needs.*

If an individual, organization, or country owns or controls something that another individual, organization or country needs to achieve its goals, then the potential for power exists. If A has or controls something B requires—technological knowledge, scarce natural resources, money, or other capabilities or competencies—then A has the potential for power and can exert influence over B. The phrase "potential for power" is used because this first condition, while *necessary*, is not *sufficient*. Another condition exists that affects power.

2. *A's power is also related to its ability to monopolize what B needs.*

If A has or controls something that B sorely needs, and B cannot get it elsewhere, then B is totally dependent on A and A has power over B. A's ability to exercise influence over B is extremely strong and compelling because of the dependency and monopoly relationship.

Power, then, is the opposite of dependency. Dependency can be observed when one individual, organization, or country provides scarce resources to others. If the degree of substitutability is low, i.e. the valued resources or similar resources cannot be easily copied or obtained elsewhere, then dependency is strong, and the power of A over B is consequently also very strong and unilateral.

Applying this logic to America, Inc. raises basic but important questions. What are the critical dependencies that affect power? Is the existence and exercise of power functional or dysfunctional? Are the leaders of America, Inc. in the White House and Congress managing power effectively? The answers to these questions are disconcerting, at best. Let's look at power and the critical dependencies supporting it to see why this is true.

A Dysfunctional Power Structure

There are a number of clear and debilitating examples of poor management and abuses of power in America, Inc. involving the White House and Congress. Let's look first at the culture of influence, bargaining, and potential corruption that pervades Capitol Hill, the lair of the lobbyist.

Lobbyists and the Road to Riches

The previous chapter bemoaned the huge amount of waste due to pork-barrel legislation and a spendthrift culture in Congress. Let's take the analysis one step further by looking at those who pave the road to waste and riches for our leaders and who facilitate an injurious and wasteful money-based culture—the omnipresent lobbyists.

Lobbying or influence peddling is a big business. It's also a growth business. The number of lobbyists in Washington has more than doubled since 2000. There are now about 35,000 registered lobbyists working mainly on K Street, the golden-yellow-brick road to riches. This represents about 65 *lobbyists for every member in Congress.* And the lobbyists must be raking in the dough, as the going rate for a lobbying shop interested in hiring a veteran Capitol Hill lobbyist is about $300,000 per year. It's no wonder, then, that Washington, D.C. has been declared a "profit center" and lobbying a growth business.[3] America, Inc. is indeed an apt title given its centrality in the lobbying or influence peddling business.

What do lobbyists do to earn the big bucks? They are mediators, linking special interest groups with the people who make and pass laws. They use their influence to support legislation and regulations desired by their interest groups. They come to be known by the company they keep and the interests they foster—e.g. the gun lobby, the oil lobby, the steel, milk, corn, or defense-contractor lobby, etc. Lobbyists affect government decisions and actions in Washington in favor of the special interests they represent. They help decide what gets done and doesn't get done at the highest levels of America, Inc. The primary basis of their power is cash, as they make lawmakers *dependent* on them and their money. There are big lobbies whose power is huge and smaller, more benign, lobbies with far less influence, and it's clearly the former's impact that deserves the most attention.

The total spent by special interests in an attempt to influence or seduce U.S. lawmakers is about $200 million. *Per Month.*[4] Lobbyists and various political action committees contribute $millions directly to members of Congress to curry their legislative favor. Lobbyists also provide meals, entertainment, "fact-finding" trips, and other junkets for executive branch personnel, legislators, and their staffs or families. Money talks and lobbyists have a very receptive audience in Washington, D.C.

It's not only the money, however. Money rules, for sure. It nurtures and perpetuates the dependency on the lobbyist, adding to his power. But there also may be a psychological force at work here, one that actually strengthens the dependency bond between lobbyists and politicians. It's the *vanity* of the politicians and lawmakers being influenced by the lobbyists and their moneyed special interests.[5] According to this view, both sides of the lobbying relationship feed off each other. The lobbyist gets his way and the favors for his special interests, but the lawmaker or politician enjoys being courted and feeling important. Politicians and lawmakers apparently have a desire to be indulged, catered to, wined and dined, and applauded. Their strong narcissistic personalities demand the attention, and they are seduced by the smooth-talking lobbyist who makes them feel important and deserving of the lavish attention.

If this view holds water, the dependency on the lobbyist is even stronger than one based solely on huge amounts of money. The lobbyist feeds the politician and lawmaker, not only in terms of vital cash, but also with a psychological catering that intensifies the dependency on the lobbyist and actually increases his power and influence over the government official. Clear-minded, objective management of all stakeholders and issues under these conditions is hardly possible.

A preponderance of data suggests that this influence peddling indeed works. The guilty plea by Jack Abramoff to three felony counts, including conspiracy to commit bribery, sent many of our leaders in Congress scurrying, trying to disassociate themselves from scandal. This suggests his widespread influence, as Abramoff's clients have contributed $millions to these leaders' coffers. The beneficiaries of Abramoff's largess included 195 Republicans and almost 90 Democrats; if there is a culture of corruption or moneyed influence in Washington, it's not owned by either political party. Other politicians and their actual or alleged tie-ins to lobbyists are by now well known, and there's no need to provide a litany of the significant allegations or cases here. I'll simply emphasize that legal contributions to lawmakers have had a major impact on the legislations passed by Congress in the last decade or so. Lobbyists definitely impact what transpires on Capitol Hill.

By Their Fruits, You Will Know Them

Consider for a moment an energy bill that gave oil companies huge tax breaks while they were reaping $billions in profits, even as gas and home heating costs went through the roof. Clearly, these companies had more influence than the consumers rocked by the high energy costs. Even the much touted bill by Nancy Pelosi and the Democrats that supposedly would really sock it to big oil wound up cutting the $32 billion in subsidies and tax breaks by only $5.5 billion, hardly a major hit on big oil's benefits. This suggests that the post-2006 Democratic Congress is open for business and is as susceptible to lobbyists' influence as its previous Republican counterpart.

Consider a bankruptcy "reform" bill influenced by credit card companies making it harder for all, including people burdened by medical catastrophe, to get out from under their debts. Or the legislation allowing U.S. corporations to open and operate offshore tax havens and escape $billions in tax liabilities. Or the formal or "informal" deregulation of certain industries, allowing them higher profits (e.g. telecommunications, banking, securities) and, relatedly, the relaxation of environmental-protection regulations that reduce corporate operating costs and move more cash directly to businesses' bottom line. Recent history is full of examples of similar pieces of protectionism.[6]

Consider the "tax reform" bills that have been passed to improve U.S. manufacturing and cure a host of other maladies including, for example, the corporate tax bill passed in Congress in October, 2004 that some have called the "No Lobbyist Left Behind Act."[7] Every lobbyist in Washington cheered this bill. Its focus supposedly was on job creation in manufacturing, but "manufacturing" included tobacco farmers, Hollywood studios, whaling captains, race-track owners, architects, and bow-and-arrow makers. The bill helped support lawmakers' pet projects and left no pork-laden request unanswered. It was a real disgrace, passed because of lobbyists' influence on Capitol Hill, not because of any clear cost-benefit analysis aimed at improving the lot of the American people.

Consider the fact that my home state of Pennsylvania has earned the dubious distinction of being one of the most productive havens for lobbyists in the country.[8] Defense contractors, for example, have learned that a quiet little place like Johnstown is a great location to set up shop and reap $millions in no-bid contracts and other goodies. Over the past decade, through 2007, one firm has received huge sums of money in military contracts, despite poor performance reviews by Pentagon auditors. Another firm has continued to receive money even though people in Washington actually tried for years to shut it down because its work was unnecessary and wasteful. A review by *The Wall Street Journal* showed that some companies' contracts were funded even though they weren't sought by military or federal agencies, the companies were inefficient, or prior work had been mismanaged or even placed under federal investigation. These and other firms' good fortunes have come about because of their lobbying of the U.S. Congressman from Pennsylvania, a Democrat who happens to be Chairman of the House Appropriations Committee on Defense, which oversees $billions in military spending. Lobbyists definitely have found a lucrative home in Pennsylvania and more money is on the way to chosen companies, even as we read the words on this page.

Look, too, at the number of new federal regulations between 2000-2005 curtailing or affecting business activities. The number has declined significantly. The number of *pending* regulations that would cost businesses $100 million or more per year has declined even more precipitously.[9] Most of these changes are due, simply, to the influence of lobbyists.

It should be pointed out before going further that citizens, of course, have the right to petition their government to redress grievances and seek equitable treatment under the law. Lobbying as a concept or right isn't the culprit. The problem stems from the size and power of certain lobbies that control decisions in the White House and Congress that clearly *create or exacerbate the social, economic, and other problems noted in this book.* There are lobbies whose exercise of power results in gross mismanagement and detrimental effects on the common good and their impact is the chief concern presently. Let's consider the nature of this negative impact in greater detail.

<u>Money rules and democracy suffers</u>. The plain facts are that money rules, large lobbies control the money, and lawmakers have become increasingly dependent on the money and the flattery that accompanies it. Lobbyists have the power and they use it. Some lobbies have more power than others, and they exercise it to affect the decisions of U.S. leaders in critical areas. America, Inc.'s Congress has become a trading floor where a "system of selling federal tax breaks, contracts, subsidies, loan guarantees, and regulatory cutbacks to the highest bidder" is the norm.[10] Money talks and the voices of lobbyists have become louder as they, through their contributions, are telling Congress what to do. In fact, an alarming practice that's becoming more common and pervasive is that *lobbyists are serving as principal fund-raisers for the very lawmakers whose opinions and votes they're trying to sway.*[11] Talk about conflicts of interest, the foxes guarding the hen house, and a biased or skewed process of management that clearly favors the interests of the few rather than the many. This suggests a major debilitating and frightening outcome of this culture of influence: *money is stifling political participation in America and negatively affecting how our democracy works.*

A culture of wealth is favoring the few. Money is choking our democracy to death, as ordinary people increasingly have little or no influence over what happens in the White House and on Capitol Hill. America, Inc. is not working for all Americans, just for the largest and richest and their lobbyists. The power or influence structure created and supported by U.S. leaders on Capitol Hill and in the White House is disenfranchising American citizens and creating a form of oligarchy antagonistic to democratic principles. Chapter 4 noted how financial and fiscal mismanagement is benefiting the few at the expense of the many and creating financial apartheid in the U.S. Lobbyists and their select, special interests are contributing further to the creation of an oligarchy in which a monied class rules and most Americans are losing influence in the democratic process.

U.S. leaders are dependent on lobbyists who control the purse strings and what money buys, including re-election. Indeed, with only a few exceptions, congressmen solicit money mainly to get re-elected, not commit felonies, but this reason hardly should make us feel better about lobbyists' influence and Congress' dependency.[12] Lobbyists have power over U.S. leaders and lawmakers—power, it is recalled, is the obverse of dependency—and the influence peddlers are affecting key management decisions in America, Inc. This strengthening oligarchy represents a biased mismanagement, and increasingly, runs the risk of creating a lack of concern with the well-being of the many.

Much like the business monopoly or oligopoly that uses market or economic power to achieve limited, self-serving ends, U.S. leaders are managing the power structure for their personal needs and goals. The power structure at the highest levels of America, Inc. is running amuck. It's costing the country $billions, contributing to profligate spending and increases in the U.S. debt, hurting the democratic process, and it's not solving major problems. Effective strategic management demands a long-term perspective and integration of strategic, long-term needs with short-term goals and tactics. This simply is not happening in the U.S., as short-term needs drive out consideration of long-term programs and solutions to huge, long-lingering problems, such as the country's horrendous oil dependency (see below). In the private corporation, power differences certainly exist, and those in power certainly use or abuse it for their own benefit. But the extent of the negative effects of power and mismanagement of influence in America, Inc. surpasses most abuses in the private sector, save for an Enron and a few similar cases of oligopolistic or monopolistic malfeasance. Changing a management system based on money, favors, vanity, and self-interest, however, will be difficult for at least two reasons: the revolving door and inertia.

The "Revolving Door." Big-bucks lobbying is luring nearly half of all lawmakers who take jobs in the private sector when they leave Congress.[13] *Nearly one half!* They enjoy a profitable second career by influencing their friends and colleagues to pass (or not pass) legislation that supports their new clients, the industries or companies they're being paid handsomely to promote and protect. This sounds like easy money, especially if the lawmakers being influenced themselves have aspirations for a future career in lobbying. This also sounds like a situation where it's very easy for the lobbyist to stray into bribery or something resembling it to get what he wants, a dangerous situation and one ripe for abuse. The bottom line is that it's only necessary to provide an incentive to one congressman to slip an extra paragraph or two into legislation to secure funding for a lobbyist's project or client. A powerful lobbyist and one or two pawns on Capitol Hill can easily take a lot of cash out of the public coffer, hardly a desirable situation and one ripe for abuse.[14] The revolving door only exacerbates this problem as it creates a dangerous mutual dependency.

Consider just one example of this revolving door. An especially flagrant or outrageous case is that of the Homeland Security Department, an organization that has hardly distinguished itself by its management prowess. Katrina was and still is an unbelievable disaster, U.S. ports still aren't secure, chemical plants and oil refineries remain inadequately protected, the inefficiency and ineffectiveness of an unwieldy organization created by lumping together 22 federal agencies and 183,000 employees provide countless horror stories, etc.—the list of management woes grows daily. Yet the department has excelled in one dubious area: generating a huge crop of government-trained lobbyists and consultants. At least 90 top Homeland Security officials had gone through the revolving door by mid 2006 to become lobbyists dedicated to influencing their former colleagues, and the number has most assuredly grown since.[15] It's truly hard to fathom how people who managed a business so poorly could find such a golden opportunity. Even Michael Brown, whose management capability and leadership were questioned or attacked by many, has started a consulting firm. Amazing.

Imagine the impact of these lobbyists and consultants on the officials remaining at Homeland Security. If these officials see the lucrative contracts being offered to their ex-colleagues by the private sector, do you think that their decisions and judgments about what companies to contract with will be affected by their own career and financial aspirations for life after Homeland Security? Clearly, there is a dangerous *quid pro quo* suggested by this golden revolving door and the influence or power attendant with it. This suggests gross mismanagement and perpetuation of incompetence at its very worst.

One more point needs mention. A focus by lawmakers on lobbyists' money, earmarks and pet projects, and possible lucrative employment some day in a lobby "shop" clearly must distract our leaders from the real problems facing the country. It takes time, after all, to become well connected and milk the system for personal gain and provide benefits to only a minority of stakeholders, leaving precious little time for other projects. It's simply easier to ignore the "big stuff," the real problems facing America, Inc., with a rationalization that someone else surely will address them some day. The costs and management problems with this should by now be obvious to all.

Inertia: oil, dependency, and mismanagement. A second and related obstacle to reform is the inertia and resistance to change that have been built up over the years in this revolving system of power, influence, and granting of favors. Consider just one egregious case—that of the oil lobby and the oil dependency of America, Inc.

The world currently consumes about 84 million barrels of oil a day, or one billion every 12 days. World oil demand is expected to reach 104 million barrels a day by 2020, a whopping 24% increase. For every two barrels consumed, only one new barrel is being discovered. And we all know what happens to price when demand is increasing and supply is decreasing or holding steady.[16]

The U.S. uses 21+ million barrels of oil a day. It produces about 7.55 million barrels, so over 60% of its oil needs must be imported. America, Inc. is clearly dependent on foreign oil, and this dependency will get worse and more problematic, as competition for oil heats up with the growth of China, India, and other countries and political instability shakes the oil-producing nations.

Who provides the foreign oil? Two-thirds of the world's proven reserves are controlled by five countries in the Persian Gulf, with Saudi Arabia alone controlling one-quarter of these valuable reserves. Other countries sitting atop of oil include Venezuela, Nigeria, Iraq, Iran, and elements of the former Soviet Union, and some of these countries clearly represent high-political-risk suppliers to the U.S.[17]

America, Inc. is clearly dependent on foreign oil, and foreign countries can exercise influence or power because of this dependency. Witness just the U.S.' treatment of Saudi Arabia over the years, despite the latter's restrictive, biased, and discriminatory political, economic, and social climate. The management of this critical dependency hasn't improved at all since 1973 when the Middle East tightened the oil spigots, drove up oil prices worldwide, and threw the U.S. into a huge recession. Virtually every State of Union address by Presidents since the 1973 embargo has argued that oil dependency is a horrific problem and viable solutions must be found, *yet America, Inc.'s leaders have learned and done little or nothing in over three decades to reverse or thwart this critical dependency and the power of Saudi Arabia and others over the U.S.*

That these problems of dependency still exist is remarkable, given the number of oil people who have inhabited or influenced the White House and Cabinet, especially in the past 6 years. Bush and Cheney are former oil company executives. Condoleezza Rice was on the board of Chevron, and Andrew Card had ties to the automotive industry, a clear ally of big oil. Cheney's company, Halliburton, has benefited hugely from the oil dependence and the U.S. presence in Iraq, but oil policy hasn't changed for the better. Cheney's White House task force set up to overhaul energy policy and boost oil production hasn't shown positive results, except on the bottom line of the oil companies. Perhaps the fact that the dependency on foreign oil still exists and is growing stronger despite the oil experience in the administration isn't "remarkable." Perhaps "predicable" is the better word.

There have been some supposed attempts to address oil dependency. For example, some U.S. officials have been making noise about drilling in the Artic National Wildlife Refuge, but this is a poor strategy and a political smokescreen to hide the mismanagement of the oil-dependency problem. There is huge danger in opening this virgin territory because of its negative impact on the environment. And even if the refuge were to be opened, it would take perhaps 10 years or more to reach full production. More significantly, the oil drilled would represent but a drop in the huge bucket of the U.S.' wasteful consumption of oil. This action simply would not solve America's oil-dependency problem, and only the oil companies and energy friends of the White House and Congress would benefit. But such a proposed action sounds and looks good. It conveys the idea that something beneficial is being contemplated and that the gross inaction by U.S. leaders may be coming to an end after decades of poor management of a debilitating oil situation.

This situation, again, reflects mismanagement and inertia of the worst kind. Everyone in a leadership position in the U.S. has known and still knows that there is a major problem with the country's oil dependency, but nothing of real substance has been or is being done. This dependency could eventually injure the country's position of power in the world, but there has been and still is no urgency to take real action and solve the problem. Our leaders are not leading or managing effectively.

This is a clear case of short-term managerial thinking. Sound management requires a good amount of strategic thinking, an ability to go beyond considerations of only short-term gratification and envision real, long-term solutions to pressing problems and areas of critical dependency. U.S. leaders are short-term thinkers, focused on the rewards provided by lobbyists and re-election at all costs, even if their actions and decisions actually injure the well-being of the majority of America, Inc.'s citizens or shareholders. Short-term thinking certainly prevails and the oil problem and decades of inaction are clearly symptoms of this defective managerial worldview.

<u>Lobbying for the status quo.</u> This is a deplorable situation that should cause widespread citizen rebellion and political action to overcome inertia and cure the oil-dependency problem, yet nothing of substance happens. It's especially deplorable and disconcerting because it is perfectly clear what must be done to help solve the problem.

The vital need is, first, to reduce demand for and consumption of oil. The next logical step is to focus on alternatives to oil and pursue them relentlessly.

There are two steps that can be taken immediately to reduce drastically the consumption of oil. The first serious and more impactful move is *to raise the gasoline tax dramatically.* Increasing taxes significantly on gasoline will drive down demand quickly. Higher prices at the pump will have an immediate effect, curtailing the wasteful habits of all but a handful of owners of gas-guzzling SUVs and inefficient cars and trucks. Gas-guzzling habits will change quickly with higher prices, a phenomenon observed every time OPEC tightened the oil spigot in the past. Raising prices would also drive people over time to buy more fuel-efficient vehicles or seek more efficient public transportation. It's time that our leaders take the lead and raise gasoline prices to reduce our oil dependency. Despite critics' screams of regressive taxation and other problems, this option has worked in other countries, including those faring at par or better economically compared to the U.S., and it can work here.

Increasing the tax on gasoline would be a bold move by U.S. leaders, signaling clearly the intention and need to drive down demand and reduce oil consumption. It would signal strong leadership in the White House and Congress and a firm commitment to solve a problem that is only going to get worse and more debilitating. Certainly, a few exceptions could be made for over-the-road truckers and others whose livelihood depends heavily on gasoline, but the impact of such a tax would be immediate and effective. It would be a real step in reducing oil dependency, not just another slick, ineffective political move that raises the flag of oil dependency but does nothing about it.

Relatedly, leaders in Congress and the White House can *support, enact, and enforce more stringent fuel-economy standards.* In this area, the U.S. has failed abysmally. The regulations have been so abused that the oil efficiency of U.S. vehicles is at a 20-plus-year low.[18] Loopholes exist that allow SUVs and trucks to waste more fuel than normal cars. Tax loopholes actually motivate and support the purchase of gas-guzzling vehicles. CAFÉ standards regulating fuel efficiency are too low and need to be raised, consistent with those in virtually every developed country in the world.

If auto makers were forced to double the fuel efficiency of their vehicles—a realistic goal if legislation and resources were dedicated to it—gasoline consumption would fall by a huge amount, reducing our dependency on foreign oil. A counter-argument—that increased efficiency would actually motivate people to drive even more, thereby wasting even more gas—is without foundation. Doubling fuel efficiency might cause a slight increase in miles driven, but an argument that people will drive twice as much, despite their work demands and other routine constraints on their time, makes little sense. It will take time, of course, before more fuel-efficient vehicles replace all of the gas-guzzlers, but the net effect of more stringent fuel-economy standards clearly will be positive. Such an emphasis on conservation is a fairly obvious and effective step, which makes one wonder why more stringent fuel-economy standards aren't being enacted and enforced. The answer is coming shortly, but it's a good guess that lobbyists and special interests are involved in the management and control of these standards and are having a negative impact.

Alternative sources of energy can be supported and synthetic fuels developed on a larger scale. Ethanol seems to be a promising additive or fuel, but huge investments are needed in production and distribution to make this work on a large scale basis and other costs are extremely high. In fact, there are contrary opinions as to the viability of corn-based ethanol as the fuel or additive of choice, from political watchers, scientists, and conservation groups alike.[19] Corn, the anointed provider of ethanol, necessitates the use of huge amounts of nitrogen fertilizer, insecticides, and herbicides. About 1700 gallons of water are needed to produce one gallon of ethanol, and each gallon of ethanol supposedly produces over 10 gallons of sewage-like effluent. Scientists like Dr. Tad Patzek at the University of California and Dr. David Pimentel of Cornell University have warned us about the downside of ethanol production and use. Pimentel, for example, claims that ethanol is a boondoggle, requiring almost 40 percent more energy to produce what we get out of it.[20] In effect, if true, this means we're importing oil to produce ethanol in a very inefficient way, and this additive is not decreasing our dependency on foreign oil at all, its much-touted benefit. Added to a negative impact on water, soil, and air from carbon dioxide releases, corn-based ethanol doesn't seem to shape up very nicely at all to these critics as the fuel additive of choice.

So why focus so strongly on corn-based ethanol? Why not rely on other crops—e.g. sugar beets—as a source of ethanol? Why hasn't there been a management analysis of the real costs and benefits of different crops as potential sources of ethanol? Because the corn lobby is big and influential.[21] It has more clout than the sugar-feet lobby, if one indeed exists. It's been pushing corn as the savior crop, while lobbying to get more and more land devoted to corn and ethanol production, including virgin land that has been set aside by the government for protection from farming and development. Can corn-based ethanol reduce America's oil dependency and not make a bad situation worse? Perhaps. But our leaders in the White House and Congress need to rely more on scientists' inputs and better cost-benefit models before committing irrevocably to only one course of action. The ethanol train or bandwagon certainly shouldn't be derailed, but it should be complemented by strategic analysis of other options—e.g. hydrogen fuel cells—before investments are fully and irrevocably committed.[22]

More management attention should also be paid to the vehicles that use the fuels. The electric car is more than a concept; it's another option that deserves additional attention. These vehicles have already been developed, sold, and proven their worth as efficient vehicles with strong performance capabilities. Toyota and others have shown convincingly that gasoline and electric fuel combinations are realistic and desirable in terms of oil consumption and performance. Methods have been and still are being developed to increase the electric component of an engine's power and reduce reliance on gasoline. The technology already exists to blow a huge hole in the oil-dependency fortress that has America, Inc. squarely in its sights. If all of this is already known, why isn't change occurring faster? What's causing resistance to the needed changes to reduce the huge problem of oil dependency and the country's weaning from the gas-combustion engine?

> *As if you haven't guessed by now, a major reason for inertia and inaction is the existence of the vast and powerful lobby machine and the special interest groups that prefer the status quo and centrality of fossil fuel.*

The *large oil companies* are benefiting from high oil prices and the U.S. dependency on oil. Profits and management bonuses are sky high. Why support changes that reduce the centrality and importance of oil and the profits and returns to shareholders? Why do anything different while $trillions of oil are still in the ground and $billions in profits are yet to be made? It's only logical for the oil companies to lobby *against* fuel-efficiency improvements and lowered gasoline consumption and *for* nice-sounding but ineffective solutions that they would control, e.g. drilling in the Artic preserve. Managers in the oil industry won't openly agree with these accusations, of course, but their actions or inactions belie their oft-stated good intentions about solving an obvious oil problem that's been around forever.

Consider, for example, how some oil companies make it difficult for their service stations to stock and sell E85, a blend of ethanol (85%) and gasoline (15%). This product seemingly should be supported by oil executives who espouse alternative fuels and reductions in oil dependency, yet their actions suggest otherwise.[23] Oil companies lose sales if their dealers sell E85, so they, in effect, try to keep it away from their retail stations. If franchises by contract must buy their fuel from the oil companies, the companies can refuse to sell E85, and consequently, the retailer can't get it from the parent organization. The stations can sell E85 if their company grants an exception and lets them buy from another supplier, but this is probably not the normal case. Similarly, the oil companies may limit advertising of E85 and restrict the use of credit cards to pay for ethanol purchases, or even require that E85 be sold only under a separate canopy, away from the oil company's main gasoline products.[24] Oil executives, then, may openly espouse alternative fuels like E85, but they manage the situation to maintain the status quo, perpetuate the dependency on oil, and maintain their own sales and profits.

Lobbyists and influence peddlers for the *big car* and *truck manufacturers* are also very active and influential. The argument is that increasing CAFE fuel-efficiency standards would hurt American car company profitability, drive massive layoffs, and create other economic ills for the U.S. That no one challenges these assertions when companies in other countries producing more fuel-efficient vehicles are profitable and supplying consumers what they want is truly remarkable. That these assertions persist when many countries supporting more efficient automotive standards are generally outperforming the U.S. in the global marketplace is equally remarkable.

Recall that GM introduced an electric car decades ago and it proved to be an efficient and attractive alternative to its gas combustion engines. The electric car was also desired by a significant number of people, despite its limited introduction and non-existent marketing. Recall, too, that GM killed the electric car, with the help of the oil companies and others in the oil lobby. There simply was too much money to be made from oil and wasteful combustion technology to allow introduction of a beneficial innovation at the time.

Worldwide *oil producers* like Saudi Arabia also make their influence felt in Washington for the status quo and against change. The oil dependency of the U.S. does much to fuel these countries' way of life. By influencing leaders in the U.S. *not* to do anything about energy conservation, the producing nations can keep the U.S. over a barrel, an oil barrel. The White House and Congress, by avoiding energy conservation and continuing to waste energy on a large-scale basis, can also continue to help generate windfall profits for Saudi Arabia, Iran, Venezuela, and other countries where the cash is used to insulate the political regimes from outside pressures to open up their economies, liberate their women, or modernize their educational systems.[25] These countries, of course, wish to maintain America, Inc.'s dependency on them and their oil at all costs, as this is a formidable basis of power, so they'll use their influence for this end.

A Sorry State of Affairs

So, where do we stand? The conclusions of the present analysis are obvious, striking, and perhaps even a bit frightening.

1. If power can be conceptualized as the obverse of dependency, then lobbyists in America, Inc.'s "headquarters" have immense power. Members of Congress, in particular, have relied on lobbyists to fund their election campaigns and junkets, making them dependent on the influence peddlers and their vast money resources.

2. Narrow, special interests often rule lawmakers' agendas, not what's good for the country as a whole. The democratic process is being increasingly thwarted by the money and power of special interests and the lobbyists who funnel their money and influence to control lawmakers and others in top leadership positions. Money rules, and it is ruining the democratic process in America, Inc. It is negatively affecting our leaders' ability to manage efficiently and effectively and achieve goals and outcomes that benefit more than a handful of select individuals and organizations. The occasional half-hearted attempt at lobbying or ethics reform up to this point in time has been a sham, a "pseudo-event" (see Chapter 6) engineered and politicized to dupe the public and make them think that steps are being taken to remove the fate of legislation from the hands of lobbyists and their dependent cohorts in Washington.[1]

3. Dependency on foreign oil is a growing and dangerous problem. Powerful providers of foreign oil, the large oil companies, their friends on Capitol Hill and in the White House, and the automobile manufacturers, among others, all are using their influence to maintain the status quo and its short-term thinking, as detrimental as it is. Real change will be difficult because of the inertia of the current power structure and a "revolving door" that unites lawmakers and lobbyists in a nefarious and dangerous economic and political bond. The foxes will certainly resist any attempts to eliminate or modify their powerful positions as guard-

---

1. A new ethics bill was sent by the Senate to the President in August, 2007. A brief analysis of it is offered below.

ians of the hen house, and the country will continue to feel the negative effects of this influence.

4. Despite these obstacles, change is absolutely necessary and vital to curtail and control the power of lobbyists and their special interest groups. The power pendulum has swung too far toward special interests and the rule of the few, and it's time to change a debilitating management oligarchy and process based on money, undue influence, excessive waste, and short-term thinking. Let's turn, then, to what must be done to rectify or reverse this state of affairs.

Controlling the Lobbyists and Managing the Power Structure Effectively

The large majority of Americans believe that lobbyists and the large companies or industries they represent have too much power and influence in Washington. Very few people believe, for example, that the Jack Abramoff case was an isolated incident. In fact, 86% of the people in one Harris poll said that they believe that he is just one lobbyist among many who just happened to get caught, and that there are many others out there actively involved in Washington's "grubby secret," the unspoken "business of the shadows," who haven't yet been caught.[26] Sad to say, the polls also reveal that people believe that the shady side of lobbying, the behind-the-scenes activity, the power of money, and the political culture in Washington won't change, *even with the passage of new lobbying restrictions.* The lawmakers, after all, would write the restrictions and the foxes guarding the henhouse aren't about to stifle their own activities, funding sources, and fun. Asking Congress to pass real lobbying and ethics reform bills is a fruitless task, according to the poll results.

The response of lawmakers to the Abramoff scandal proves sadly that these assertions and opinions have some validity. When the House Ethics Committee and Speaker Dennis Hastert called for a total ban on junkets financed by favor seekers, the lawmakers rebelled and killed the ban outright.[27] Other potential restrictions on lobbying activities have met a similar quick demise. The bills that have been proposed seem to be a symbol of lobbying reform that lawmakers can hold up to impress constituents that their representatives are noble people, intent on reform and the highest ethical standards.[28] In all fairness, there are undoubtedly some on Capitol Hill who are sincere in their efforts at reform. The predomident feeling or attitude of the public, however, supported by the empirical poll data referenced earlier, seems to be that these sincere lawmakers are clearly in the minority.

To reinstate confidence in government in light of the Abramoff scandal and other Congressional misdeeds, a real reform bill is needed. This is the *minimum* action that must be taken. It is not the only action, but it is a needed basic step to implement change. A real reform bill would ban or tightly control all gifts to politicians and lobbyists' paying for politicians' travel. It would post all contributions to lawmakers on websites where public access is uninhibited. A real reform bill would eliminate or tightly control earmarks and the stealthy passage of legislation that only benefits the lawmaker or a select group of his or her constituents or lobbyists. The bill, that is, would reduce or eliminate wasteful spending on pork-barrel projects. It would slow the revolving door drastically by not allowing lawmakers to become private lobbyists and influence their former colleagues for at least five years, with no exceptions, and would limit the amount of private money in political campaigns. An effective bill would create an independent ethics-oversight committee to police lobbyists and their dealings with lawmakers and other politicians. For obvious reasons, the committee would not be staffed by lawmakers who have benefited immensely from the largess of the very lobbyists whose actions they must scrutinize.

With this in mind, let's take a look at the most recent ethics bill that the Senate sent to the President in August, 2007.[29] The bill calls for bans on gifts, meals, and travel paid for by lobbyists, and requires lawmakers to identify lobbyists who raise $15,000 or more in contributions to lawmakers' coffers. It increases the visibility of earmarks by letting lawmakers see exactly what they and others are receiving. Given the 6,500 or so earmarks already this year totaling $billions, this suggests that the bill provides some needed additional scrutiny. The bill is ostensibly aimed at reducing the number of earmarks for pet projects that members of Congress can add to spending bills and aims to shed light on the stealthy practice of diverting public funds for personal projects that's done routinely by lawmakers. This all sounds positive, but let's look more closely at the bill and early reactions to it, including by members of Congress who would have to abide by its provisions.

Closer examination of the bill reveals major problems, especially in the area of earmark reform. Earmarks that benefit *only* the sponsor and his or her family are prohibited, but those that also benefit others—a sponsor's friends, colleagues, or lobbyist pals—are not prohibited, and this hardly seems restrictive or effective. The Senate Majority Leader unilaterally can decide what indeed is an earmark and whether it complies with the new disclosure statements. So, the leader can determine whether the bills *he brings to the floor* comply with the rules, ostensibly another case of the fox guarding the hen house. The bill also eliminates the requirement that earmark lists be searchable, which seemingly allows bad bills to hide and survive in a throng of other bills.

For an earmark or special (read "pork") project to be approved, lawmakers would be required to make their plans and a bill's provisions known at least 48 hours before the Senate votes on them. 48 hours? Given the number of bills that routinely come up on the floor and given the fact that lawmakers don't read most of the bills they vote on, what's the likelihood of sufficient scrutiny and attention to detail of the bill being presented? In addition, there's a nice loophole that enables lawmakers to sneak things through without scrutiny: if lawmakers say that full and early disclosure is not "technically feasible," the Majority Leader could *waive the restrictive requirement*. This hardly suggests a real attempt to curtail the flow of pork-barrel projects or earmarks.

The new transparency and publicizing of earmarks to lawmakers—who is getting what—may actually be motivating the *wrong* behavior. Seeing what one is getting relative to one's colleagues may actually foster competition to outdo others in generating earmarks. The visibility of earmarks, in reality, may increase their value as measures of a lawmaker's clout, standing, or influence, and thus motivate even *more*, not fewer, earmarks. If true, this suggests that even more wasteful spending and pork-barrel projects will be the rule rather than the exception as a result of the reform bill.

The bottom line is that the new ethics reform bill seems to be toothless, preserves the status quo, and is trying to fool people into thinking that real change is occurring and things are being fixed in Washington. While some Senators have expressed enthusiasm for the reform bill, others, most notably, Jim DeMint and John McCain have stated that it guts reform and is nothing but a sham and cover-up that changes little to reduce the power of special interests and the wasteful mismanagement of U.S. funds. All in all, it seems that it will be business as usual on Capitol Hill, despite the reform bill, if not because of it.

A related problem: "donor bundling". While emphasis has been on the power of lobbyists and their money, there is a relatively new problem that must be mentioned along with lobbying, namely, *donor bundling*. Bundling has grown in popularity and presents yet another area of potential abuse in the power-based process of funding and controlling lawmakers and politicians seeking high office.

Bundlers are integrators and conduits of funds. They are individuals who act as middlemen, asking friends, family, co-workers, and other business acquaintances for contributions that they, in turn, bundle and pass on to candidates for use in their election campaigns. Bundling is legal, candidates need not identify their bundlers, and the process is becoming increasingly popular. While bundling accounted for only 8% of campaign funds in 2000, the number rose to 18% in 2004, and solid estimates show it already accounting for 28% of the record $379 million raised overall for the 2008 campaign. The *Wall Street Journal* reports that the major presidential candidates are using bundlers—mainly lawyers, well-known business people, even lobbyists. Hillary Clinton (223 bundlers), Barack Obama (263), Mitt Romney (307), Rudy Giulliani (138), John McCain (442), John Edwards (543), and Fred Thompson (77) all use bundlers (the numbers reported are those as of the date of the *WSJ* article), and the usage will likely increase because of bundling's success in raising funds.

Bundling, like lobbying, is clearly becoming big business and, more importantly, consistent with the theme of the current chapter, potentially another source of undue influence over candidates for high public office. Bundlers have already been accused of surpassing the legal limits of individual contributions by secretly *reimbursing* their contributors for the donations they bundled together, thereby increasing their own contributions illegally while still currying favor with their chosen candidate. The reward for bundling is access to candidates and increased influence over their positions and campaign platforms. As Fred Wertheimer, the president of Democracy 21, a nonpartisan group dedicated to reducing the influence of money in politics, said: "This has opened the door to anything-goes bundlers pursuing anything-goes fund raising."[30]

The 2007 ethics reform bill contained no suggested controls over bundling activities or their funding limits. Bundling has quietly been growing more prevalent and influential and, to this point, political candidates have kept the details and results of bundling very hush-hush. The result, again, is that money talks, a wealthy oligarchy is being strengthened quietly, influence peddling and dysfunctional dependencies flourish, and the average citizen loses yet more control over the electoral process in America, Inc.

A better solution. A strong ethics reform bill would have been a step in the right direction. If done properly, it would have added accountability to lawmakers' and other politicians' actions and negate a portion of the influence peddling based on the power of money. A strong ethics reform bill, however, even if one had been passed, is only one move to curb lobbying- and bundling-related excesses. There is another approach: a system based in part on the *public funding of major elections*.

Even a strong ethics bill will be subverted by politicians and lobbyists, as it's in the best interests of both parties to do so. Public funding of elections would help reduce the lobbyists' power over lawmakers and give some control over the politicians back to the people where it belongs. Federal funding of Congressional and Presidential elections would help to renew the democratic or participative management approach to government that the original managers of a fledgling republic envisioned. Even public funding, of course, would have to be aided and supplemented by additional controls or limits on the amount of lobbies' and bundlers' contributions to political campaigns. Public funding would do little good if U.S. leaders could supplement their public funds with unlimited amounts of cash from special interests. So, public funding still needs help from bills and ethics rules governing lobbyists' money and influence, and the two in concert can produce positive change.

Consider for a moment the critical notion of management control. Control involves an evaluation of performance against predetermined goals or metrics, and then sponsoring changes or reforms if actual performance falls short of desired levels. In America, Inc. presently, management control lies in the hands of the politicians who write and evaluate legislation, who control and evaluate themselves, and who with the help of big money and gerrymandering often control their own re-election. In this process, the politicians become increasingly dependent on the lobbyists and bundlers who, in turn, control the purse strings and much of what the politicians do, hardly a effective model to produce change and reform. A more effective process *would take some of the control out of the hands of those who have a vested interest not to change*, who prefer business as usual and the self-serving model just described. A better management control process would ensure that representatives in Washington can't let the public down or sell them out for personal gain. Public funding of critical national and Congressional elections would provide some leverage over the politicians who supposedly work for the public good. Some of the control of the purse strings would be taken away from those who presently monopolize those strings and use them for personal benefit, not the common good.

Public funding would likely help restore public trust in big government. It would probably make key political races into more competitive affairs and help attract a broader more qualified slate of candidates compared to the few who presently benefit from nepotism, friendship ties, political connections, or coalitions of moneyed interests. For a very few dollars per capita, major U.S. elections and more political power could be put into the hands of the people than is currently the case.

Can federal financing work as a form of management control? It's already worked in a few states and municipalities, and clean-money campaigns are under way in a significant number of others. Still, much more work needs to be done.[31] Yet the effort definitely seems to be worth it. The situation in America, Inc. will only get worse until enlightened citizens and lawmakers force needed change and reduce the power of the lobbyists, bundlers, and their narrow interests. Hiding one's head in the sand and saying "that's the way it is in Washington" will only perpetuate a costly and wasteful system of management and influence.

People get the leadership and management they deserve. If people are satisfied with wasteful leaders in Congress and the White House, they need do nothing to maintain the present sorry state of affairs. If citizens wish to stop wasteful spending, outlandish pork-barrel legislation, undue influence by huge lobbies and their money, a harmful dependency on foreign oil and governments, and an erosion of the democratic process in America, Inc., they need to speak out and get involved to restore a power balance more in favor of the common good. They need to *scream* for reform—in the press, on blogs, on direct lines to their representatives, etc.—and use their votes before the mismanagement and abuse of power leads to even greater problems in the U.S. Better leadership and management are needed in America, Inc., and they are affected and driven by effective *followership* and more intense *citizen involvement*, a point I return to in Chapter 7.

CONCLUSIONS

Lobbyists have power and use it to run America, Inc. Lawmakers and other politicians depend on lobbyists and bundlers and their special interests for funds to support a host of things, including their re-election campaigns, and this dependency is at the heart of lobbyists' influence.

The mismanagement of the power structure is having pervasive and deep effect on and in America, Inc. The country is becoming an oligarchy run by those with money or access to it. The democratic process and related values are being subverted badly, as increasingly the man in the street has little say over government legislation or policy. There indeed is a real danger that a culture of corruption and unethical behavior will become the norm if the excesses of lobbyists' power remain unchecked.

U.S. leaders have become very short-term oriented. Short-term thinking is supported strongly by the quest for rewards provided by lobbyists and bundlers and, relatedly, by a fear of not being re-elected. Biting the bullet and doing the right thing are not as attractive options as making the bucks now, having fun, and staying in elected office. Avoiding the tough, but necessary, long-term decisions is the result of the present system of mismanagement and influence on Capitol Hill and elsewhere in America, Inc.

Corrective action must be taken soon. At minimum, a strong ethics-reform bill must be passed and an independent ethics-oversight committee created to police lobbyists and their dealings with politicians and lawmakers. A stronger and more lasting solution would be the public funding of Presidential and Congressional elections. A "clean money" system of public funding would renew the democratic process, reduce the need for and power of lobbyists and bundlers, and go a long way toward reducing the gross mismanagement of power and influence at the highest levels of America, Inc.

Endnotes

1. Lawrence G. Hrebiniak, *Making Strategy Work* (Wharton School Publishing, 2005). For earlier discussions of dependency and power, see R. M. Emerson, "Power-Dependence Relations," *American Sociological Review*, 27, 1962; David Jacobs, "Dependency and Vulnerability: An Exchange Approach to the Control of Organizations," *Administrative Science Quarterly*, 19, 1974; and Robert Dahl, *Modern Political Analysis* (Prentice-Hall), 1963.

2. See *Making Strategy Work*, Ibid. Chapter 9.

3. Jeffrey Birnbaum, "The Road to Riches is Called K Street," *Washington Post*, June 22, 2005.

4. Bill Moyers, "A Culture of Corruption," *Washington Spectator*, April 6, 2006; see also www.commondreams.org for a reprint of Moyers' article.

5. Alfred Lubrano, "Lobbyists Know it's All in the Vanity," *The Philadelphia Inquirer*, January 17, 2006; Philip Lacovara, *The Ethics of Lobbying* (Georgetown University Press, 2004)

6. "Culture of Corruption," op. cit.; Tom Hamburger and Janet Hook, "Lobbyists Find New Congress is Open for Business," *Los Angeles Times*, January 22, 2007; "Better Ways to Attack George Bush," The Economist, April, 3, 2004; "From Bad to Awful," The Economist, November 27, 2004.

7. "Lobbyists' Delight," The Economist," October 16, 2004.

8. For a discussion of the facts contained in this paragraph, including a discussion of "Murtha Inc.", see John Wilke, "How Lawmaker Rebuilt Hometown on Earmarks," *The Wall Street Journal*, October 30, 2007.

9. "Road to Riches," op. cit.

10. Public Citizen, "Lobbyists Contributed $103 million to Lawmakers Since 1998," May 23, 2006; see, too, Common Dreams Progressive News Wire, May 23, 2006, www.commondreams.org.

11. Brody Mullins, "Growing Role for Lobbyists: Raising Funds for Lawmakers," *The Wall Street Journal*, January 27, 2006.

12. "Hobbling the Lobbyists," The Economist, January 28, 2006.

13. "Road to Riches," op. cit.

14. "Hobbling the Lobbyists," op. cit.

15. Editorial, *New York Times*, June 21, 2006; Eric Lipton, "Former Antiterror Officials Find Industry Pays Better," The New York Times, June 18, 2006.

16. Jeffrey Ball, "Efforts to Reduce U.S. Addiction to Oil Are Few," *The Wall Street journal*, September 28, 2004; Jeff Gelles, "Predicting the End of Oil Age," *The Philadelphia Inquirer*, February 19, 2006; Jeffrey Ball, "As Prices Soar, Doomsayers Provoke Debate on Oil's Future," *The Wall Street Journal*, September 21, 2004; "What if?" *The Economist*, May 29, 2004; "The Oil-holics," *The Economist*, August 27, 2005.

17. "Efforts to Reduce U.S. Addiction to Oil," Ibid.

18. "The Oilholics," op cit.

19. Jeremy Rifkin is a well-known author whose previous works include *The Age of Access* and *The Biotech Century*. His latest book, *The Hydrogen Economy*, questions the logic and feasibility of corn-based ethanol as a fuel addictive and argues instead for the use of hydrogen cells as a better, cleaner, and more efficient fuel source. Conservationists and scientists have also been vocal about corn-based ethanol and its problem. See, for example, Ted Williams' article, "Ethanol Is Not the Answer to Our Energy Problem," *Fly Rod and Reel*, Vol. 29, June 2007. Don't be misled by the publication. Williams is its Conservation editor and guru and his work is always researched and written carefully. He has published his work in other conservation-oriented magazines and journals, including *Audubon* and *Sierra Magazine* and is an authority on most conservation-related issues. For more on Williams, see note 19 below.

20. The work by Williams, op. cit., contains quotes and the results of interviews with well-known scientists like Tad Patzek and David Pimentel. Their research and publication records suggest that their opinions on ethanol and other fuels are well founded based on rigorous scientific methods and sound empirical evidence. See also "Ted Williams on Conservation," *Winds of Change* (Ohio Valley Environmental Coalition, July 2004); Ted Williams,

Wild Moments, (Storey Publishing, 2004); He is Editor-at-Large of <u>Audubon</u> magazine and has contributed extensively to <u>Sierra Magazine</u> and other conservation-minded publications.

For more by Tad Patzek, see "The Disastrous Local and Global Impacts of Tropical Biofuel Production," <u>Energy Tribune</u>, March 2007; "A First-Law Thermodynamic Analysis of the Corn-Ethanol Cycle," <u>Natural Resources Research</u>, Vol. 15, February 2007; "A Statistical Analysis of the Theoretical Yield of Ethanol from Corn Starch," <u>Natural Resources Research</u>, Vol. 15, December 2006.

David Pimentel and Tad Patzek published "Green Plants, Fossil Fuels, and Now Biofuels," <u>Bioscience</u>, Vol. 56, 2006, and "Producing Ethanol and Biodiesel from Corn and Other Crops is Not Worth the Energy," <u>Natural Resources Research</u>, Vol. 14, 2005; David Pimentel is the author of 290 scientific papers and 20 books whose Curriculum Vitae is posted on the Cornell University website, College of Agriculture and Life Sciences.

21. Rifkin, op cit.

22. Ibid.

23. Laura Meckler, "Fill Up With Ethanol? One Obstacle is Big Oil," *The Wall Street Journal*, April 2, 2007.

24. Ibid.

25. Thomas Friedman, "No Mullah Left Behind," *The New York Times*, February 13, 2005.

26. "Large Majorities of U.S. Adults Continue to Think that Big Companies, PACs, and Lobbyists Have Too Much Power and Influence in Washington," Harris Poll, November 8-13, 2005; "Very Few U.S. Adults Believe the Jack Abramoff Case is an Isolated Incident," Harris Poll #9, January 24, 2006; Rupert Cornwell, "The Lobbyists' Scandal: The Secret World of Washington," *The Independent* (UK), June 30, 2005.

27. Editorial, "Razzle-Dazzle 'Em Ethics Reform," *The New York Times*, June 21, 2006.

28. Lee Drutman, "Lobby Reform: Worse than Window Dressing," *Providence Journal*, April 27, 2006; see, too, Common Dreams News center, www. commondreams.org, April 27, 2006.

29. Not a whole lot has been written about the new ethics reform bill as of this writing and the present book's going to press. For some information and analysis, see: David Rogers, "Congress Approves Lobbying Overhead," *The Wall Street Journal*, August 3, 2007; Jeff Zeleny and Carl Hulse, "Senate Sends Ethics Bill to Bush," *The Philadelphia Inquirer*, August 3, 2007; and Edmund Andrews and Robert Pear, "A Rule to Deter Earmarks Instead Helps Them to Flourish," *The Philadelphia Inquirer*, August 6, 2007.

30. "Donor Bundling," Ibid.

31. Brody Mullins, "Donor Bundling Emerges as Major Ill in '08 Race." The Wall Street Journal, October 18, 2007.

6

More Power-Related Problems: The Attack on Science, the Press, and Other Management Abuses

The last chapter emphasized that the power of lobbies and their special interests is a scourge on the U.S. political process and that it must be confronted and reduced. Mismanagement of large, influential, well-heeled lobbies by leaders in Congress, it was argued, has already created a host of ills, including massive pork-barrel waste and major damage to the democratic process in America. There are other areas, however, where power (or the lack thereof) is creating major dysfunctional consequences. There are still other areas where mismanagement of power rules, creating and exacerbating problems that will hurt the country if present trends continue. This chapter will consider these alarming trends, including attacks on science and the press led and supported by many U.S. leaders.

Science Under Siege

Influence in scientific matters should be with scientists and their proven methods of data collection and analysis. History has shown us clearly what happens when politics, pseudo-science, or religion tries to control, negate, interpret, or repudiate sound science, and the lessons aren't pretty. The sad facts, however, are that science presently is under attack in the U.S., the country is losing its dominance in the sciences, and non-science-based explanations of important phenomena are threatening and eroding the creation and sharing of scientific knowledge. This real and pervasive attack on science is putting America, Inc. at a disadvantage in an increasingly competitive world. The mismanagement of science is also leading to disastrous results, if not addressed and corrected. Let's consider what's behind this attack and the dimming of the scientific aura and then discuss what remedies are necessary.

An Economic and Political Time Bomb: Losing the Edge in Science

Foreign advances in science now rival or exceed those in the U.S. Looking at patents, for example, reveals that while Americans still win a goodly number of them, the percentage of patents won is falling, as foreigners, most notably, Asians, have seized the lead in many areas.[1] The U.S. share of industrial patents has been declining steadily over the years, an alarming trend. Significantly, there has also been a decline in published scientific research. Looking at the top physics journals, for example, reveals that American output in two decades fell from a majority to a minority of papers published, falling from 61 percent in 1983 to just 29% in 2003.[2] Other countries' scientists are gaining an advantage in this area of basic research, a reversal of form that clearly spells problems for the U.S. This decline can also be seen in the number of Nobel Prizes won, an obvious icon of scientific excellence. The American share, having peaked from the 1960s through the 1990s, has fallen significantly since, opening the door to scientists in other countries.

Part of the problem is due to the fact that too few Americans are attracted to technical or scientific fields of work. There simply has been a decline in interest in scientific careers in the U.S., a trend that clearly indicates problems for the long-term economic welfare and political security of the country.[3] A federal panel, established by Congress, issued a number of reports about the critical problem of declines in the science and engineering work force and labeled the trend as extremely troubling.[4] One report points out that the dominance of the U.S. in its share of 18-to-24-year-olds who earn science and engineering degrees has fallen drastically. While it was third in the world in 1975, the U.S. ranked 17th in 2004, behind Taiwan, South Korea, China, Japan, even Ireland and Italy.

Other studies report related, very unsettling findings. U.S. teens are among the world's worst at math, according to a major international study.[5] The percentage of top-achieving math students in the country is about half of that of other industrialized countries, including Finland, Korea, Japan, Canada, Australia, Iceland, France, Germany, the Slovak Republic, Poland, and Spain. The U.S., in fact, ranked 24th among 29 countries that are members of the Organization for Economic Cooperation and Development, hardly an impressive figure or cause for optimism.

In what is surely an ominous sign for U.S. technical prowess and progress, American universities have been slipping lower in a prestigious international programming contest.[6] In 2005, the University of Illinois finished in 17th place in the Association for Computing Machinery International Collegiate Programming contest, the lowest ranking in the 29 year history of the competition. U.S. colleges used to dominate this type of programming "olympics," but an American school hasn't won since 1997 and the results have grown increasingly negative since. The conclusion of experts in the field is unmistakable: the U.S. is falling behind in computer science and technology and the world's technical leadership is shifting away from America and primarily to Asian nations. The data also suggest the deterioration of the country's educational system in science and technological leadership.

Data such as these bode poorly for America, Inc.'s future position in an economically- and politically-competitive world. Like the global corporation, the country can only compete if it has resources and capabilities that can give it a competitive advantage or equality in a changing political and economic environment. The present situation, however, suggests a time bomb ticking slowly and inexorably toward an inevitable catastrophe or denouement that will result in America, Inc.'s *competitive disadvantage* in a world where other countries have made significant scientific leaps.

Other data suggest similar trends in the sad state of science in the U.S., and this alarming state of affairs is no longer a secret, but a known fact. The critical question is why this is happening. Why is such a sound scientific and engineering tradition being reversed? What is causing a decline in scientific inquiry and creating such a dangerous economic time bomb? The present contention is that many of the critical causal factors underlying this problem can be placed squarely on mismanagement by America, Inc.'s leaders and the growing and countervailing power and popularity of "non-science" explanations of scientific phenomena. The two facts or trends, moreover, are not totally independent. Let's examine the sad facts impacting the standing and importance of science in the U.S.

The Attack on Science

The attacks on science are occurring on a number of fronts, some more obvious than others. One simple explanation derives from laws of *supply and demand*. As more countries expand technologically, the global demand for scientists and engineers increases. Attractive job markets grow and prosper in other countries, not predominantly or only in the U.S. as had been the case for years, and this siphons off talent and distributes it to growing competitor nations. America, Inc., after all, is definitely in a global marketplace competing for a relatively limited talent pool, just like the global corporation.

In the past, shortages in key personnel could be made up by attracting a good number of foreign students, scientists, and engineers and offering them lucrative university fellowships or high-paying positions. But this source of a relatively easy and quick supply of scientists and engineers has been drying up. Many of America's top universities have suffered deep declines in foreign student enrollment.[7] For example, the number of Chinese students applying to U.S. graduate schools dropped 45 percent from fall 2003 to fall 2004, according to the Council of Graduate Schools. Significant drops in foreign student enrollment have been reported by U.S. universities that traditionally have relied heavily on foreign students to fill student and job-related roles.[8]

While supply and demand explanations have merit, federal government policies haven't helped the situation. In fact, they've exacerbated the problem. Since 9/11, foreign students have had difficulty in acquiring visas for study in the U.S. Students and job seekers from all countries face scrutiny and long clearances from the FBI, CIA, and others involved with homeland security. There very likely exists a perception in the world that the U.S. since 9/11 has become increasingly hostile to foreign talent. There likely is a strong belief that student or work related visas in the U.S. are very hard to get, so why bother going through a difficult and unrewarding process? It's simply easier to pursue opportunities in other countries with growing and lucrative scientific and engineering programs.

The fact that some American universities may be in decline only exacerbates the problems noted. Public colleges and universities are being undermined by budget cuts and a mood of legislative indifference or even combativeness.[9] Insufficient funding leads to increased class size and the elimination of key classes and electives, thereby making graduating with the required courses difficult and reducing the attractiveness of the entire educational experience. This may cut down on student enrollments, especially among foreign students seeking the tougher engineering and scientific curricula. Such financial and management policies can also result in faculty turnover and the devaluation of degrees, leading further to an inability to attract and retain the best students.

Management decisions by U.S. leaders and effects on science. The attack on science by U.S. leaders—formal and informal, intended or unintended—is even more worrisome. The effects of management or mismanagement have already been suggested when discussing the U.S.' reactions to 9/11 and the tightening of restrictions on foreign students and job applicants in the name of homeland security. But this example only reflects the tip of the iceberg. Other policy changes have even greater impact on science.

The Defense Advanced Research Projects Agency (DARPA) at the Pentagon has long underwritten "blue-sky" research and long supported basic research at universities that wasn't tied to strict, short-term payoffs. This practice over the decades has paid off handsomely in terms of innovations and useful technologies, for both the private and public sectors. This policy, however, has been changing drastically.[10] In recent years, there has been a major shift away from basic research and support of "blue-sky" research in universities. In fact, the portion of research dollars going to universities has dropped a whopping 43 percent in just the last few years. And there are more strings attached to the dollars still going into basic research: DARPA now demands, for example, that only graduate students with American citizenship be allowed to work on its grants to universities, bringing us back to the previous discussion of the paucity of science-trained students and personnel. And DARPA is not hiding its shift in research focus. In response to a query from the Senate Armed Services Committee, it revealed its change in policy away from long-term, basic research to short-term projects with more immediate payoffs. The reasons DARPA cited for the change in policy included the need for faster weapons systems development and for more classified projects since 9/11. (Everything, it seems, can be explained by 9/11). So, the policy shift is real, and there was little or no objection to it by the Senate committee.

There has been a strong negative reaction to DARPA's change in policy, especially at the leading research universities. Professors and research scientists are afraid that basic research will get squeezed out in this attack on "blue-sky" projects. Some universities have consequently cut back on the number of positions in computer science departments and basic research facilities, which further exacerbates the problem of basic research without government support. The bottom line is that the government seems to be walking away from its research role and its support of basic science which, to some scientists, is like "killing the goose that laid the golden egg."[11] Although DARPA has disputed this and similar claims, many still feel that its actions represent an attack on basic science or, at minimum, a redefinition of science to focus more on short-term deliverables, most notably, those needed to wage war.

Another example of the indirect government attack on science is the funding of the National Institutes of Health. The budget of NIH had more than doubled from fiscal 1995 to fiscal 2003, rising to almost $10 billion from $4.3 billion.[12] In 2004, because of fiscal pressures due to highly debated tax cuts, military costs, and a growing deficit, the federal government cut NIH's funding. Since 2004, adjusting for inflation, NIH's budget has been reduced, affecting the funding of promising projects: the chance of a scientist's work being funded fell from 27% to 22% overall, and to less than 10% in some fields, during this period. This downward trend is continuing, making it more difficult for scientists, even those with good track records, to fund promising research, and the prognosis of any reversal in policy any time soon is bleak.

Under these conditions, grant reviewers are increasingly reluctant to gamble scarce money on "speculative/bold (pick your adjective) approaches to understanding and treating diseases."[13] Innovation, however, demands risk-taking and occasionally funding the risky, speculative project. Not all risky projects come to fruition; some are mistakes that will cost NIH money, but this is the price of innovation. Innovations and breakthroughs in the treatment of disease demand that some ideas or projects that are out of the ordinary be funded and tested in the name of sound science and controlled experimentation. Without risk-taking and occasional funding of the black-sheep project, research becomes more ho-hum and ordinary, suggesting a future slippage of innovative work in the medical sciences.

There are other, more subtle attacks on research that surely can affect scientists' ability to stay abreast of critical trends and findings. The Environmental Protection Agency announced in late 2006 that it was sharply reducing the number of technical journals and environmental publications that EPA scientists and other employees could access online.[14] Coupled with other actions by the EPA—e.g. closures of agency libraries—the outcome is that agency personnel are increasingly being denied access to hard copies or electronic versions of important scientific publications. This represents an attack on scientists' capability to stay abreast of developments in the scientific community, including the latest empirical findings and evidence that are so crucial to remaining at the leading edge of scientific research.

The lack of funding across many fields of science—direct or indirect, overt or subtle—reduces the number of available government scientific positions and the financial support for academic professorships and research personnel at the universities, detracting further from the country's scientific capabilities. The funding cutbacks hurt scientific progress, providing an example of how government decisions can affect science, even if in an unintended way. These and many other similar examples also reinforce the points made in Chapters 4 and 5 about government priorities, spending, and waste. For example, an emphasis on spending on "guns" negatively affects not only "butter," but also ultimately scientific innovation, basic research, and the control or elimination of disease. Financial and fiscal decisions by leaders in the White House and Congress that favor excessive military spending and needless pork-barrel earmarks and waste reflect the mismanagement of America, Inc.'s scarce resources, jeopardizing its position in an increasingly competitive economic and scientific world. The cost of wasteful, profligate spending is much greater than it might seem on the surface.

Some attacks on science are even more obvious and disconcerting than the erosion of funding for long-term, basic research. For example, there have been accusations of *purposeful distortions or suppressions* of scientific information by the government. One report argues: that safe-sex information was purged from the Centers for Disease Control website; that there was posting of misinformation on the National Career Institute site indicating an increased risk of breast cancer among women who had abortions; and that the government suppressed information about global warming, prescription drug advertising, and water pollution caused by the oil and gas industries.[15]

Accusations by a former Surgeon General of the U.S. support the fact that the government tried to suppress or distort scientific information. Dr. Richard Carmona, Surgeon General from 2002-2006, said that he was blocked routinely from speaking out on controversial issues like sexual abstinence, stem-cell research, sex education, and emergency contraception, and was pressured to support an "ideological, theological" agenda in his work and public statements.[16] He also said he was prevented from releasing a report on global health because he refused to make it a political statement touting positive actions by the U.S.; barred from attending a special Olympics event because it would benefit a politically-prominent Democratic family (the Kennedys); and had his speeches regularly vetted and changed by political appointees to be consistent with accepted ideology. Only time will tell if these actions are those of the current administration or a more general repression or distortion of scientific facts.

In February 2004, the Union of Concerned Scientists released a detailed two-part report, documenting the "Suppression and Distortion of Research Findings at Federal Agencies" in areas of climate change, air quality, reproductive health, airborne bacteria, Iraq's aluminum tubes (erroneously claimed by the administration to be part of that country's nuclear weapons program), endangered species, and forest management.[17] By December, more than 5,000 scientists had signed on to and agreed with the statement and the facts contained therein. Among the signers were 48 Nobel laureates, 62 National Medal of Science recipients, and 135 members of the National Academy of Sciences, which renders any counter-argument of selective perception, bad science, or pure "politics" impotent and useless.[18]

These are striking data, but the scientists went even further. They wrote in a second part of their report about "Undermining the Quality and Integrity of the Appointment Process," which described the purging of qualified scientists from federal advisory panels, the appointment of less qualified "political" substitutes for scientists, and the reliance on political questions as appointment criteria (e.g. had they voted for President Bush). The facts smack heavily of cronyism, mismanagement, and direct attempts to suppress or distort science in favor of a political agenda, which clearly represents an attack on science and an attempt to diminish its influence in all matters political, social, and economic. The long-term impact of these abuses and mismanagement are not hard to imagine.

Another problem area in which many scientists and lay people alike saw an attack on or repudiation of science was that of global warming. Decisions in the White House, Cabinet, and by many in Congress about this threat for many years clearly indicated a strong disbelief in the scientific principles underlying it and its consequences. There had been much written about global warming and the validity and urgency of the threat, including some dissenting opinions. But while opinions and feelings about global warming ran the gamut from belief to disbelief, cold to hot, the actual objective data largely supported the phenomenon in scientific terms.[19] Most studies in refereed scientific journals overwhelmingly supported the existence of a global-warming trend that some day would have negative repercussions on the planet.

Despite the preponderance of support for the phenomenon of global warning, the scientific data were still attacked and the scientists espousing them were muzzled or pressured not to speak up on the issue. Government agencies routinely misrepresented, suppressed, or distorted scientific data and hampered scientists' efforts to report their findings.[20] NASA's lead climate scientist revealed that he had been pressured by a political appointee to cease talking about the dangers of global warming. He was warned of the "dire consequences" by NASA officials if he didn't keep quiet on the subject. The department of Commerce was found to have blocked the release of a scientific document developed by personnel at the national Oceanic and Atmospheric Administration on the effects of global warming on the frequency and strength of hurricanes. The EPA suppressed data on climate change because of political pressure to do so. Etc. Despite the scientific basis of global warming and its correlates or consequences, there routinely was an attack on science and scientists and the clear suppression or mismanagement of vital information on the subject, a clear case, again, of U.S. officials not allowing data to get in the way of their opinions or party-line propaganda.

All or most of this resistance was hopefully put to rest in early 2007 when hundreds of the world's leading climate scientists representing 113 governments reported from Paris that global warming has begun and is very likely caused by humans. Their 20 page report concludes unequivocally, with more than 90 percent certainty, that global warming is caused primarily by the burning of fossil fuels and its effects will be devastating, including increased hurricane activity and huge rises in sea levels around the world. However, U.S. leaders as of this writing still have rejected mandatory limits on greenhouse gases, perpetuating the mismanagement of a very serious problem and, in so doing, continuing to denigrate the positions and influence of sound science. Some large companies have even been accused of funding research whose goal it is to refute the scientific evidence and create uncertainty about the validity of such evidence. If true, this would represent an additional attack on scientific integrity.

To refuse to do anything about global warming on economic grounds also exhibits a faulty logic. The U.S. withdrew from the Kyoto Treaty or protocol, arguing that it was fatally flawed and would cost the U.S. economy as much as $400 billion and 4.9 million jobs.[21] Yet at least 157 nations have ratified the protocol with little economic turmoil. The administration's "facts" of money and job loss, furthermore, were not backed by rigorous statistical and economic analysis. The administration was doing exactly what it had been accusing environmentalists of doing: presenting facts with little, no, or weak supporting evidence or data. Also, a negative economic argument is rendered totally laughable, given the gross financial mismanagement and lack of concern with debt and deficits documented in Chapter 4. How could anyone cite a global-warming-caused deficit when the cumulative national debt is passing $9 billion, a fiscal gap of $63 trillion is projected, and no one seems to want to do anything about them? The $400 billion is most certainly an overstated sum and the real cost, if any, pales in comparison to the yearly deficits being created by war, pork-barrel legislation, and other programs that hardly raise a bit of debate or discontentment.

So, the beat goes on. Environmental issues still aren't being confronted adequately, and the scientists who espouse them still have little influence. A "Healthy Forest" initiative made the clear-burning and logging of forests easier, a "clear-skies" bill doesn't have the touted effect, and regulations on mining have been ignored or changed to allow companies greater access to the extraction of raw materials. Regulations dealing with clean air and water similarly have been voided or ignored. Science is increasingly being left out "in the cold," creating a devastating mismanagement of the environment and its scarce resources. While the current administration provides recent egregious examples of the attack on science, the facts presented suggest a broader-based cultural, political, even theological repudiation of the value of science.

Let's consider two more "down to earth," everyday examples of the attack on science. Take, first, the interesting case of snowmobiling in Yellowstone National

Park.[22] A Clinton-era proposal called for the elimination of this form of travel in the park, and the EPA and National Park Service strongly agreed with the action at the time. The growth in the popularity of snowmobiling had created a host of problems. Air pollutants at times were higher than "those over a Los Angeles freeway," and park rangers literally had to don respirators and ear plugs as protection against carbon monoxide and noise."[23] Wildlife was stressed by the commotion and wild riders and placed at risk; over 1000 bison were killed because they wandered outside the park on the convenient snowmobile trails. Research done by the National Park Service concluded that snowmobiling damaged the park and its wildlife and should be banned.

Snowmobile manufacturers, riders, and their various lobbyists cried foul, and their cries fell on the ears of a sympathetic administration. "New" scientific tests were done at a high cost to American taxpayers, and the administration then decided to ignore scientific facts it found "inconvenient."[24] In effect, the White House ignored the old scientific data in favor of the new, flawed, more convenient data, and reopened the park to snowmobiling. Various administration officials, including Interior Secretary Gale Norton, tootled through the park, in effect, providing personal endorsements for the new flawed science and upsetting the park rangers who were choking on the acrid blue smoke emitted from the machines.[25] The administration ignored scientific data and its duty by favoring the snowmobiles over preservation of the park, its animals, and other features of its habitat.

Luckily, a federal judge overruled the politicians and lobbyists active in the case and told the administration to "get back to the core mission of protecting parks for generations to come."[26] Still, this was a sorry spectacle indeed, and one that clearly showed an attack on science in favor of special interests. Other writers, including Christie Whitman, one-time head of the EPA who resigned her post in frustration, pointed out how Bush, Cheney, and some Capitol Hill Republicans had little use for environmental regulations built on a foundation of solid science.[27] The conclusion is obvious: even objective science and facts can be manipulated for the good of the few, not the many, which clearly is an example of gross mismanagement and an abuse of power.

One other example deserves a brief mention. In the Department of Education, there are federal monetary grants-in-aid available for low-income college students. Students apply for the grants and choose a field of study or major area as part of the application process. In August 2006, it was reported that *"evolutionary biology" had mysteriously vanished from the list of acceptable majors.*[28] Why?

A spokesperson for the Department of Education said that the omission was an inadvertent mistake, that "evolutionary biology" would be put back on the accepted list of major study areas. Yet, many scientists and individuals in universities, the American Civil Liberties Union, and other organizations expressed grave concerns about the omission, and felt that it was awfully coincidental that this major was dropped during a time when the teaching of evolution was under attack in some public schools. What would have happened if someone hadn't spotted the omission? Would students continue to be turned down for the grants, without knowing why, without knowing that they had chosen a suddenly invalid field of study? Why was the study area dropped so quietly, without warning to new applicants? Cynics might argue, even if evolutionary biology is put back on the list of valid majors for grant purposes, that something more than an inadvertent mistake occurred in this case. To some, such an action may signal just one more example of a quiet, subversive attack on science. To some concerned citizens, it represented a move by leaders in America, Inc. to define or sway the course of sound science.

"Alternatives" to Science

Yet one more attack on science has been developing in the U.S. in recent years. This attack on science comes from increasingly popular *pseudo-science* or *non-scientific explanations of scientific phenomena*. These include religion and its spawn, e.g. intelligent design, and they are gaining power and leading potentially to mismanagement of America, Inc.'s capabilities and strategic choices.

This is difficult territory to negotiate, in that it is fraught with strong personal beliefs and religious values. At one extreme, there are the fanatical evangelical Christians who reject virtually everything not contained in the Bible, who espouse theocracy in government, and who offer divine explanations of worldly phenomena that directly confront and contradict science. At the other extreme, there are those who believe that religion is the root of all evil and that mixing religion and politics or religion and science only breeds major problems, including war, bloodshed, suffering, and a lack of technological progress and innovation.[29] History clearly seems to favor the latter school of thought by providing countless examples of religion-borne strife and the dangers of organized religion over the centuries. Still, individuals in the U.S. have a right to various freedoms, including personal choices about religion, and no one is suggesting that this right be suppressed. However, when individuals' beliefs create widespread political, social, economic, or philosophical rifts that lead to the rejection of valid scientific principles, the cumulative effect of which is to place America, Inc. in jeopardy in an increasingly competitive and hostile world, then this signals a problem that must be addressed.

Centrality of religion. In 1782, a French immigrant named Hector St. John de Crevecoeur predicted that America was clearly destined to become a much more *secular* place than Europe.[30] Religious "indifference" would become the rule, he predicted, as passion over all things religious would disappear. De Crevecoeur, of course, was totally wrong: just the opposite has come to pass. Most European politicians would rather "talk about sexually-transmitted diseases than their own faith in God."[31] Some American policymakers, in contrast, seem to talk of little else, directly or indirectly. Our leaders and even our courts discuss abortion, the inception of life, stem-cell research, gay marriage, the right to live or die, school prayer, etc. with constant reference, explicitly or implicitly, to religious beliefs or principles. America, it sometimes seems, is moving toward a theocracy where the final word about right and wrong and even decisions about running for major public office come *directly* from higher, heavenly sources. Indeed, election to high office in the U.S. is virtually impossible without belief in, and public witness of, the importance and munificence of God and religion.

This embracing of religion in the U.S. is growing stronger. From what was basically a godless constitution, more and more politicians and people in the street believe that the country and its constitution were founded on Christian principles. Not so. In the eighty-five essays of *The Federalist*, God is mentioned only twice, and in the sense of "only heaven knows." In the Declaration of Independence, God gets a couple of brief mentions. "In God We Trust" appeared on coins during the Civil War era, and "under God" was put into the Pledge of Allegiance during the McCarthy debacle in 1954. In all of this, Jesus Christ is a non-existent player.[32]

Despite these very humble and inauspicious beginnings, religious beliefs are strengthening and are very real. One Gallup poll showed that roughly one-half of Americans believe in creationism, while only 28% believe in evolution. Americans are more than twice as likely to believe in the Devil (68%) than evolution. An article in *Science* showed, relatedly, that of 34 countries surveyed, only Turkey had fewer people who believed in evolution than the U.S.[33] George Bush won 80% of the "values voters" in 2004, and the polarization of politics based on religion is probably getting even stronger with every passing day.[34]

The emphasis on religion is contributing to the attack on science. Intelligent design has been proposed as a substitute for evolution, Darwin's elegant discussion of natural forces affecting life-form changes over time. (The arguments about intelligent design have appeared in court cases, newspaper articles, school-board hearings on curriculum and textbooks, etc. and consequently are well known and need not be repeated here). Others have suggested facetiously that it's silly to stop with an attack on evolution. Other attacks on science and substitutions for science are also possible: e.g. replacing chemistry with alchemy, neurology with phrenology, physics with magic, and astronomy with astrology in our high schools and universities can easily accompany and support the new emphasis on intelligent design over evolution.[35] Why stop, after all, with just one area of pseudo or bad science? Sadly, there are probably some who take these tongue-in-check recommendations seriously.

The critical question presently is "what's wrong with all of this?" How does the increasing centrality and importance of religion and pseudo-science reflect or lead to mismanagement and/or abuses of power that can affect America's standing or competitive position in the global arena? Let me begin answering these questions by relating a discussion that fueled major trepidation in my mind about the relationships between religion and science and the effects on sound management of America, Inc.'s resources and competitive strategies.

Years ago, I was doing some work with the C.I.A.—above board programs on management, organizational design, and strategy implementation, nothing "spooky" related to spying or covert operations. During the course of the work, I had the opportunity to talk informally with C.I.A. participants on all sorts of subjects. One discussion proved to be particularly interesting and troublesome.

The discussion centered on recruitment of personnel for work in the C.I.A. Eventually, talk turned to recruitment on college campuses as the agency, like many other large organizations, turns to the campuses to find people in many academic areas or disciplines to ensure a pool of human resources and continuity of work. After a while, the discussion focused on the schools that the C.I.A. employees thought were the best places to recruit and hire young people for entry into "the company." I was surprised when the same few college names came up as representing "recruitment heaven," schools that were touted as consistently providing the best people for the agency. My surprise turned into mild shock when I realized that the top schools mentioned were religion-based or religious-order universities, well-known institutions with strong religious ties and reputations. I, of course, asked why these schools are such recruitment gems, and at the time wasn't fully ready for the answer I received.

The schools are great, I was told, because their kids fit easily and quickly into the C.I.A. system. They don't question things. They accept tasks and information as fact and without hesitation. They've been trained to accept dogma and tenets of faith that defy reason, but represent the official position of their Church.

They don't debate or seek an informed exchange of ideas when ordered to do or not do something; they've been trained by Church superiors or elders who know best and who, consequently, shouldn't be challenged. The young students are programmed to be perfect followers of orders and top-down doctrine, and few of them ever cause problems once they join the agency with its structured rules, routines, and modus operandi.

Once I recovered from the initial surprise, it was obvious why recruits from the religion-based schools were such desired additions to the agency. They would fit in perfectly. They followed orders, even shaky ones, because theirs was not to reason why, but to do or die, so to speak. Authority rules in all matters and superiors must be obeyed. Period. Thinking about the C.I.A. example reminded me of reading or hearing a Jesuit slogan years ago that said, basically, "Give me a child for his first seven years, and I'll deliver you the man, mind, body, and soul."[36] Good "company" employees, then, like proselytized church members, are team players who go along with superiors and don't question their motives, knowledge, or "facts."

Clearly, this is only one example with a very small sample size. Nonetheless, I believe it's one whose logic could easily be extended to a larger population. The example helped to highlight for me the antithesis of religion and science, dogma and logic, and helped explain why reliance on the former can lead to attacks on the rationality of the latter. Science involves the formation and testing of ideas and hypotheses and demands an informed exchange or debate on those ideas and the data that represent them. Religion often eschews this intellectual process and replaces scientific inquiry with ideological or dogmatic certainty, fear, "truth," and faith. Different religions have different ideologies and matters of faith, hence creating ideological rifts, even warfare, among religions, but the one element that even different religions share in common is that they appear to be antagonistic to the curiosity, inquiry, debate, and testing of data and information that mark the scientific method.

It's easy to see why a management based on theocracy and tenets of faith would be antagonistic to stem cell research, evolutionary biology, or other types of technological or biological experimentation that challenge accepted religious dogma and faith-based principles and truths. It's understandable why scientists and other creative people in a global talent pool would not find such a climate to their liking: *creativity is vital to innovation and economic progress, but authoritarianism and blind faith are stifling and antagonistic to creativity.* It's easy to see why management based on religious tenets can lead to a serious case of mismanagement and an abuse of the power of religion in political, social, and economic matters in America, Inc. or elsewhere in the world.

The attack on science is real and it must be stopped. The independence of the scientific model must be reinforced, and the funding of sound science must be maintained. A brave new brand of leadership and management is badly needed to focus on the real issues facing the country, including the reinstatement and centrality of science and technological innovation as cornerstones of America, Inc.'s greatness in a competitive world. This and other aspects of sound leadership are vital, and they are discussed in detail in the next chapter.

The Press Under Siege

"The only security of all is in a free press."

"The press [is] the only tocsin [alarm bell] of a nation. When it is completely silenced ..., all means of a general effort are taken away."

Thomas Jefferson

Attacking the Press

The attack on the press and other news media is another real, nefarious, and dangerous problem. Like a CEO and top-management team who wish to silence critics and control, embellish, and slant all information about corporate performance and strategy, some U.S. leaders too are trying to control information and silence critics and the "tocsin" of the press. Unlike the CEO and top-management team who ultimately must face critics and account for measurable performance outcomes, control of the press and other news media by U.S. leaders allows them to define performance and create a "spin" or web of propaganda that insulates them from the same type of accountability their CEO counterparts face. This quest for control is clearly fomenting an ongoing attack on the news media, especially the press.

Paradoxically, the attack on the press represents examples of both effective management and severe mismanagement, depending on point of view and the goals or outcomes attained. Those attacking the press are doing so very effectively; the results of this attack, however, are hurting political and social outcomes in the country and leading to the control of information and news by politicians and a few dominant organizations. This oligopolistic control can cloud distinctions between "spinning" and searching for truth and between information and misinformation, which can undermine the power and utility of the Fourth Estate, which according to Edmund Burke and others, is more important than the other three estates or branches of government.

Defining exactly the independence or freedom of the press has been somewhat problematical since the founding fathers, most notably, Jefferson, extolled the virtues and critical importance of a free press to a democratic society. Recent history in the U.S. has raised the salience of the issue to new levels and renewed argument about just what this freedom entails, especially in times of a war on terrorism. This modern attack began with the Nixon administration's going to federal court to halt publication of the Pentagon papers and winning its case, citing national security and charging two newspapers with treason. This was the first time in the history of the American republic that newspapers had been restrained from publishing a story, and it really proved to be a hallmark decision that put the press in continued jeopardy, right up to the present time.[37] The hostility toward and desire for control of the press and other media by the executive, judicial, and legislative branches of government has grown even stronger since 9/11 and declaration of a war on terrorism. Let's consider the main weapons, tactics, and battlefronts in this modern attack.

Management by fear. The context or climate within which the attack on the press and other news media is occurring is a critical first factor to a full understanding of why the attack is working. Since 9/11, "management by fear" is a major weapon used by leaders in the White House and Congress. This is an aspect of management or leadership style that I return to in Chapter 7, but it must be mentioned presently as a factor in the attack on the press and other news media.

As bad as the Vietnam and Watergate era was, U.S. citizens never felt that their safety was directly at risk. The war was being waged far away. After 9/11, however, all of this changed drastically. Americans had been attacked and killed at home. The U.S. was vulnerable, and safety was a major concern. In this climate of apprehension and fear, it was pitifully easy to pass the Patriot Act with no debate or amendments. It was easy to detain hundreds of people and violate their personal rights, as this was necessary to protect Americans from harm. It also was not at all difficult to institute controls on free speech and pass draconian security measures, as these were absolutely critical to the ability to manage an effective war against the terrorists. This was top-down, unilateral management at its very best (or worst).

This climate of fear and paranoia led logically to the government's classifying or reclassifying information supposedly vital to waging the war. Within six months of 9/11, access to government records was limited by executive order in 300 separate cases.[38] The government could *hide information and classify or reclassify its mistakes* in waging its battle against terrorism. By classifying and controlling more and more information, leaders of America, Inc. could shield themselves from critical reviews by stakeholders, including the press, other media, and the public. It could also hide some spending from public scrutiny. The Department of Defense, for example, requested $30.1 billion for fiscal 2007 for classified or "black" programs that have little or no Congressional oversight or public scrutiny. Billions could disappear down a black hole with secrecy and precious little accountability.[39]

While all of this was happening, the Congress, press, indeed, all the media, rolled over and played dead.[40] Nary a complaint was heard. It was a management and politics of fear, and silence on the government's tactics supported what was going on. American flags sprouted everywhere. In such an atmosphere, it was considered unpatriotic, un-American, even treasonous, if the tactics were questioned or challenged. The top-management tasks in Washington became easy; it was possible to do virtually anything, including attack the Constitution, in the name of war and patriotism.

When the press began finally to monitor a powerful government and not serve as its mouthpiece; when the press began questioning the need to invade Iraq; when it began questioning government mistakes and competence in a poorly-fought and suspect war on terrorism; when the press and other media finally woke up and became more aggressive and feisty in doing their job—challenging the rationale of the war and informing the public what exactly was going on—they were attacked by some as *traitors*. They were drawn, quartered, and skewered over the hot coals of government enmity and public opinion. The ultra conservative majority took the press and the "liberal" media to task, especially when certain "secret" or delicate information was leaked and published, e.g. evidence of wiretaps without the necessary warrants to engage in this activity.

Management by fear had indeed worked, is still working, and will continue to be used to control the press and public opinion. Some U.S. leaders, for example, said that the 2006 mid-term elections were about "security," which is another way of saying about "fear." September 11 will be invoked time and time again to raise the public's fear and justify countless actions and tactics—past, present, and future—e.g. spying on Americans; a ruinous war, poorly planned and executed; torture; the right of the press to leak "classified" information; even the right of the press and the people to dissent. Fear is the administration's "get out of jail card"[41] and, because of its effectiveness, could become part of the routine or *modus operandi* of administrations yet to come.

Creating Pseudo-Events and News. *The government is also attacking the press and undesirable media indirectly by creating its own news stories and pseudo-events for public consumption. It's a way to "beat them by joining them."*

A pseudo-event or pseudo-news story possesses certain characteristics:[42]

1. It is not spontaneous, but occurs because someone has planned or planted it. An earthquake is an event, but a series of interviews on terrorism is usually a pseudo-event.

2. A pseudo-event is planned and planted primarily for the purpose of being reported or used immediately. It is propagandistic. Its occurrence is arranged for the convenience and needs of the people producing the pseudo-event, and the question, "is it real?" is less important than "is it newsworthy?" The planted information is repeated over and over, a way to "catapult the propaganda," a term used by President Bush, with the effect that, with repetition, the event and related information become real, become the truth, and worthy of belief. But as George Orwell warned: "Political language ... is designed to make lies sound truthful and murder respectable, and to give an appearance of solidity to pure wind."[43]

3. A pseudo-event's relation to reality is often ambiguous. The news interest in an earthquake is what happened and what are the consequences, which can be measured and documented. The interest in a series of interviews with political leaders is on whether something is really happening, what it really means, and what are the "real" underlying facts, all of which are not easily measured or documented and some of which must be taken on faith.

4. A pseudo-event, finally, is often a self-fulfilling prophesy. The person who argues that his job for years has been to keep the wild lions out of Washington D.C. can point to a distinguished and successful career. So, too, can the political leader who argues that a major terrorist event hasn't occurred on his watch since 9/11, despite the fact that little has been done in a cause-effect fashion to prevent such an attack.

The government has created pseudo-events since 9/11. The 9/11 attacks were certainly real events. Continuing reports about the war on terrorism, however, are often pseudo-events. What is the war and on whom is it being waged? Declaring war on Japan or Germany identified a foe clearly. Declaring a war on terrorism or Islamofascism is less clear, even if emotionally charged. Terrorism and fascism suggest an ideology, a method or modus operandi, so the "war" is a struggle against something ideological or methodical in nature and hard to define. This certainly sounds brave when it is trumpeted by U.S. leaders, but in reality, it is also fraught with ambiguity as to what's really happening, who the real enemy is, and what the real progress and consequences are. Indeed, a real question deals with whether the "war" is actually reducing terrorism and fascism, or whether it is really nurturing and increasing them in the world.

Interviews and press conferences are surely planned and managed often to create pseudo-events that can be used immediately for propaganda purposes. Certain statements, claims, or "facts" are repeated constantly—e.g. "Keeping America Safe." This is certainly newsworthy, but is it true? Has the war on terrorism really accomplished what the countless press conferences, interviews, and other news events claim, or has it been due to good luck, the incompetence of terrorist groups, or their slow, deliberate planning that there hasn't been a major terrorist event on U.S. soil since 9/11? Such claims or statements have been a self-fulfilling prophecy of sorts, but the likelihood of another attack is certainly higher than the likelihood of lions invading Washington, D.C., so many of the claims and facts put forth in interviews and press conferences should be scrutinized very carefully and challenged as to their validity.

In fact, news and public relations work often go hand-in-hand. At least 20 different federal agencies, including the Defense Department, have produced and distributed hundreds of television news segments in the last four or five years, and these are routinely reported in the press.[44] Most of these pseudo-events or stories were broadcast without acknowledging the government's role in their production and distribution. Stories about the fall of Baghdad, progress in the Iraq war, the drive to strengthen aviation security, the opening of markets for American farmers, regime change in Iraq, Medicare reform, etc. were all feel-good propaganda materials created by the government. In some cases, the reporters of the news stories were under contract with the administration and being paid to hype White House news and "objective" accomplishments that smack of subjective bias and definition, just like pseudo-events.

Consider just one example of how news and public-relations messages can be skillfully intertwined for an intended purpose—a case of packaging 9/11, terrorism, and the war in Iraq.[45] Television ads in my home market—Philadelphia—and elsewhere were run around the sixth anniversary of the 9/11 attacks, not coincidentally, at the same time Gen. David Petraeus was delivering his report to Congress on the progress of the war in Iraq. One ad featured a woman who said that she lost two relatives to Al Qaeda—a firefighter uncle who was killed in New York on 9/11 and her husband who was killed in Iraq. There's an implicit connection between Iraq and Al Qaeda here: terrorism and Al Qaeda are inextricably linked, Iraq and terrorism are linked, therefore, Iraq and Al Qaeda must be linked. The invasion of Iraq wasn't done to fight Saddam Hussein and Iraq, but to fight and defeat terrorism, i.e. Al Qaeda. The intended message or implication is obvious: Saddam Hussein was behind or connected to the 9/11 attacks, so the invasion of Iraq was necessary and justified to defeat terrorism and Al Qaeda and avenge 9/11.

This and similar messages are working. Despite ample evidence to the contrary, people still believe that Saddam Hussein was behind the 9/11 attacks. In a New York Times/CBS News poll in September 2007, a full one-third of respondents said that Hussein was personally involved. In June 2007, Princeton Survey Research polling for Newsweek found that 41% of those asked said that Hussein was directly involved in planning, financing, and pulling off the terrorist attacks.[46] Entangling the war in Iraq with 9/11 and threats of terrorist attacks has been effective, providing a clear mandate to some to win in Iraq. It also certainly aids, abets, and feeds management by fear, discussed above, and contributes to a management approach based on anxiety, control of the news, and the creation of pseudo events and PR sound bites for public consumption.

This is more than a case of managing the news. Using paid-off pundits, passing off press releases disguised as news telecasts, and even press access being granted to pseudo-journalists working under phony names have led some to conclude that the government "is not simply aggressively managing the news, but is out to sabotage the press corps from within, to undermine the integrity and reputation of journalism itself."[47] Care clearly must be taken to heed once more the words of Thomas Jefferson:

"[A despotic] government always keeps a kind of standing army of news writers who, without any regard to truth or to what should be like truth, [invent] and put into the papers whatever might serve the ministers."

Creating news and pseudo-events are part of an effective attack by U.S. leaders or "ministers" on the press and the brainwashing of the American public. But there are even more weapons in an arsenal being aimed purposely at the independence, usefulness, and integrity of the press and other media that are part of an overall approach to the management and control of news and propaganda.

Media consolidation. The General Accounting Office (GAO), an arm of Congress, looked at oil company mergers between 1994 and 2000 and came to the conclusion that the mergers and the attendant increased industry concentration actually drove up gasoline prices for consumers. Consolidation was linked clearly to higher prices at the pump, according to the GAO analysis. Greater concentration also increased the power of the large oil companies over consumers.

Industry forces play a major role in corporate strategic management, and companies try to control or take advantage of them. Organizational size and market share can lead to effective control over suppliers and customers, create huge entry barriers for potential competitors, and reduce the intensity of competition in a market or key market segment, leading to excess profits. Industry consolidation via merger or acquisition usually leads to oligopoly and, often, to effective control of industry forces. It allows the larger, merged companies to cut costs via scale and scope economies, thereby increasing margins. The savings, however, are not passed on to consumers. In fact, the increased power of the large players over consumers in the oil and other industries allows them to actually raise prices, increasing margins even substantially higher. Anti-trust legislation and regulations exist theoretically to regulate this market power, but the regulatory climate in the U.S. of late has not been focused on regulation but, rather, supports corporate power and control of industry or market forces. The bottom line is that, more often than not, the consumer loses at the hands of consolidation and increased industry concentration, especially when government controls are weak. These clearly are the implications of the GAO study.

Turning to the government, its support of corporate power is evident in the increasing concentration and consolidation of firms in the news media, including the press. When Michael Powell was FCC Chairman, he began the process of relaxing rules and regulations about ownership of TV stations and newspapers, creating a climate ripe for media mergers and consolidations. His logic basically seemed to be that (a) concentration of the media isn't that strong, and (b) the internet with its numerous blogs and websites adds competition and increases the number of news sources, thereby working against the powers of increased concentration. The information or news market shares many of the characteristics of a perfectly competitive market, according to this view.

The real facts, however, negate or dilute Powell's logic. Many sources of news and information indeed do exist, on the internet, in print, on radio, and on network and cable TV. There are countless blogs offering news and analysis, and there are 24-hour news outlets on radio and TV (e.g. CNN, Fox News, CNBC, Limbaugh, and Franken). There are many newspapers, including the large well-known national publications. The problem is that *the sources are more partisan than ever before*.[48] Fox News appeals to conservative Republicans, while the majority of CNN viewers are Democrats. There are many blogs but, again, they are usually preaching to a choir made up of like-minded people. Large numbers of news sources don't necessarily create many, varied, and extremely balanced or nuanced points of view. Self-selection rules, as people see, read, and listen to only the news sources they choose to see, read, and listen to. And often it is the few large news companies that create and disseminate the facts and opinions that the many blogs respond to, attack, or play with. The perception of large numbers is misleading, then, and suggests information variety and competition that simply aren't there.

This segregation of information or partisanship of sources permits listeners, viewers, and readers to filter out news they don't believe or care about and focus only on the "facts" they choose to believe. But the viability of democracy depends on *people being exposed to news and views they would not necessarily choose for themselves.*[49] Democracy's health depends on debate and consideration of all sides of an issue before a choice or consensus is reached. The large number of supposed news sources is misleading, as they stifle debate and preach to a choir of avid enthusiasts with limited or narrow points of view. Michael Powell's notion of competition from numerous news sources, then, is invalid. It's also dangerous, as it encourages increased concentration and consolidation of news sources while preaching competition.

The government allowed increased concentration in the oil industry, and the GAO study reported the negative consequences for the consumer of this *laissez-faire* policy. U.S. leaders appear to be making the same offer of industry consolidation and concentration to the large news media companies. The result will likely again be an increase of power of the large corporation, more concentrated control of the creation and distribution of news, and another dangerous and costly blow to the American consumer who, despite the many blogs, etc. that exist, is beholden to a news oligopoly.

Is this trend toward concentration real and is it a threat? One study of the 150 largest media markets in the U.S. concluded that 140 or 93% of them are over-concentrated according to traditional antitrust standards,[50] and concentration limits and controls information diversity and flow. If one huge corporation controlled both the production and distribution of all information, news, and entertainment, it could rule the country. Such a monopoly would be seen by most people as dangerous, and surely this concentration of power couldn't possibly happen in the U.S. Or could it? There already are only a handful of corporations that control this production and distribution (e.g. CBS-Viacom, Murdoch-FOX, GE-NBC, Disney-ABC-ESPN, and Comcast) and, as of this writing, Rupert

Murdoch just finalized the deal to purchase Dow Jones and add the prestigious *Wall Street Journal* to his stable of companies, increasing the size and clout of his News Corp.[51] How much more consolidation needs to occur before people get nervous and see oligopolistic, if not monopolistic, competition as dangerous to information production and distribution?

Let's take just one small example of the effects of consolidation, vertical integration, and approved control over the marketplace—namely, Comcast in Philadelphia. Comcast owns the basketball team, and it owns the cable sports channel that televises its games. It also owns the lines or broadband "pipes" that bring the signal for all basketball games and other sports broadcasts into homes in the city and surrounding suburbs. Comcast can choose which channels to carry in these pipes, and it already has blocked consumers' access to sports programming in Philadelphia, despite subscribers' objections. Comcast controls access to sports via cable in the city and it uses its power in many other matters, as witnessed by the huge tax breaks it wrangled when it negotiated the terms for its new high-rise building, the Comcast Center in Philadelphia.

A good example of Comcast's attempt at additional influence can be seen in its and other media giants' long battle over network neutrality being waged in the nation's capital.[52] Cable companies have the right to control their broadband networks. Network neutrality denotes open access to the internet by all companies. If Comcast and others have their way, networks wouldn't be neutral; cable companies would like to turn the internet into a "proprietary fiefdom," a place where they could control other companies' business conducted through their broadband pipes.[53] They could deny access to some companies and charge different rates, thereby taxing some companies' access more than others, informally controlling what it broadcasts, and determining what people see and hear on TV. Free-market proponents argue that market power would allow Comcast and like-minded giants to favor certain content suppliers and discriminate against others, which could destroy the intent and bias usage of the internet. Comcast would be in a position, then, to control not only sports, but news and flows of information to a community in which it enjoys a monopoly. Comcast, of course, is not alone in its attempt to control news and entertainment—other huge players listed above are also in the game—but it's one example of market power due to size, oligopoly, and preferential treatment by the government or the rule of law. Increased concentration in the industry would definitely exacerbate the problems even further.

Another example of attempts at government control of the media can be seen in the attacks on public broadcasting. With the ideological media fostering limited, political points of view and given the pseudo-events often provided by government sources, it's important to have vigilant independent media, including the press, radio, and TV, whose interests are more objective and favor a broad swath of the American people. This independent, objective role has traditionally been assumed by the Public Broadcasting Service, among others.

PBS, however, has been under attack. (PBS is not the press, but a loose confederation of 350 or so public stations. Still, the issues of control and power nonetheless are the same as for all news organizations). There are those in the executive and legislative branches of government who feel that the PBS is straying too far from accepted political ideology. Some well-known PBS types—most notably, Bill Moyers—have been accused along with the Corporation of Public Broadcasting of being too liberal and "populist."[54] Kenneth Tomlinson, the Chairman of the CPB, allegedly doesn't want anything aired on PBS that is too anti-corporate or anti-Republican.[55] If true, the traditional role of PBS is being attacked. "Public" broadcasting would disappear in favor of a more political agenda. If the large players in oligopolistic media industries are indeed becoming more politicized and powerful because of size and consolidation, it would appear that an independent PBS system that challenges those in power and states conclusions based on data or evidence, not political ideology, is extremely important to a well-informed public and sound democratic principles.

If the PBS continues to be attacked and weakened, then, this would represent a major blow to the flow, quality, and objectivity of information. The situation would move closer to the scary picture laid out a few years ago in an editorial cartoon by Jack Ohman in *The Oregonian*.[56] One frame shows "Orwell 1984," with a picture of a mean-looking face and the well-known words, "Big Brother is Watching You." A second frame refers to a different sort of Orwellian reality that shows the same mean face but now says: "You Are Watching Big Brother," "You're Listening to Big Brother," and "You Are Reading Big Brother." Far fetched? If the present trend toward consolidation, oligopoly, politicization, and market power continues, the press and all independent media would be seriously compromised and the new Orwellian situation would become reality.

Make no mistake about it: market power and control increases profitability in the private sector, and market power due to consolidation and the ever decreasing number of large players is leading to increasing, ever-tighter political and economic control of the media, including the press. This oligopolistic control leads to increased power—dependency on the few, see Chapter 5—which allows the few to control what's read, heard, and seen. If large news purveyors hook up with the government propaganda machine discussed previously, and if the government continues to create pseudo-events and "news" stories slanted toward its view of salient "facts," this management and control of information will not serve the American public well. Such a strategic alliance between government news makers and large news distributors that convey the party line will hurt the press, other news media, and ultimately American democracy.

If the media giants have their way, organic growth and growth by merger or acquisition will continue, and fewer huge companies will control news and entertainment in the U.S. Leaders of America, Inc., much like their brethren in corporate management suites, can continue to foster and support this consolidation which, in turn, will limit how people hear, see, and read the news. Or U.S. leaders can take actions to restore balance in the news or information gathering and distribution industry in the country. As usual, the prognosis varies with the enlightenment of U.S. leaders and the general public and the latter group's making known its wishes to elected representatives about abuses of power and control of information. Without a strong public outcry and demands for reform impressed upon the White House and Congress, the attack on the press and other news media, including the PBS, will continue, drastically reducing the quality of life in America, Inc. This will prove to be mismanagement of the very worst kind, as it will again benefit the few at the expense of the many and result in dogma or biased beliefs driving out real news and objective fact.

◆   ◆   ◆

The dire need, then, is twofold: (1) the need for effective leadership in the White House and Congress to address the vital issues laid out in this and previous chapters; and (2) the need for effective "followership," with U.S. citizens pressuring their leaders for effective reform and change. The next chapter considers these needs and demands in greater detail.

CONCLUSIONS

The last chapter showed how lobbyists have power and use it to run America, Inc. Dependency on lobbies and their money, it was argued, is creating dysfunctional mismanagement in the country as special interests rule and decisions in the White House and on Capitol Hill favor the few, leading to profligate spending, pork-barrel waste, and even threats to the democratic process. This chapter adds to the list of problems caused by poor management and a dysfunctional power structure by showing how leaders in the U.S. are attacking science and the press, directly and indirectly, and what the negative outcomes of this assault might be.

Science is under attack in America, Inc., and the country is losing its position of scientific and technological dominance. Funding decisions, tax cuts favoring the few, military spending and the predominance of "guns" over "butter," a decline in sponsored basic research, controls on immigration of scientists and students wishing to study science or engineering, and the general climate of fear and apprehension in the country are creating a situation hostile to science and the scientific method. This situation, the result of top-management policy decisions, bodes poorly for the economic and political well being of the U.S. in years to come. The precarious position of science is being threatened further by non-scientific or pseudo-scientific explanations of worldly events or changes, e.g. the attack on evolution by those fostering "intelligent design."

There is also an ongoing attack on the news media in the U.S., especially the press. Government leaders' reliance on management by fear, the creation of pseudo-events and pseudo-news stories, the development and distribution of news and propaganda by government-employed "reporters," and the support of media consolidation and concentration, *inter alia*, are leading to control of the production and distribution of news in the U.S. and control over what people see, hear, and read. This is an especially serious attack in a democratic country in which the press and other news media have played a dominant informational and educational role.

This mismanagement of power and the attacks on science and the press are surely leading to major problems, and they must cease or be seriously tempered. Nothing will change, however, unless the general public becomes outraged and demands reform. If people don't want to live in an Orwellian nightmare in which science, knowledge, and all the news that's fit to print, read, hear, or see are controlled by "big brother" or huge corporations, they had better make their wishes and demands known to their elected representatives and demand significant reforms. People get the leadership they deserve; if they don't demand change and reform, the present system of waste, control by lobbyists and monied interests, attacks on science and the press, and the consequent erosion of democratic principles will only get worse and more debilitating.

Endnotes

1. William Broad, "U.S. Is Losing Its Dominance in the Science," *The New York Times*, May 3, 2004.

2. *Physical Review*, a series of top journals in physics, tracked this downturn in published papers. The editor remarked that other journals are also seeing this downward trend. See the "U.S. is Losing Its Dominance" Ibid.

3. The National Science Board report, "An Emerging and Critical Problem of the Science and Engineering Labor Force," was published May 4, 2004, at its headquarters in Arlington, VA. The key aspects of the report can be found in William Broad, "National Science Panel Warns of Far Too Few New Scientists," *The New York Times*, May 5, 2004; also see Kevin Hall, "Engineers: Foreigners Get Most Degrees," *The Philadelphia Inquirer*, August 13, 2005.

4. Ibid

5. June Kronkolz, "Economic Time Bomb: U.S. Teens are Among Worst at Math," *The Wall Street Journal*, December 7, 2004; Floyd Norris, "U.S. Students Fare Badly in International Survey of Math Skills," *The New York Times*, December 7, 2004.

6. Ed Fracienheim, "U.S. Slips Lower in Coding Contest," CNET News.com, April 7, 2005.

7. Sam Dillon, "Foreign Enrollment Declines at Universities, Surveys Say," *The New York Times*, November 10, 2004.

8. Ibid.

9. Editorial, "Universities in Decline," *The New York Times*, August 27, 2003; see also "State College Cuts Make Graduating a Struggle," *The New York Times*, August 24, 2003.

10. John Markoff, "Pentagon Redirects Its Research Dollars," *The New York Times*, April 2, 2005.

11. Ibid.

12. Sharon Begley, "A Smaller NIH Budget Means Fewer Scientists and 'Too-Safe' Studies," *The Wall Street Journal,* September 1, 2006; see also Bernard Wysocki, "National Institutes of Health is Under Fire," *The Wall Street Journal,* June 22, 2004.

13. "A Smaller NIH Budget," Ibid.

14. Carol Goldberg, "EPA Scientists Losing Access to Journals," *Common Dreams Progressive Newswire,* October 9, 2006.

15. "Politics and Science in the Bush Administration," a report prepared for Rep. Henry Waxman, U.S. House of Representatives, Committee on Government Reform, August 2003; see also Marjorie Heins, "The Attack on Science," *ZNet,* December 22, 2004.

16. Laura Meckler, "Former Surgeon General Says White House Edited Speeches," *The Wall Street Journal,* July 11, 2007

17. Union of Concerned Scientists, "Scientific Integrity in Policymaking: An Investigation into the Bush Administration's Misuse of Science, February-March, 2004 (go to http://www.ucsusa.org); also see "Attack on Science, Ibid.

18. Ibid. The "Attack on Science" article has additional reference items in its Notes section that deal with the integrity of government interventions in the science community.

19. There literally are scores of articles dealing with the topic of global warming, and many are in highly respected academic and professional journals and follow the tenets of sound scientific inquiry. Al Gore's book *An Inconvenient Truth* published in 2006 (Rodale Publishing) and his world tour of the book's main findings helped popularize and disseminate the important issues related to global warming. See also Lauren Etter "Global Warming: A Cloudy Outlook," *The Wall Street Journal,* December 10-11, 2005; "Hotting Up," *The Economist,* February 5, 2005; "The Sound of Distant Howling," *The Economist,* December 3, 2005; and Nicholas Kristof, "I Have a Nightmare," *The New York Times,* March 12, 2005.

20. Mary Brumder and Kathleen Rest, "Muzzling of Federal Scientists Must Stop," *The Philadelphia Inquirer,* February 8, 2007; Brumder is Executive

Director of the Government Accountability Project (www. shistleblower.org), and Rest is Executive Director of the Union of Concerned Scientists (www.ucsusa.org).

21. "Global Warming: A Cloudy Outlook," op. cit.

22. "Smog Over Old Faithful," *The Philadelphia Inquirer*, December 27, 2003.

23. Ibid.

24. Ibid.

25. Felicity Barringer, "Secretary Tours Yellowstone on Snowmobile," *The Wall Street Journal*, February 17, 2005.

26. "Smog Over Old Faithful," op. cit.

27. Chris Mondics, "Whitman Criticizes Bush Administration," *The Philadelphia Inquirer*, January 27, 2005.

28. Cornelia Dean, "Evolution Major Disappears from Approved Federal List," *The New York Times*, August 25, 2006.

29. See e.g., Richard Dawkins, "Is Religion the Root of All Evil," *The Philadelphia Inquirer*, January 29, 2006; Dawkins' TV series, "The Root of All Evil," appeared in January 2006, in the U.K. See, too, Sam Harris, *The End of Faith*: Religion, *Terror, and the Future of Reason*, (W. W. Norton & Co., 2005).

30. Lexington, "Purgatory Without End," *The Economist*, May 28, 2005.

31. Ibid.

32. Brooke Allen, "Our Godless Constitution," *The Nation*, February 21, 2005.

33. Nicholas Kristof, "God, Satan, and the Media," *The New York Times*, March 4, 2003; Jon Miller, Eugenie Scott, and Shinji Okamato, "Public Acceptance of Evolution," *Science*, August, 2006.

34. "Purgatory Without End," op. cit.

35. Cartoons by Tony Auth depicting these kinds of "substitution" for science and the attack on scientific theories or knowledge appeared in *The Philadelphia Inquirer* and other syndicated newspapers on June 22, 2005, and August 4, 2005. They were tongue-in-cheek "shots" against intelligent design and other silly substitutions for real science, but some people, remarkably, took them seriously.

36. I was taught by Jesuits in high school (a religious school, but one believed to be the best academically in the city) and I remember seeing or hearing a slogan like this first hand. A similar quote appears in Dawkins', "Is Religion the Root of All Evil," op. cit., which reinforces my recollection of this saying or boast.

37. "Clamping Down on Freedom of the Press" *The Center For Public Integrity,* February 17, 2005.

38. Ibid.

39. Molly Ivins, "The Great Bush Reclassification Project," *Truth Dig* April 27, 2006; "Down the Black Hole," *The Philadelphia Inquirer,* June 18, 2006.

40. See, e.g., Gael Murphy, "The Guards Are Sleeping," *AlterNet,* May 2, 2005.

41. Leonard Pitts, "Fear the 9/11 Hammer," *The Miami Herald,* January 29, 2006.

42. Daniel Boorstin, *The Image* (New York, Vintage Books, 1961).

43. George Orwell, "Politics and the English Language," 1946.

44. David Barstow and Robin Stein, "News or Public Relations? For Bush It's a Blur," *The New York Times,* March 13, 2005.

45. Janet Elder, "Packaging 9/11, Terror, and the War in Iraq." *The New York Times,* October 17, 2007.

46. Ibid.

47. Eric Boehlert, "Tearing Down the Press," *Salon.com,* March 2, 2005.

48. Andrew Kohut, "More News Is Not Necessarily Good News," *The New York Times*, July 11, 2004.

49. Cass Sunstein, *Republic.com* (Princeton University Press, 2001).

50. Mark Cooper, "Analysis Shows Media Markets are Already Highly Concentrated—Consumer Groups Question Wisdom of Further Concentration," *Consumer Federation of America*, May 12, 2003.

51. William Safire, "The Five Sisters," *The New York Times*, February 16, 2004.

52. Jeff Gelles, "The Battle to Enact Network Neutrality," *The Philadelphia Inquirer*, June 25, 2006.

53. Ibid.

54. "Politicizing Public Broadcasting," Editorial, *The New York Times*, May 4, 2005; Frazier Moore (Associated Press), "Bill Moyers Retiring from TV After Tonight," reported in *The Philadelphia Inquirer*, December 17, 2004; "Bill Moyers' Speech to the National Conference for Media Reform," *Free Press*, May 16, 2003.

55. "Politicizing Public Broadcasting," op. cit.

56. Jack Ohman, "1984 Orwell, 2004," *The Oregonian*, May 15, 2003.

7

Dysfunctional Leadership: Compounding the Problems of Mismanagement

Leadership at the top is critical to the performance and viability of organizations. Leaders work and provide guidance in many important areas—strategic, operational, and cultural—and their poor performance can hurt an organization. Poor planning, excessive short-term thinking, a focus on personal gain over the common good, an inability to learn and adapt, not leading by example, and failure to choose and develop the right resources and capabilities for the organization, including critical human resources, are just a few of the leadership or top-management failings that can negatively affect organizational performance.

Previous chapters in this book suggest strongly that the leadership of America, Inc. in the White House and Congress is sorely deficient and leading the country into serious trouble. The management failings noted in the previous paragraph represent the defining characteristics of America, Inc.'s leadership. It's a deplorable situation, and one that cannot continue.

The prevailing message to this point is that management decisions, actions, and even inaction at the very top are sowing the seeds of economic, social, and political problems that, unless addressed, can put our present financial, governance, and security systems at risk. The motivation for personal gain, refusal to think strategically and address long-known problems, and even the incompetence of some U.S. leaders and their close cohorts have clearly been highlighted or suggested in previous discussions. This chapter expands upon this notion of poor leadership and shows how problematic and worrisome the situation at the top really is. The chapter also discusses briefly the notion of poor "followership" in the U.S., and how it's supporting and nurturing the shortcomings of leadership in the country. It makes a strong case for public rejection of and revolt against the long-standing policies and tactics of leaders in the White House and Congress.

Let's begin by summarizing briefly the leadership shortfalls I've been referencing or implying throughout the book.

DYSFUNCTIONAL LEADERSHIP

What does effective leadership look like? What are some of the attributes or characteristics of sound leadership? There are many opinions and data that deal with these questions, as leadership has been studied and discussed extensively.[1] Let me try to borrow from this vast literature and my own experience to state succinctly what I believe to be effective leadership in top-management positions.

Effective leaders are *objective, capable, eclectic, above board*, and *open-minded*. They surround themselves with people who bring different, even opposing, points of view to the table. They welcome disagreement and constructive criticism and thrive on developing decision processes that lead ultimately to agreement and consistent courses of action. They are honest, rely on sound data and the judgments of others, and don't conceal facts that are not to their liking. They rarely, if ever, ignore data that get in the way of their own opinions.

Good leaders value *sound planning*, but they are not wedded to rigid bureaucratic approaches to the process. They collect and analyze multiple forms and sources of *timely and valid information*, and they are adept at "connecting the dots" and inferring what the data are indicating or suggesting. Good planning involves *long-term* or *strategic thinking*, and effective leaders build this into their planning models and processes. All of us live in the short-term and worry about the here-and-now and immediate problems to some degree, and so do effective leaders and managers. However, they don't let *only short-term thinking* and myopic views rule their judgment on critical issues. They are aware of the importance of the long haul and attempt to ensure that short-term decisions and actions aren't inconsistent with or antagonistic to important long-term, superordinate goals.

Effective leaders also implement or execute well. They don't only focus on strategy making, but also on *making strategy work*. They understand the critical aspects or components of execution—sound *organizational design*, effective *methods of coordination, feedback, and controls*, the importance of good *incentives* that motivate and reinforce the right things, and the need to develop the *resources and capabilities* to achieve strategic and short-term goals.[2] The last item includes the choice and nurturance of *qualified people*, as the effective leader knows that there's much he or she doesn't know and, consequently, there's a need to employ knowledgeable people to complement the organization's other resources and capabilities.

Effective leaders place a premium on *learning*. Sound planning and execution are vital, but rarely do things go according to plan. Feedback about performance—both positive and negative—must be analyzed to explain the performance and facilitate learning and adaptation. Learning from past mistakes and miscalculations is vital to a continued trajectory of growth and success and avoidance of the expensive and ineffective plans and programs of the past. Without learning, organizations cannot change, adapt, or cope with new challenging environmental conditions.

Effective leaders can also *inspire* others to stretch and achieve challenging goals. Inspiration can be important and occasionally a charismatic personality is helpful, but in the absence of the previous capabilities or characteristics discussed—e.g. strategic thinking, sound planning, open-mindedness, etc.—it can lead to followers pursuing the *wrong ends*, resulting in ineffective, inconsistent, or poor organizational performance. Inspirational leaders can lead an organization or country astray, and history provides many examples supporting this point (Hitler, Ghengis Kahn, and others, I'm sure, were inspirational and charismatic leaders to many of their followers).

Given this brief overview, what kind of leadership does America, Inc. enjoy? How do our leaders or managers in the White House and Congress stack up? The fact is that they don't stack up very well at all. Discussions in previous chapters have identified a number of serious shortcomings and debilitating problems when held against the criteria or benchmarks just noted. Let's review a few of the leadership shortcomings previously discussed.

Like any large global organization, America Inc.'s survival depends upon sound planning and intelligence gathering to defend it against competitors and protect its financial assets, citizens, and intellectual capital. It's abundantly clear, however, that America's planning and intelligence mechanisms are severely flawed. Planning in the financial and fiscal domain is a travesty. Total U.S. debt is $9 trillion, and shows no signs of abatement. Leaders in the White House and Congress are spending like drunken sailors, and their penchant for red ink and pork-barrel projects is leading to serious troubles. Critical problems—e.g. the huge looming fiscal gap due to increased spending and reduced taxes or the looming financial crisis in social security and Medicare/Medicaid—are being ignored. Exorbitant levels of debt can eventually drive away investments in the U.S., making the country increasingly vulnerable in a global economy that demands continuous investments in new technologies. Solving these problems will take planning and "biting the financial bullet," but our leaders to date have shown no taste for real decisions and actions, especially unpopular ones.

The intelligence community is an organizational and management quagmire that virtually precludes the possibility of sound planning and adequate preparedness on the intelligence front. Too many intelligence organizations with different agendas and a lack of clear responsibility and accountability militate against sound planning, effective coordination across agencies, and a focus on common goals or a united thrust. Incentives are inappropriate, creating massive competition rather than cooperation among top management in key intelligence areas. Appointments of czars and other "leaders" to head the intelligence effort are useless and impotent methods that simply cannot address the underlying problems that plague the intelligence community. U.S. leaders are failing miserably in this vital area of planning and national security.

Leadership must be objective, consider all options, reflect open-mindedness, and include many, if not all, interests or points of view to be effective. The power structure in America, Inc. is sorely defective in all of these areas. Lobbyists and their special interests rule Capitol Hill. Money talks and U.S. leaders in Congress listen intently and act according to the lobbyists' demands and desires. The republic is being turned increasingly into a management oligarchy in which the wishes of the powerful few clearly override the needs of the majority of Americans. Lobbyists and their moneyed interests are actually destroying participation in the U.S. democratic process. Leaders in Washington are taking the lobbyists' money and spending it on pet projects that benefit themselves and a chosen few of their constituents. Increased dependency on lobbyists and their money is increasing their power and influence well beyond the limits of safety and sound political process. Easy money is contributing to profligate spending and waste, which exacerbates the problems of increased debt.

Poor human resource policies and a failure to cultivate and use critical capabilities, knowledge, and personnel skills also are increasingly the norm in America, Inc. The stature of scientists is slipping badly, victims of a power structure in the U.S. that is attacking or ignoring science with increasing fervor. The distortion and outright suppression of scientific research and data have become all too commonplace. The replacement of scientists in important leadership positions by political hacks and insiders is having major debilitating effects that, if continued, will exacerbate the current downward trend of the U.S. in the worldwide scientific and technological communities.

The appointment of people to key leadership or functional positions at the highest levels based primarily on loyalty, friendship, or political leanings is perpetuating a system that ignores or destroys the critical technical and managerial competencies needed to compete and prosper in an increasingly complex economic and political world. This is a leadership problem that must be fixed but, at best, it will be a difficult chore. "To the victor belongs the spoils," including high level jobs to loyal cronies, is a long-standing aspect of the Washington culture. Its negative impact on the appointment of qualified managers, though fairly obvious to any student of management and organization, will be hard to combat and negate, but future leaders, especially in the White House, will have to face up to the task.

Leaders must not only plan effectively, they must also directly or indirectly affect the conditions or factors that lead to the successful execution or implementation of their plans. Effective management involves both planning and doing, and support of the latter begins with top management. But, again, U.S. leaders are not up to the management task. U.S. leaders in Congress and the White House apparently know little or nothing about organizational structure and its impact on performance. The White House Cabinet organization is unwieldy, with a lack of clear responsibility and accountability. A lack of clarity in roles, responsibilities, accountability, and authority at the very top of America, Inc. surely translates into problems down and throughout the entire management structure.

The organization (or lack thereof) of the intelligence community is a good example of an unwieldy and poorly performing organizational structure. Such a structure simply defies sound organizational and management principles and cannot work effectively. How U.S. leaders could have allowed such an important function of government like intelligence to evolve over the years into an organizational structure marked by competing agencies with overlapping and conflicting missions, little agreement on responsibilities and accountability, poor coordination, and no or little formal authority to control a large and diverse set of agencies or organizations is totally beyond logical comprehension. This is an example of gross mismanagement and leadership at their very worst.

A word about management incentives and controls is also in order. Incentives and controls tell people what's important and what should be supported in an organization. They reinforce certain behaviors and drive out others, which ultimately helps to define an organization's culture and *raison d'etre*. So, what does analysis of America, Inc.'s incentives and controls at the highest levels reveal? It reveals an organization whose leaders or top managers think only about short-term gratification, *not* long-term needs or programs for the common good. It reveals behaviors that support profligate spending, amazing waste, and even borderline unethical performance in support of narrow, personal goals and the wishes of a few biased interests or groups. Analysis of incentives uncovers a fabric of programs, actions, and decisions into which is woven long strands of self-interest and personal gratification. It reveals a system of rewards that totally eschews the tough decisions that are necessary to support the long-term needs of the country.

Why should leaders in Congress fix Social Security, Medicare, or other programs in which they happily don't participate? Why worry about and fix health care if leaders are immune to and unaffected by the shortcomings and vagaries of the present system? Our Congressmen have separate, but certainly *unequal* retirement and health-care plans, which provide no positive incentive to cure the major ills in these areas. One only has to look at *what hasn't been done* in certain areas—social security, Medicare and Medicaid, oil dependency, debt reduction, etc.—to see this myopic approach to management and the lack of willingness to bite the bullet and solve the real problems facing the country. *Real leadership demands strategic thinking and a will to attack formidable problems, even unpopular or difficult ones, for the common good. Our leaders certainly have not, and are not, exhibiting the needed will and determination.*

A final and potentially fatal flaw of U.S. leaders is the apparent inability to learn from past experience. Despite the Iraq debacle, sabres are again rattling in the White House, Cabinet, and some corners of Congress, and the sound bytes and news messages suggest that U.S. leaders are actually preparing plans for a possible war with Iran. Everyone by now knows how unprepared the U.S. was for the invasion of Iraq and its aftermath. Generals involved in the combat have listed the mistakes and informed the public of the ongoing mismanagement of the post-invasion situation. General Ricardo Sanchez, for example, a former U.S. Commander there, denounced the "catastrophically flawed, unrealistically optimistic" war plan for Iraq.[3] Others have warned that we're in over our heads, bogged down hopelessly in Iraq and Afghanistan, and that getting into a conflict with yet another country in the region would be a military and economic disaster, while also turning other countries in the Middle East and elsewhere against us and out militant ways.

Never mind the shortage of military resources, the real Al Qaeda threat our leaders seem to be ignoring, the support of terrorism by our allies, Pakistan and Saudi Arabia, the bolstering of radical terrorism in the world that additional military action by the U.S. is found to motivate and support, etc. It seems that action against Iran is on the table as a viable option. The messages coming out of Washington sound eerily familiar to those preceding the invasion of Iraq.[4] The way to avoid World War III, according to President Bush, is to prevent Iran from gaining knowledge about how to harness nuclear power. Or V.P. Cheney's words that the U.S. wouldn't "permit a brutal dictator" with terrorist ties and weapons of mass destruction to threaten the U.S. Does this sound familiar? The invectives and accusations aimed years ago at Saddam Hussein clearly have been recycled and are now being redeployed against the leadership of Iran, suggesting that we haven't learned from the Iraq debacle at all and we're ready to make the same mistakes again.

Many data and the opinions of others support my accusations about dysfunctional U.S. leadership.[5] Critics of leadership argue that there isn't a culture of candor and openness at the top of America, Inc. Rather, dissent and debate are seen to reflect disloyalty and, thus, are avoided. Members of Congress ignore facts and data that don't agree with their biases and party positions, and Congress and the White House are venues where many people "never let the facts get in the way of their opinions." The credibility of U.S. leaders is suffering, both abroad and at home, and approval ratings for the White House and Congress continue to plummet. The qualifications of political appointees are often called into question and there is a strong opinion that many high-ranking officials can't handle complex issues and jobs. Stubbornness to admit mistakes and an inability to learn and adapt are the hallmarks of many U.S. leaders' management style, especially in recent years in the White House and Congress. This certainly isn't a pretty picture of leadership and top management in America, Inc. Actually, it is a sad state of affairs that is leading to major debilitating consequences, as this book has been emphasizing. Something must be done soon to reverse the trends and ensure a higher-quality leader in the top management positions in the U.S.

Before talking about cures, however, there is yet one more critical question: *how can U.S. leadership continually get away with this behavior?* In most organizations, performance reviews and analyses of goal achievement that are negative lead to major change. Why, then, can U.S. leaders get away with behaviors, policies, and decisions that fly in the face of efficient and effective management and perhaps even ethical standards? Why do their abysmal planning and execution results virtually go unchallenged, despite national elections, regime changes, and constant attacks by one political party or the other with a stated resolve to make things right in Washington? The Democratic victories in the mid-term 2006 elections, for example, held the promise of major change. Quite frankly, however, little if anything of importance has resulted save for an increased demand to pull out of Iraq, which likely would have also resulted even if the Democrats hadn't prevailed. Why, then, do we let our leaders "do their thing" in Washington to the detriment of the many? Why do problems like oil dependency still exist, despite leaders' promises for decades to right a dangerous situation?

Based on my experience, there are at least *three interdependent explanations* of the poor and dangerous leadership in America, Inc., three highly related reasons why this ineffective leadership or management survives and why inertia and the "same old, same old" persist, despite the problems attributable to top management incompetence that this book has identified. The three can be summarized as follows: (1) an effective use of "management by stealth," (2) a heavy emphasis on management by fear, and (3) dysfunctional followership, including citizens "giving up" and not holding leaders accountable for their decisions and actions. The first two factors, of course, contribute mightily to the third condition. The obverse, however, is also true: creating "good" followership can combat and negate the first two management styles noted, while poor followership only reinforces poor leadership. Let's consider these points further.

Management by Stealth

U.S. leaders in the White House and Congress have gotten quite adept over the years at "managing by stealth," doing things and making decisions that fly under the radar of public scrutiny and, thus, contribute to public forbearance. Stealth relies on decisions or actions by leaders that are not easily detected and, hence, not usually publicized, scrutinized, and challenged. It often involves incremental decisions or changes, none of which alone attracts attention, but which cumulatively add up to major policy and operating shifts. In short, management by stealth usually implies sneakiness and pulling the wool over the public's eyes.

Hercule Poirot, the famous fictional detective created by Agatha Christie, once noted that the easiest way to hide something heinous and purposeful is to place it amongst other heinous acts that appear random and unpurposeful. In the middle of a skein of random, senseless murders, for example, a planned or premeditated homicide would also appear to be unplanned and random, hiding the murderer's true motives. Murder by stealth, so to speak, and ordinary people with fewer "gray cells" than Poirot surely wouldn't discern what was happening.

Members of Congress usually don't commit murder, at least not literally, but they are nonetheless very good at hiding things. Unlike Poirot's cagy murderer, however, they often hide bad things among the good. Thousand-page bills are brought to the floor for a vote, with little or no notice or warning. Reading the bills is impossible, so they are passed without debate and usually without publicity and public scrutiny of all the bills' provisions. Or, more commonly, wasteful or "heinous" bills or rule changes are attached to other bills that are desirable and important, e.g. when a pork-barrel project or wasteful earmark is attached to a bill on Medicare or Medicaid. Killing the bad bill or rule change would mean voting against the entire package, including the desirable legislation, and no one in Congress wants to be known as the lawmaker who stood in the way of increased benefits for elder citizens. So the earmark or wasteful bill, in lamprey fashion, hitchhikes on the good bill, goes along for the ride attached to it, and passes quietly with ease, with no public scrutiny or debate.

Hiding something bad among things that are good is an example of management by stealth, and it is done routinely on the floors of Congress. Earmarks are added to bills to allow lawmakers to fund pet projects that help themselves or vulnerable colleagues facing re-election problems. Multiple earmarks or add-ons that appeal to a host of lawmakers often grease the skids for other legislation, including less popular bills, and the use of these stealthy add-ons is increasing. President Reagan vetoed a transportation bill in the 1980s because it contained a *few hundred earmarks*. Amazingly, last year's version of a transportation bill *included more than 6000 add-ons*. In the fiscal year ending September 30, 2005, there were 15,818 earmarks attached to all of the federal spending bills, and the same process is still running rampant today.[6] Most of these add-ons, of course, are intended to escape public scrutiny and pass without notice or fanfare, providing wonderful examples of a management style based on stealth and furtive processes.

There are countless other examples of stealthy management exhibited by our leaders in the White House and Congress in all sorts of matters, including environmental rules and regulations, energy programs and initiatives, worker safety standards, health rules, and product safety requirements. Consider the changes in the rules governing environmental protection, of which there have been many. For example, in late 2002, new rules were proposed to manage 192 million acres of federal forest lands and grasslands to better "harmonize the environmental, social, and economic benefits" of land usage. This is code or doublespeak for making it easier to log, mine, drill, and rape federal lands.[7] The new rules allowed logging and other uses without the need to study the effects on wildlife, water quality, or the public's access to the lands for recreational purposes. Similar changes the year before negated previous rules that prohibited timber harvesting and road building on 60 million acres of forestland.[8] Still other rule changes relaxed the need for environmental reviews before forests could be thinned "to prevent wildfires."[9] These rule changes were done quietly, without fanfare or the careful public scrutiny that the National Forest Management Act had legislated and assumed would occur as part of the law. And there's more, lots more.

The Wednesday before Thanksgiving 2004, while most Americans were thinking of turkey, dressing, gravy, and pumpkin pie, the administration was quietly relaxing clean-air rules in industry's favor. Similarly, just a few days before announcing protections for scenic Utah rivers—the Colorado, Dolores, and Green, including protections from hard rock mining claims for 112,000 acres of land surrounding river valleys—the Interior Department opened up almost 5,000 acres of the preserved area to oil and gas drilling.[10] The former "protections" were publicized, while the latter changes were done quietly and surreptitiously, hiding among the favorable-sounding protections. The latter rule changes allowing oil and gas drilling presented a greater threat to these peaceful river areas than hard rock mining (few companies had expressed a wish to pursue this option and thus protections really weren't needed), but they were implemented quietly, without drawing attention to them or scrutinizing and challenging their potential devastating results. The areas affected are home to a number of endangered or threatened species, many prehistoric sites, and a huge recreational industry, so these rule changes were potentially extremely impactful and deserved more public attention, but they were implemented in the quietest fashion with no due diligence or public participation.

A disconcerting story about wild horses barely received any attention in the news media. Wild horses, it seems, had been protected under laws and rules passed by Congress years ago. These magnificent creatures roamed free on the plains, a wild resource that in some ways symbolized the spirit of the Wild West and America. But things changed for these animals when they began to encounter the ire of influential farmers and ranchers. Quietly, with no hearings, debates, or public notification, there was a change in the rules that supported the law protecting the horses. The horses—the pests—could be rounded up (even slaughtered, according to some accounts) with no consequences or repercussions to those carrying out the carnage. Another case of managing scarce resources with stealth.

These stealthy attacks and quiet management-change processes are not confined to the area of the natural environment and its waters, fauna, and flora. There, indeed, are many other examples. The alternative minimum tax (AMT) is a clear case that shows the devastating effects of stealth. The AMT was instituted over three decades ago by Congress to ensure that very wealthy people couldn't use the myriad tax loopholes at their disposal to avoid paying any income taxes. It was aimed at the "fat cats" to ensure that they anted up some share of taxes, even if not a fair share. But the impact of the AMT has been mushrooming in a quiet way, and only recently has some attention (though not enough) been paid to it.

The original AMT was aimed at only a few hundred households. By the year 2000, this had grown to roughly one million taxpayers, a high percentage increase but still not a huge number in a rich nation like America, Inc. But, amazingly, this number will have grown to about 35 million households in 2008 by some estimates. Even more staggering is the fact that the vast majority of these taxpayers are families with children who make $75,000–$100,000 per year, while only about 30% of taxpayers who make $1 million or more will owe the AMT. All of these facts and trends, of course, have been kept fairly quiet by our leaders in Washington. They are fully aware of the repercussions of this far-reaching and onerous tax, but they've been silent, quietly letting the tax ax fall on more and more middle-class Americans while the truly wealthy wage earners escape the AMT's wrath. Why this silence and quiet approval by our leaders? Because the government desperately needs the money to pay for its exorbitant spending, including funds for the waging of war, to make up for financial losses due to recent tax cuts and maintain the low capital gains and dividend tax rates that primarily favor the wealthy.[11] Given the fiscal gap and financial problems noted earlier, U.S. leaders need the money and the AMT is turning the trick. It's silly to kill or draw attention to the goose laying the golden eggs, especially when the goose isn't complaining very loudly and no one has publicly stood up to fight for the goose's rights.

The AMT will definitely affect more and more Americans in a certain but quiet way, and our leaders have shown little motivation to bring the economic injustices caused by it to light. This is a good example of management by stealth: keeping people in the dark as long as possible, letting the tax base expand, collecting monies from individuals who never were the targets of the original tax bill, and quietly ignoring the highest-end taxpayers the bill was aimed at decades ago.

There are countless other examples of the stealthy approach to managerial decision making by America, Inc.'s leaders. By now it is well known that the Bush White House had for a significant time a secret spying operation that authorized the NSA to tap overseas phone calls by U.S. citizens, an operation that defied the provisions of the 1978 Foreign Intelligence Surveillance Act (FISA). The justification for the secrecy or stealth was that the White House was only spying on "terrorists," although no evidence or proof of terrorism has even been shown for the thousands of citizens who were the victims of the eavesdropping.[12] Never mind, too, that obtaining a warrant under FISA could be expedited to take hours, even minutes, and could even be done legally 72 hours after the spying had already begun. Secrecy, obviously, could be maintained while following the tenets of due process, which eliminates the need for illegal stealthy activities. Still, due process was routinely ignored, consistent with a management approach that basically eschews openness and debate. President Bush recently agreed to follow FISA rules and procedures about obtaining warrants, but the example is still an effective one that shows how rules can be quietly broken or bent over a period of time.

Similarly, the FBI has secretly sought information about thousands of U.S. citizens and legal residents from their banks and credit card, telephone, and internet companies without court approval or a subpoena, according to the Justice Department.[13] The justification given was the Patriot Act, the sweeping anti-terror law that seems to allow all sorts of fact-finding activities without disclosure. This secretive style of U.S. leaders is particularly distasteful, given the lousy track record in Iraq, our deficient intelligence capabilities, inability to find Osama Bin Laden, etc. Secrecy and stealth, without results, is especially grating when the impotent secret activities are finally brought to light.

Other examples of management by stealth that were brought partly to light include the "torture taxi," the largest covert CIA operation since the cold war era. This program, run by shadowy government contractors in Afghanistan, Europe, and elsewhere, kidnapped people and sent them to secret prisons around the world, where they were held and tortured.[14] The justification for these actions was derived from the Military Commissions Act which, in effect, "codifies racial and political discrimination, legalizes kidnapping and torture of those the government deems its political enemies, and eliminates *habeas corpus*," the ancient precept that prevents the authorities from arresting and detaining someone without cause.[15] Hundreds of people were held without cause, tortured, and never charged with a crime as part of this furtive program that seems to embody the worst aspects of a management style based on stealth.

Many other examples abound. New rules on publishing auto-safety information, requiring hospitals to protect workers against illness, protecting coal miners from black-lung disease, and increasing the hours truck drivers operate, thereby increasing the probability of fatigue and accidents, were enacted with little or no public scrutiny.[16] The nation's energy policy was discussed behind closed doors with oil executives and Vice President Cheney, an "on-leave" oil executive, making critical decisions. Cheney actually went to court to keep the membership of his elite energy-policy group a secret. A meeting of like-minded, unknown cronies with a clearly biased point of view, decided energy policy to their own chosen specifications and needs behind closed doors, hardly an objective, open process of decision making. To this day, the data, processes, and results of this meeting have never come to light, a wonderful example of management by stealth and the public's need-not-to-know. It suggests that Dick Cheney, a very powerful VP, is not a great fan of openness in government but, rather, prefers a more furtive, closed approach. One could also argue that this is a clear case of appointing the foxes to guard the hen house without open discussion or debate, including inputs from the hens.

These and other examples basically suggest that, over time, our leaders in the White House and Congress have been gradually and quietly eliminating constraints on their exercise of power, whether by rule changes, law, regulations, or even the abrogation of treaties and agreements in the international arena. They suggest that, increasingly, management by stealth has become and still is an accepted modus oprandi by U.S. leaders. Making decisions, changing rules and regulations, and holding meetings veiled in secrecy seem to be the preferred managerial approach to addressing complex problems.

Is this growing secretive or stealthy approach wrong? Should we all be increasingly concerned about the number of rule changes and regulations being made and the covert actions being taken by U.S. leaders in the White House and Congress? I'll let George Bush answer. In an April 2004 news conference, when Iraq's weapons of mass destruction (WMD) were being discussed, Bush stated that Iraq was definitely hiding something and "… a country that hides something is a country that is afraid of getting caught" doing something wrong. Forgetting the tautological elements of his reasoning (a country that hides something is afraid of getting caught, and a country afraid of getting caught must be hiding something) and extending the argument beyond Iraq and WMD, a White House or Congress that engages in management by stealth with its furtive and secretive approach clearly *must* be hiding something that it doesn't want to get caught doing.[17] Ignoring due process, abrogating the law, annulling existing rules, and quietly attaching bad earmarks to good bills in the legislative process *certainly suggest wrongdoing and a desire to skirt or avert the public's need to know, debate, and approve.* So, management by stealth is wrong, inappropriate, misleading, and inefficient, to answer the question raised above.

The final question, of course, is why the public has been acquiescent, in effect, rolling over and playing dead even when they occasionally are told that these changes in policy and operations are occurring. The obvious first answer—the public doesn't know what's happening until it's too late—has already been offered. But the answer goes a bit deeper, rooted in 9/11 and another leadership approach or tool closely aligned with or subsumed under management by stealth—namely, "management by fear." The fact is that the public is fearful, has abrogated its responsibility as watchful citizens, and is relying on and trustful of

U.S. leaders to keep doing the right things, and this is supporting the dysfunctional leadership of America, Inc.

Management by Fear

Managing by fear has long been and still is an effective approach to quiet the masses and get them to acquiesce to changes that leaders propose or sneak through. Management by stealth keeps people in the dark; management by fear tries to ensure that people are deathly afraid of the dark and look to a select few leaders who are the sources of light or truth that must be believed, trusted, and followed.

The first ingredient in the process is the creation of real fear and apprehension. The 9/11 attacks took care of this critical ingredient. Management by fear has long been a useful tactic, but 9/11 was the recent event that contributed mightily to its use and effectiveness. America had never been attacked on its home soil. Previous attacks and wars were foreign affairs. Even Pearl Harbor, as heinous an attack as it was, was not perpetrated at home, on the continental U.S. It happened "over there," miles away in the Pacific. But 9/11 hit home hard. These attacks were on the home front. Enemies were no longer mysterious, foreign creatures; they were here and we were vulnerable before their terrorist attacks and methods. They could strike again, at any time, killing or maiming thousands of innocent, hard-working people, and this was very frightening. The eminent psychologist, Abraham Maslow, told us years ago that people concerned primarily with basic security needs and frightened by physical danger cannot function at a higher cognitive or psychological level. They are afraid and, like lemmings, will follow anyone who reduces the fear and tells them what to do to avoid danger. This is the basic ingredient, the *sine qua non*, underlying management by fear.

The next critical element or step is to *perpetuate and grow the fears*, even if this means creating phony issues and fake enemies. It's important to fan the fires that have been created. It's necessary to elevate the terrorist-warning index occasionally from "yellow" to "red" to generate fear, concern, and apprehension, and to remind people that danger is imminent and only the leaders raising the warning can provide the road to safety and security. I'm not suggesting that real dangers and threats don't exist, just that *faux* issues must be created when the real things are absent for a period of time.

Another critical element, closely aligned with the perpetuation of fear, is to create "camps" or factions that are simple, yet effective, tools in explaining who's responsible for the dangers or sources of fear. The simplest approach is to create binary distinctions or groups—"good guys" and "bad guys." There are people who are against terrorism, and those who are all right with it. There are those who want to win in Iraq and stop terrorist activities, and those who don't. There are people who love the U.S. and those who don't, those who support our troops, and those who obviously won't. There are those who question the leadership in the White House and Congress, and those enlightened people who don't and who will follow the leaders' path to glorious victory. If you vote in elections for the wrong people, surely calamity will befall you and the nation, so it's imperative to vote for the right people who, of course, are the people telling you all of this. In other words, it's important for leaders to be *divisive*, separating followers into simple groups and playing them against each other, while clearly extolling the virtues and patriotism of one chosen group.[18] If you're not with us, you obviously must be against us and should be dealt with harshly.

These, then, are the essential components of management by fear. Coupled with management by stealth, leaders can keep followers in the dark, create fear and apprehension by creating and controlling information, be divisive, and convince followers that only their leadership can maintain safety and security. As simplistic as this sounds, it's always worked effectively. As Hermann Goering, Hitler's Reich-Marshall, told us at the Nuremberg trials after WWII:

> "… the people can always be brought to the bidding of the leaders. This is easy. All you have to do is tell them they are being attacked, and denounce the pacifists for lack of patriotism and exposing the country to danger. It works the same in every country."

Management by stealth has been a tactic used by the White House and Congress for years, and it's become more prevalent in the last two decades. Management by fear, too, has been around for a long while, as witnessed by Goering's comments, but it's been especially prevalent and extensively used by U.S. leaders after 9/11, a perfect catalyst for a management approach founded on insecurity and a fear of terrorism.

This management style or approach, with its reliance on stealth and fear is dangerous. It disenfranchises many citizens in America, Inc., and it divides them into groups or factions hostile to each other. It revises rules or regulations supporting laws, thereby resulting in emasculation of the law and due legislative process. It frightens people and uses their fear to lead them to support decisions and actions that are not always beneficial for the country as a whole. A corollary in corporate America would be an executive team that: (1) openly professes support for an agreed-upon mission or strategy, but then institutes rules, incentives, or procedures that slowly but assuredly create behavior and results contrary to stated goals; and (2) uses motivational tactics based on fear and job insecurity to get subordinates to fall into line and go along with their plans, even if they're destructive of shareholder value and organizational culture. Luckily, the tactics of these ineffective or unethical executives are usually uncovered and they are ousted by shareholders or the legal system. Yet, the same or similar management tactics by those on Capitol Hill or in the White House are usually tolerated for a longer period of time. Why are U.S. leaders allowed to persist in their dysfunctional or sneaky ways, without facing a revolt of the citizenry?

In addition to the management techniques already noted, there is yet one more explanation for this inertia and tolerance for our leaders' perversions and shaky tactics, namely, *poor or dysfunctional followership in America, Inc.*, which results from and nurtures a management style based on stealth and fear. Management by stealth and fear is effective at destroying criticism and negative reactions to bad policies and decisions, and poor followership allows the dysfunctional leadership to continue and flourish.

Dysfunctional Followership

Poor leadership can only survive and prosper with poor or dysfunctional *followership*. People truly get the leadership they deserve. Alexis de Tocqueville, in his wondrously insightful work, *Democracy in America*, warned us about a number of things that resonate strongly today. He worried that the federal government's power would become so strong and concentrated that U.S. citizens could be reduced to "nothing better than a flock of timid and industrious animals, of which the government is the shepherd."[19] He feared that the majority would trample on minorities—the "tyranny of the majority"—and that a strong government could reduce the "independence of mind" of the U.S. citizenry. He feared too that an avowed lover of liberty and freedom could quietly and furtively become a "hidden servant of tyranny." If the public acquiesced and allowed its leaders, its lovers of liberty, to overcome them psychologically and emotionally and reduce their willingness to provide the needed checks and balances on leaders' actions and decisions, then surely this tyranny would result.[20] The tyranny of poor leadership is inevitable if followers roll over, play dead, and allow government officials to have their own way, without challenges, checks, and needed balances.

Management by stealth and fear, coupled with the dysfunctional power structure noted in Chapters 5 and 6, is leading to a form of this tyranny in America, Inc., and deficient, ineffective followership is paving and easing the way. U.S.

leaders on Capitol Hill and in the White House couldn't easily get away with a power-stealth-and-fear-based management style if followers were more vigilant and cared about critical decisions that affected them and their progeny. As mentioned previously, the 2006 mid-term elections were the cause of some optimism and hope that voters are getting tired of the "same old, same old" in Washington. A Wall Street Journal/NBC News poll in December 2006, likewise showed public discontent with U.S. leaders' performance on Iraq and other issues and indicated that voters want Congress especially to take the reins and actively set a new policy course for the country.[21] Other articles occasionally have addressed financial and fiscal problems and the deplorable state of health care in the U.S., implying that the general public wants reform. Still, despite these signs of some unrest among U.S. citizens, the country is far from being out of the woods. Poor followership is still the rule and much more needs to be done to eliminate the dysfunctional leadership at the highest levels of America, Inc. The general citizenry is quiet, obedient, and still rolling over and playing dead, allowing U.S. leaders to continue their flawed policies at will.

The "Perfect Customer." Years ago, I heard a marketing executive in a well-known automobile company describe the "perfect customer" from the industry's and his company's point of view. He said that perfect customers are "plentiful, rich, and awfully stupid." Plentiful? Sure. It's better to have many potential buyers than just a few, big powerful buyers. Rich? He really meant "price insensitive," willing to add on expensive options to the cars they purchased. But "stupid?"

His point was that the more informed a customer is, the more demanding he or she can be. Today's car buyer can go to the internet, locate cars, and get information about dealer invoice, selling price, product availability, and profit margins. The customer is motivated by self interest to educate herself to get the best deal possible. The customer of yore whom the marketing executive was describing didn't have this access to information. He or she knew little and the car salesperson knew everything. There as yet was no widespread use of the internet. The salesperson, then, had power, as the customer was totally dependent upon him and his knowledge. The former executive and his sales staff presumably wouldn't like today's well-informed customers who only make their sales job tougher.

Intelligent, informed stakeholders—board members, customers, shareholders—have influence in the private corporate sector. They can hold management's feet to the fire because of their knowledge of products, services, costs, industry forces, and options available to the organization. They can judge the effectiveness of management's actions and hold them responsible for transgressions and poor decisions. While there certainly are weak and uninformed stakeholders in the private sector, for the most part they are sufficiently informed to have a say on the important issues confronting management. Unfortunately, the same isn't true in the political arena, where the "customers" of America, Inc. act as if they don't care about dysfunctional leadership and poor management in the White House and on Capitol Hill. America, Inc.'s leaders have carte blanche in most matters, and U.S. citizens often act like "stupid" consumers, letting their leaders get away with the dysfunctional, inefficient, and even dangerous behaviors noted in previous chapters of this book. Some of this passive behavior clearly results from the management by stealth and emphasis on fear by U.S. leaders; citizens don't know what's happening and they place their unconditional trust in leaders to keep them safe. But the explanation for poor followership goes even deeper than this.

Voters today seem bored or intimidated by complex national issues. They would rather judge and pick a candidate the way they choose a breakfast cereal—based on catchy TV advertising and brief slogans. So, is it in the politician's best interest to give the public complicated issues to ponder before an election or a major budget hearing? No way. Better to reduce the issues to crisp, poll-tested sound bites. Talk about the causes and effects of global warming, the real costs of reducing the country's dependency on foreign oil, or the ultimate disastrous effects of huge deficits and profligate spending? Better to spoon feed the public cute slogans and preposterous exaggerations. Better to treat people like a "nation of nitwits," as Bob Herbert of the New York Times once put it. It's simpler and it works. It also creates anomie, a lack of urgency or caring in political and economic matters, and a climate in which U.S. leaders have free rein to do as they wish. Even with such a crucial contest between Bush and Kerry in the 2004 election, only about 54% of eligible voters went to the polls. And this is not atypical; despite its espousal of democracy and freedom, the U.S. is marked by one of the worst records among all nations in terms of the percentage of eligible voters who actually go to the polls and exercise their constitutional right to choose their leaders. Voters may feel intimidated or, worse yet, they simply don't care, and this only nurtures dysfunctional leadership in Washington, D.C. To be sure, there is a minority of citizens who are active politically, who track and try to influence what goes on in the White House and Congress, but the majority of Americans act consistent with the unflattering description of uncaring or disenfranchised stakeholders or "perfect customers."

De Tocqueville warned us that citizens must stay involved in government matters to maintain checks and balances and control their leaders. To do this, early citizens read newspapers, pamphlets, the printed content of speeches, and anything else that provided different sides of controversial issues. For a democracy to work and to maintain some control over leaders' decisions and actions, citizens, the consumers of America, Inc.'s products and services, must be aware of the issues. But one problem today is that Americans don't read. Newspapers ("Dinosaur Blogs") are in trouble; fewer people read them or rely on them for news or editorial analysis. A recent study by the National Endowment for the Arts, "Reading at Risk," reports that reading in the U.S. is down—for every age group, income level, educational level, and every region of the country.[22] Only 57% of the people surveyed said that they had read a book in the previous year. But "book" included anything—diet books, novels, fiction or nonfiction, mechanics manuals, etc. *And all a person had to do was read three pages to get credit for a full book.* Only 57% of the people surveyed had read even three pages of a book—an amazing statistic with serious implications.

If people don't read, where do they get their news and "facts?" From the TV and the Internet, of course. But can't they be effective substitutes for reading books and newspapers? We've already discussed in a previous chapter the problems of media bias, sound bites, and selective tuning into internet blogs and TV programs that don't convey all sides of political, social, and economic issues. It was argued then that Americans usually log on to internet sites or watch TV news programs that convey the "party line" only and don't provide balanced food-for-thought around key questions. Judging by their popularity, it seems that many people prefer the escape of "reality shows," while eschewing the real but boring issues that affect the quality of their lives. The result is anything but a learned or well-rounded citizen who can effectively understand and challenge the complex problems in the nation's capitol, which again contributes to poor followership and a lack of effective concern or control over what U.S. leaders can do.

A survey of over 112,000 high school students to determine their level of knowledge about the First Amendment and the rights it guarantees adds greatly to the concerns being raised presently.[23] One out of five kids felt that they shouldn't disagree with authority—the government knows best. Thirty-three percent felt that the press should have *more restrictions* placed on it, not fewer, and that government should approve newspaper stories before people read them. The group felt that the press enjoys *too much* freedom, despite First Amendment guarantees of a free press. A full 75% said that it should be illegal to burn a flag, despite the Supreme Court's ruling in 1989 that flag burning is free speech. One half of the students believed that the government can censor the internet, and one third said the First Amendment *goes too far* in the rights it guarantees. These data suggest, among other things, that these young minds know little about First

Amendment rights, including the all important freedom of the press, and that they, as adults, will not confront and challenge their leaders in Washington to maintain these rights and prevent dysfunctional leadership and management from hurting the country. Hopefully, this scenario proves to be invalid; the signs, however, are that a next generation of quiet followers stands ready to abrogate their responsibility to hold leaders accountable for their decisions and actions, again like the perfect customer described above.

A "blot" on democracy. There is another major blot on democracy in America that creates uncaring and ineffective followership—*redistricting* or *gerrymandering*. This is simply a way to divide, design, or redesign a voting area or location in such a way as to give one political party a huge advantage in an election. In the U.S., gerrymandering has been done on a grotesque scale, with incumbents safeguarding re-election by designing absurd voting districts that look like "doughnuts, sandwiches, and Rorschach tests."[24] Gerrymandering has made a joke of many elections to Congress. In the 2004 elections, no more than 30 seats of the 435 in the House of Representatives were competitive and, in 2002, four of five congressmen won their races by more than 20 percentage points.[25] It's far easier to reconfigure voting areas to guarantee results than it is to convince voters and other skeptics that one's political and economic programs have merit and that they alone justify re-election.

This is more than unfair and not right. Gerrymandering puts people off voting and destroys needed interest in politics and U.S. leaders' policies and decisions. Is it any wonder that, in 2004, voters in over 400 congressional districts may have been turned off because the result of the vote was a given, a *fait accompli*? If only 30 or so seats out of 435 are indeed competitive, why bother voting at all? Guaranteeing election results is not what the founding fathers had in mind when they discussed the responsibilities of citizens and leaders in the voting process. The focus should be one of issues, checks and balances, and performance, not the ability to draw up favorable election districts.

Redistricting is all too common in the U.S. and it's helping to create and support dysfunctional followership. Voters simply give up—why bother getting involved politically and exercising the right to vote if an election is "cooked" and the result is a foregone conclusion? This represents leadership, management, and followership of the worst kind, as it reinforces the power of elected officials, destroys the motivation of voters, and creates a climate of *ennui*, a "who cares" approach to politics among the majority of citizens. This climate, of course, supports the dysfunctional leadership and management style this book has been railing against, and it should be a concern for all U.S. citizens.

Major Changes are Needed

The time has come for major changes and reforms in the leadership and management of America, Inc. Leaders in the White House and Congress have exhibited myopic thinking, made ineffective, costly, and even dangerous decisions, and have avoided critical economic and social programs for too long a period of time. And, truth be told, the current administration has brought this dysfunctional leadership to its ugly head. While earmarks, pork-barrel legislation, profligate spending, government waste, etc. have been the norm for quite a while in government, the handling of the post 9/11 war on terrorism has raised the bar and the world's awareness of poor leadership and management. The war in Iraq alone has done wonders to highlight these top-management problems. Poor planning, cooked or biased intelligence, and a faulty, close-minded, ideological rationale coalesced to fuel the start of the war, and horrific management has resulted in a campaign that has been inefficiently and ineffectively conducted, resulting in a financial, political, and ideological quagmire and a degradation of America's influence in a changing, increasingly hostile world. Other management debacles like Katrina have only added to the negative perception of U.S. leaders, at home and elsewhere. It's time to hold leaders accountable and motivate followers—the citizens and major stakeholders of America, Inc.—to get more involved in shaping the future course of their democracy. It's time, as has often been done in public corporations, to hold our leaders, our top managers, accountable for their deeds, misdeeds, and lack of action in areas critical to the well-being of the country.

There are many changes or reforms that are needed, some more difficult than others to implement. Many of the necessary reforms are large and encompassing and deal with problems that go beyond those considered under the topics of leadership or followership treated in this chapter. These changes have been suggested in previous chapters, and have included financial and fiscal reform, reduction of lobbyists' influence, organizational design and effectiveness issues, and addressing the abuse of power. These and other recommendations for change, integrating critical material from the entire book, will be summarized in the concluding chapter.

Still, there are few changes or reforms in the area of leadership and followership that are germane to the present chapter's discussion. First, the activities of leaders in Washington must *become more visible or transparent*. All voting and spending bills and rules changes by Congress should be posted on a website, with a clear description of the substance of the bills and rules changes. If, increasingly, people are relying on the internet for their information, posting data on a website might actually attract needed attention to our leaders' spending and voting habits. This extension of the "sunshine" mentality can begin to inform citizens of key votes and stances, while doing much to reduce management by stealth.

Second, *all earmarks must be eliminated.* The practice of sneaking through earmarks as addenda to positive legislation must be voided. If a funding request cannot stand on its own merits, it should not be able to sneak by under the radar of public attention and scrutiny. This seems basic to a full disclosure of U.S. leaders' spendthrift and sneaky ways and a significant reduction in yearly deficits. It was argued previously (Chapter 5) that the ethics reform bill of 2007 did nothing to reduce onerous and wasteful earmarks. It's time for real leadership in the White House and Congress to finally address this problem and redress the countless wrongs that are being perpetuated.

Third, the *laws, practices, or rules regarding gerrymandering or redistricting must be changed.* Elections imply contests and the discussion, dissection, and analysis of key issues. Voters lose interest when an election is decided *before* the election, not on the issues, but by a person or persons controlling and modifying voting districts to favor incumbents. Federal laws and increased centralized controls over state gerrymandering laws and practices would be a huge step in reducing the inequities and atrocities that currently exist.

Fourth, a way must be found to *make high-level government positions attractive to more of the brightest and the best minds in the country.* The most qualified Americans are rarely summoned or attracted to public office, or so it seems. Cronyism, nepotism, loyalty, connections, and, of course, money, often drive candidate selection, cabinet appointments, and nominations for other high level positions.

Consider for a moment the Department of Homeland Security, ostensibly a vital part of an effective war on terrorism and the furthering of national safety. At present, there are many top-level jobs unfilled, negatively affecting the agency's performance. Even more significantly, the prospects are strong for a huge "brain drain" after the 2008 election (using the term very loosely). In 2004, 360 of its top employees and managers were politically appointed, with little regard for qualifications or capabilities, which helps explain the gross incompetence of the department. But if the majority of these appointees and other more qualified personnel leave a sinking ship at once, then what? The danger is that a new administration will act quickly, focus again on loyalty and cronyism in replacing key people, and incompetence will be perpetuated, even celebrated, and the "normal" situation maintained.

Something else is surely preferable. Certainly, plans can be formulated to attract qualified career people from within the government and from outside organizations to serve in key roles in such a supposedly important agency. Surely, certain key people—security experts, department heads, etc.—can be kept in service based on their skills and capabilities, regardless of how politically incorrect this will seem to the Washington insiders and the political hacks who are emasculating our government's ability to perform. Some U.S. leader(s) must finally stand up to make high-level government positions attractive to qualified people rather than maintaining the status quo with its overabundance of unqualified political appointees.

Fifth, lobbyists and their money must be controlled. Americans have the right to "petition" their government to redress grievances or seek equitable treatment, of course, but the pendulum of influence has gone too far with increasing benefits to the few. A handful of major lobbies effectively control huge sums of money that are affecting major decisions by U.S. leaders and creating a management oligarchy in Washington. Political "looting" is running rampant in the U.S., as both Republicans and Democrats are feeding at the trough. Both parties' leaders and candidates for high office are happily seeking easy cash, and both sides are engaging in a kind of "pay-to-play" corruption and supporting lobbyist-written deals and bundlers' activities that benefit the politicians, not the general public.[26] More attention clearly needs to be paid to publicizing and controlling this flow of cash and influence.

Relatedly, lobbyists' control of the Congress and the "revolving door" between Capitol Hill and K Street help ensure that many politicians become pawns of monied special interests and, later, lobbyists themselves, not qualified analysts or adjudicators of critical issues challenging the republic. Under these conditions, effective leadership and management cannot exist; major policies will again reflect the wishes of a management oligarchy and their minority supporters, not those of the vast majority of the stakeholders and citizens of America, Inc. Laws simply must be enacted to slow down and control this revolving door and eliminate a form of "inbreeding" that is affecting important decisions in the nation's capital.

Sixth, the mention of lobbyists, bundlers, and their special interests suggests that Congressional elections and national elections for President and Vice President should be *financed more by public funds provided by taxpayers*, not primarily by the private donations of the moneyed interests. If citizens had greater control of the purse strings, they would have a greater propensity to listen to competing candidates on the issues. The present system disenfranchises the majority of Americans in the voting process and creates a political oligarchy; public funding of major elections would renew the franchise and motivate many voters to participate more actively in the choice of leaders on Capitol Hill and in the White House. It's definitely time for this to be considered as a viable option.

Finally, building on the discussions of power and influence in previous chapters, the press and other media must get more involved and publicize the transgressions, stealthy practices, and dangers being created by U. S. leaders. Too many of these problems are simply not known or publicized. Poor followership is fueling dysfunctional, ineffective leadership, and an active news media, especially the press, must become the watchdog for control and accountability of the country's top management and an informed provider of vital information to U.S. citizens. The problems being identified presently will not go away magically with regime change and a new administration in Washington. They need to be publicized and debated, and this is the job of an active media.

Of course, the general public must do its part. U.S. citizens have been too quiet and reticent, allowing dysfunctional U.S. leadership to flourish. It's definitely time to rebel and protest. It's time to petition U.S. leaders to change their positions on debt, spending, health care, etc. Dysfunctional followership cannot continue to support bad policies or acquiesce in the face of horrific leadership in the White House and Congress. Regime change must soon be associated with real leadership and management change before it's too late and America, Inc. faces a bankruptcy of sorts—political, economic, and social. It's time, finally, for action and change and the general public must do its part.

CONCLUSIONS

The leadership at the very top of America, Inc. in the White House and Congress is inefficient, ineffective, and dysfunctional, creating major problems. Poor planning, a lack of emphasis on clear responsibility and accountability, excessive myopia or short-term thinking, an inability to confront and treat long-standing, critical problems, and incompetent fiscal and financial performance that almost borders on the criminal or unethical are just a few of the negative characteristics of the top management or leadership in the U.S. This dysfunctional leadership and the profligate spending and waste that results from it has caused, and will continue to cause, major problems in the economic, political, and social spheres of America, Inc. It is even creating a dangerous situation in some areas, e.g. the poor organizational design of the intelligence community and the real threats to the nation's security that could result from this organizational hodgepodge.

The top leadership in the country gets away with its dysfunctional and ineffective behavior because of three interdependent activities or phenomena. *Management by stealth* represents processes of decision making and management actions that are designed not to be easily detected and, hence, not open to public scrutiny and analysis. The trick here—which U.S. leaders in the White House and on Capitol Hill have mastered—is one of sneakiness and deception aimed at hiding things—from rules changes about environmental protection to hidden taxes that injure the majority of taxpayers, including people the taxes weren't even intended to affect; from slinky ways of eliminating the time-honored precept of *habeas corpus*, to ways of making important policy decisions in the dark, e.g. regarding energy and the waging of war; from ways to attach bad bills and earmarks to worthwhile legislation, to ways of controlling the outcomes of elections. Management by stealth is flourishing at the very top levels of America, Inc.

Management by fear supports the clandestine activities of U.S. leaders. By creating fear and then perpetuating it, even with phony issues and fake enemies, the leadership team tries to ensure a pliable base of citizens ready and willing to trust its policies with no questions asked. Management by stealth keeps people in the dark, and management by fear tries to ensure that the leaders acting stealthily and creating the fear are seen as the only sources of light and truth in this dark world of political ignorance.

Finally, there is *dysfunctional followership*, which allows poor leadership to survive and prosper. Intelligent, informed citizens have influence or clout, but dysfunctional followership is characterized by uninterested, uncaring, or uninformed citizens who seem bored or intimidated by complex national issues or who prefer hearing about politics via quick sound bites or brief, catchy phrases and slogans more suitable to reality shows or product advertising on TV. These apathetic consumers of government services certainly support the nation's leaders' reliance on stealth and fear, thereby perpetuating what can be called dysfunctional leadership or poor management.

This chapter has identified some reforms or changes that are needed, including the elimination of earmarks, controls on gerrymandering or redistricting, and the financing of critical national and congressional elections with public funds. But this book has suggested additional important reforms and needed changes to improve the management of America, Inc. The next and final chapter summarizes the key reforms and changes that are necessary, acting as a kind of glossary or reference list to conclude and integrate the material that has been presented in this book and to show how it is possible to improve the management of America, Inc. before it's too late.

Endnotes

1. For good discussion of leadership, see: Gary Yukl, *Leadership in Organizations* (Prentice Hall, 1994); Keith Grint, *Leadership* (Oxford University Press, 2001); Larry Berman (ed.), *The Art of Political Leadership* (Rowman and Littlefield, 2006); Edwin Locke, *The Essence of Leadership* (Lexington Books, 1991); Michael Useem, *The Leadership Moment* (Three Rivers Press, 1998) and *Leading Up* (Crown Business, 2001).

2. See L. G. Hrebiniak, *Making Strategy Work* (Wharton School Publishing, 2005) for a good discussion of strategy implementation or execution and management's role in this process.

3. For an excellent discussion of the dangers and problems of an attack on Iran and why the U.S. seems to be heading in this direction, see Trudy Rubin, "On the Brink of a Blunder," *The Philadelphia Inquirer*, October 27, 2007.

4. Rubin makes this point convincingly. See "On the Bunk of a Blunder," Ibid.

5. See, for example: Albert Hunt, "Bush's Credibility Canyon," The Wall Street Journal, April 1, 2004; Charlemagne, "We Told You So," *The Economist*, May 15, 2004; Jackie Calmes, "Questions of Leadership Style," *The Wall Street Journal*, May 19, 2004; "Still Not Loved. Now Not Envied," *The Economist*, June 25, 2005; "Approval Ratings for President and Congressional Leaders Continue to Drop," *The Harris Poll*, #66, August 24, 2005; Steve Benen, "Is President Bush Learning?" *Alter Net*, August 30, 2006; Trudy Rubin, "Retired Generals Speaking Out," *The Philadelphia Inquirer,* April 12, 2006; Trudy Rubin, "Bush Out of Touch With Mideast Vision," *The Philadelphia Inquirer*, July 30, 2006; Tom Hundley, "No-Confidence Vote in U.S. Leadership," *Chicago Tribune*, reprinted in *The Philadelphia Inquirer*, September 10, 2006; Matt Taibbi, "The Worst Congress Ever," *Rolling Stone*, October 25, 2006.

6. Brody Mullins, "As Earmarked Funding Swells, Some Recipients Don't Want It," *The Wall Street Journal*, December 26, 2006;

7. "Timber-r-r-r-r-r! One By One, The Safeguards Fall, "Editorial, *The Philadelphia Inquirer*, December 8, 2002; Joel Brinkley, "Out of Spotlight, Bush Overhauls U.S. Regulations," *The New York Times*, August 14, 2004.

8. Ibid.

9. "Timber-r-r-r-r-r-r!" *The Philadelphia Inquirer*, op. cit.

10. "'Protections' for Utah Rivers Emerge as Gift to Oil and Gas Industry," bushgreenwatch.org, October 1, 2004.

11. "Mr. Bush's Stealthy Tax Increase," Editorial, *The New York Times*, March 13, 2005.

12. Jonathan Schell, "The Hidden State Steps Forward," *The Nation*, December 24, 2005; Mark Sherman, "FBI Investigated 3,501 People Without Warrants," *The Associated Press*, April 29, 2006; "Bush as Nixon," *The New York Times*, December 20, 2005.

13. Ibid.

14. Ted Rall, "America's Nuremberg Laws," *Common Dreams news Center*, October 12, 2006; Onnesha Roychoudhuri, "Tracking the Torture Taxi," *Truthdig*, September 19, 2006.

15. "Out of the Spotlight," *The New York Times*, op. cit.

16. "Mr. Cheney's Imperial Presidency," Editorial, *The New York Times*, December 23, 2005; Bob Herbert, "Masters of Deception," *The New York Times*, January 16, 2004.

17. Others have remarked on the tautological argument, e.g. see William Saletan, "Trust, Don't Verify," *Slate*, April 14, 2004.

18. See "The Great Divider," Editorial, *The New York Times*, November 2, 2006, for a good discussion of divisive leadership and its relation for management by fear.

19. Alexis De Tocqueville, *Democracy In America*, (Signet, 2001); see also Adam Cohen, "Democracy in America, Then And Now, a Struggle Against Majority Tyranny," *The New York Times*, January 23, 2006, for an excellent application of De Tocqueville's ideas to modern America.

20. "Democracy in America, Then and Now." Ibid.

21. John Harwood, "War-Weary Public Wants Congress to Lead," *The Wall Street Journal*, December 14, 2006.

22. National Endowment for the Arts, "Reading at Risk: A Survey of Literary Reading in America," July 8, 2004.

23. John S. and James L. Knight Foundation, "The Future of the First Amendment," Spring 2004.

24. "No Way to Run a Democracy," *The Economist*, September 18, 2004.

25. Ibid.

26. See, for example, the excellent discussion by David Sirota, "Democrats Kiss Up to K Street," *AlterNet*, July 18, 2007, which shows clearly the influence of "honest" and "dishonest" graft on leaders in both major parties.

8

Keeping America, Inc. From "Going Out of Business"

The preceding chapters have laid out a host of problems in America, Inc. due to mismanagement and ineffective leadership. The basic premise of the book—and by now, hopefully, an observable and believable fact—is that the country is marked by severe problems of mismanagement at the very top—in the White House, Cabinet and Congress—and that they will soon take their toll, negatively affecting the country financially, socially, and politically in an increasingly complex and hostile world. Hiding mismanagement and its costly policies and decisions behind the popular notion that government is "different" and can never be expected to run efficiently and effectively might have deterred critics from revealing and correcting top management shortcomings in the past. However, the looming situation is quite different: without major changes in management methods and leadership, serious repercussions will surely make themselves felt and tax the economic, social, and political underpinnings of the country.

Steps must be taken by U.S. leaders to keep America, Inc. from these inevitable hard times. It's time, finally, to address problems that have been festering and soon will become open sores. It's time for our leaders to think about huge impending problems and their solutions and spend less time focusing on earmarks, personal gain, re-election funding, the use of steroids in baseball, the integrity of N.B.A. officials, future jobs in a lobbyist shop, etc. It's about time to drop the "politics is different" mantra and the "this is the way things are done in Washington" smokescreen and focus on real leadership and imminent problems before it's too late.

In many respects, America, Inc. is just like the large global corporation. It's necessary, more than ever before, to focus on sound management and organizational design to compete effectively and remain viable in an increasingly complex and turbulent world. The U.S. is not a business, of course, but there certainly are important lessons in management that can be borrowed from the private sector to address and solve the impending problems, and this is exactly what this book has done. Chapter 1 introduced the concept of America, Inc. and showed how the growing complexity of the global economic and political environment demands a new focus on sound management and effective organizational design. Chapters 2-7 discussed the major issues that need attention by our leaders in the White House and Congress, as well as possible decisions and actions that can help the country regain a strong position domestically and globally. Let's summarize these points presently to serve as a guide for action by our leaders and U.S. citizens alike.

Develop the Right Focus

In the corporate world, top management must focus its resources and energies effectively to achieve desired goals. Focus requires sound planning (strategy, goal setting) and effective execution to support the chosen strategic and short-term plans. Effective execution includes decisions about organizational structure, coordination, clarification of responsibility and accountability, the incentives needed to motivate desired results, and the controls to support learning, knowledge sharing, and organizational change. Top management in America, Inc. must also focus its resources and energies effectively and worry about similar planning and execution issues.

It's important and beneficial, first, to focus on sound management and organization by *starting at the very top*, in the White House and Cabinet (Chapter 2). With 30 or more Cabinet-level officials under the President, it's necessary to clarify roles and responsibilities, authority, interdependence, spans of control, and coordination around critical tasks to give some semblance of order and logic to decision making. Poor management and organization in the White House and Cabinet certainly aren't the most critical problems identified in this book, but they indeed can affect or exacerbate the impact of those problems. A lack of management and organizational clarity at the top can translate into a lack of clarity at lower levels and create additional problems of responsibility, accountability, and inefficient and ineffective decision making.

Chapter 2 argues that mismanagement at the very top represents "the start of something bad" and it, accordingly, must be addressed. The steps to improved management are laid out in the chapter, and they represent the first actions for a President, Cabinet, and Congress to consider. The chapter also emphasizes the critical need for capable people in top-level management positions. The job requirements and capabilities needed by Cabinet members should dictate the choice of people, not the cronyism and political loyalty that has often dominated this choice in the past.

Reorganize the Intelligence Community

A real need for focus, managerially and organizationally, is indicated in an analysis of the intelligence community where planning and execution are extremely problematical and may be contributing to a dangerous situation (Chapter 3). The community desperately needs focus to reduce the number of organizations, improve planning, coordination, and cooperation, and develop a supportive culture in order to handle future intelligence-related challenges. In the absence of a major overhaul, the intelligence community's performance will only degenerate.

The intelligence community really numbers around 64 or more agencies at the present time, not just the 15 or 16 that are commonly mentioned. A large number of organizations and agencies is difficult enough to manage and control, but their relative independence, separate budgets, and competition for scarce resources greatly reduce the probability of cooperation and knowledge sharing. Effective coordination is non-existent. The establishment of an Intelligence Czar and other roles is meaningless and ineffective without supporting those roles with authority and legitimate coordinative responsibility that agency personnel recognize and accept. An "industry" culture presently works against interdependence, cooperation, and collaborative decision making, and the incentives that exist support this negative culture and the prevailing competitive *modus operandi*. Poor management and inadequate organizational design prevail and the current system of intelligence simply cannot work effectively, and this poses a real threat to the country, as Chapter 3 noted in detail.

So, what can be done by our leaders in the White House and Congress? The first critical need is a *reorganization of the intelligence community*. Nothing less will work. Fancy titles like "czar" sound impressive and productive, but really mean little or nothing for actual intelligence performance. Reliance on informal coordination methods, inter-agency good faith, the existing "tradecraft," etc. simply are not sufficient to generate effective intelligence in the future. Although opposition to reorganization within the intelligence community surely will be vast and strenuous, the time has come for U.S. leaders to consider the option. Reorganization is absolutely necessary to achieve focus and improve performance.

Chapter 3 presented one possible reorganization, realigning the intelligence community into *three main divisions or groups*—Foreign Intelligence, Domestic Intelligence, and Military Intelligence. These represent three logical strategic and operating foci or thrusts under which to subsume the large member of existing agencies or organizations. The present array of intelligence agencies simply cannot function effectively, and the escalating cost of this inefficient community must be halted and its organization and coordination mechanisms changed and rationalized drastically. The three divisions or groups can be supported by centralized functions that service them while achieving both increased efficiency and effectiveness. Methods or processes for coordination across the three divisions or groups can also be developed to support knowledge sharing and more effective performance, as Chapter 3 showed.

Structural change is necessary, but alone is not sufficient. Other changes are required to support the new organization and these three units. Chapter 3 argued that responsibility and accountability must be clarified along with areas of interdependence across the three areas. Incentives must be developed to support cooperation rather than conflict and competition across intelligence units and to nurture a new culture that recognizes common goals. These are difficult tasks but, as the chapter indicated, the present incentives and culture do not support cooperation but, rather, pit agency against agency in competition for resources and status, and this only detracts from the overall intelligence capability.

Other reorganizations are possible, not just the one offered in Chapter 3. The point being emphasized is that something must be done and done soon. Reorganization is necessary and critical to future performance. Regardless of the option chosen, the reorganization must be real, with emphasis paid to *a more parsimonious, focused set of intelligence divisions or groups; clarification of responsibility and authority; development of methods for improved coordination and cooperation across divisions; and changes in incentives, structure, and people within the intelligence community to affect a change in culture over time.* The crying need, in an increasingly hostile world, is to develop an intelligence system with the right focus and set of capabilities to get the job done, and how to respond to this need is the essence of Chapter 3.

Putting the Financial and Fiscal Shop in Order

Chapter 4 pointed out in no uncertain terms that the U.S. will face severe economic troubles if present financial and fiscal policies continue to rule. The country is facing a financial and fiscal mess that sorely needs attention. Problems include: a $9 trillion debt that keeps growing; a frightening fiscal gap of $60+ trillion due to future obligations in Social Security and Medicare that are being ignored; a huge amount of foreign debt that's been funding U.S. purchases, lifestyles, and even our wars; a weakening dollar and potential loss of economic clout and status in the world; an overindulgence in earmarks, pork-barrel projects, and other forms and methods of wasteful spending; and a growing overemphasis on "guns" over "butter" in the country's spending habits.

These and other problems identified in Chapter 4 demand that U.S. leaders finally think strategically and address the country's financial and fiscal woes. This advice won't be received well by many of our leaders who spend like drunken sailors; nonetheless, there are actions or steps that absolutely must be taken to avoid severe economic problems in the near future.

The first necessary step mentioned in Chapter 4 is to *reduce and control government spending, borrowing, and waste.* Passage of a strong *balanced-budget constitutional amendment* would be a logical and important step. Efforts have been made along these lines in the past, but they have failed or were undermined by U.S. leaders. It's time to rethink the constitutional issue to curb and control the level of waste and spending in a spendthrift leadership group in America, Inc.

Another step would be to *eliminate all earmarks,* many of which constitute "pork"—frivolous, wasteful projects that serve only a small minority of beneficiaries. If funding requests can't face public scrutiny and stand on their own merits, they shouldn't be attached to other spending bills and snake through Congress in a stealthy way. Not all earmarks are bad—some help children, hospitals, universities and they will easily pass the increased scrutiny. But forcing all funding requests to make it on their own would certainly reduce the number of hidden earmarks from the 16,000 or so that routinely escape public scrutiny and certainly contribute $billions to wasteful, even silly spending.

The ethics reform bill of August 2007 did nothing to attack and reduce the number of earmarks. If anything, the legislation will actually motivate an *increase* in their use and popularity, as Chapter 4 stressed. U.S. citizens must let their leaders in Congress know that *they won't put up with such mismanagement and waste.* It's time for citizens to hold lawmakers responsible for their spending decisions and actions; it's time to become aggressive and vocal and vote the "knaves and fools" out of office if their wasteful spending habits persist.

On the fiscal side, *a revision or revamping of the tax code* would help to eliminate the huge problems and inequities under existing tax laws and even lead to increased revenues for the country. To begin with, the present tax code is hopelessly complex, with tens of thousands of pages of rules and gobbledygook that can best be described as a rambling maze of mammoth size that provides an extremely fertile ground for lawyers to uncover loopholes and other tax-avoidance "goodies." The tax system is simply too complicated and unfair in its impact, as Chapter 4 showed, and it must be revised significantly.

The present tax system is also contributing to a growing form of financial apartheid in the U.S. Wealthy Americans and corporations are paying a smaller share of the income tax burden, while middle-class wage earners are making up for it by paying a greater percentage of the total tax receipts. Tax cuts have generally favored the wealthy, but the cuts haven't raised additional revenues as has been advertised. The Alternative Minimum Tax, while aimed originally at "fat cats" to ensure that they paid a fair share of the tax burden, is presently hammering the middle class while, relatively, the fat cats are escaping the growing AMT massacre. The AMT has not been repealed simply because of the revenue it's generating, but the time has come to eliminate this tax and its inequities and revise the tax code.

Chapter 4 considered some reform options, including a *flat-tax* system that would simplify things and very likely generate additional revenues for the country. A flat tax would eliminate the many hours and $100 billion or so spent annually by citizens on tax preparation and would be easier to manage. Of course, the financial analysts, tax consultants, and lawyers who currently manage the tax code certainly would be against a move toward simplification, but it's time for U.S. leaders to think of the majority of their constituents and finally take needed action on the tax front.

It's also time for U.S. leaders to show some gumption and challenge the ways of the Pentagon. It's time to bite the bullet, so to speak, and *rethink and reduce military spending.* Despite a war on terrorism, which suggests quite different methods of waging war, the military budget keeps growing due to the funding of traditional warfare methods and equipment. The Pentagon's requests for weapons systems and ordnance are granted with nary a whimper or challenge from U.S. leaders. Military spending in the U.S. is presently equal to that in the rest of the world combined, and it's consuming more and more of available U.S. income to the detriment of other needed programs. "Off-budget" spending is growing and actually increasing the relative amount dedicated to war, and the total military budget is consuming more and more of the available funding to the detriment of social, educational, and health-care programs, as well as infrastructure rehabilitation projects that are sorely needed.

The military budget is loaded with earmarks, contributing to wasteful spending and increases in debt, and it definitely needs seriously reining in by U.S. leaders. The military-industrial complex surely will go "ballistic" over any proposal for cutbacks, but military spending has benefited from inertia or momentum over the decades and it cannot be allowed to continue to grow out of control. Surely, the cuts can be done without sacrificing America, Inc.'s military might and increasing the country's vulnerability in a hostile world.

These and other actions mentioned in Chapter 4 are needed to put America, Inc.'s financial and fiscal shop in order. Our leaders' spendthrift ways must change, and serious thought must be given to a *Constitutional balanced-budget amendment, the elimination of earmarks, major tax reform, and reduction of the military budget.* The debt picture and growing fiscal gap facing the country are surely leading to an economic earthquake and these problems cannot be ignored any longer. Confronting issues like the looming bankruptcy of Social Security, the reduction of total debt, and placing budgetary controls on the Pentagon won't be easy, but they must soon be done to avoid a huge negative impact on the majority of U.S. citizens.

Confront Power and Reduce Dysfunctional Dependencies

Chapters 5 and 6 pointed out that the power structure in the U.S. is creating a host of serious problems that need attention. The main thrust of Chapter 5 was directed against the power of lobbies and lobbyists and the dysfunctional outcome of their huge influence. The chapter emphasized how the power of money (over $200 million spent per month to seduce lawmakers) and the vanity and greed of lawmakers are turning the legislative process into a grab-bag of sorts that is primarily benefiting and serving minority interests. It explains why major problems, e.g. a huge dependency on foreign oil, haven't been addressed or solved, despite the amazing amount of rhetoric and promises over the years by Presidents and other politicians to reduce this malevolent dependency.

Chapter 5 presented a host of examples of pork-barrel legislation and earmarks that are sucking up scarce resources and detracting lawmakers' time and attention from the real problems facing the country. It points out the negative impact of a "revolving door" between lawmakers and lobbyist shops and how this relationship is perpetuating $billions in waste and affecting the legislative agenda. The chapter warns, too, how the power of lobbyists and various dependencies associated with it are actually creating a management oligarchy in the country and disenfranchising the majority of citizens from participation in critical decisions and the legislative process.

Chapter 5 presented a number of action items to address the power of lobbyists, slow down the "revolving door," and refocus our leaders' efforts in the right direction. These include creation of a real and powerful *ethics reform bill* that bans or controls gifts to politicians and sets up an independent ethics-oversight committee to police lobbyists and lawmakers alike. The bill would *publicize all spend-*

ing bills and open them up to public scrutiny. Another important aspect of the bill would be to *ban all earmarks* that are attached to other pieces of legislation and currently work their way stealthily through law-making channels. This was mentioned in Chapter 4, but it was worth repeating in Chapter 5. Forcing all projects to pass muster and public scrutiny on their own merits in the legislative process would reduce the number of pork-barrel projects and their associated waste and, more importantly, would add visibility and illumination to the sneaky business dealings involved in the "earmark trade" and the unhealthy influence of lobbyists. It's about time for Congress to pass and support a *real ethics reform measure*, not the ineffectual sham of August 2007 that actually provides loopholes to protect and motivate the increased use of earmarks.

Chapter 5 focused, too, on solutions to the critical oil dependency problem that's plagued the country for decades. With only promises from U.S. leaders over the years to do something about it, but with nothing actually resulting from their supposed good intentions, it's time for our leaders to take real action. To eliminate or reduce this terrible dependency, drastic steps are needed. First, lawmakers should *raise the gasoline tax dramatically*. This hasn't been done for decades and it's about time to use this aggressive tool again. Increasing taxes on gasoline will drive down demand very quickly and curtail the wasteful habits of most drivers. It will, over time, motivate the purchase of more fuel-efficient vehicles and even the increased use of public transportation. The message of a significant tax increase is also clear: leaders will have finally found the gumption to attack the oil lobby and do something about a wasteful and dangerous dependency.

U.S. leaders also should enact and enforce *more stringent fuel economy standards* for vehicles, standards that presently have sunk to abysmal lows. This move won't have as immediate an effect as raising gasoline prices, but it will help over time. Experience in other countries has shown that more efficient vehicles will cause an overall drop in the demand for fossil fuels. To support these actions, funds should be dedicated to finding and supporting *alternative sources of energy*, e.g. hydrogen fuel cells.

Resistance to these moves by established members of the oil lobby—oil companies, Middle-East oil barons, automotive companies—will be huge, and many tales will be told as to why few or none of the corrective measures will work. U.S. leaders must see through this smokescreen and finally exhibit the courage and determination to reduce the oil dependency. If existing leaders don't exhibit the guts to take on the task, they should be removed from office and replaced by those willing to do the right things. Without such a resolve and emphasis on action, the huge troubles that lie ahead will certainly challenge the viability and progress of the country.

Chapter 6 enumerated various elements of an attack on science, the press, and other news media. It showed how these attacks are undermining what Americans see, read, hear, and believe, and how control of information is leading inexorably to a new and dangerous "Big Brother" scenario in the U.S. The attack on science can be seen in the growing number of non-scientific explanations of scientific phenomena, explanations of natural phenomena that directly confront and contradict science, and funding cutbacks that are having a negative effect on the centrality of science in the U.S. Reduction in sponsored government research is reducing the attractiveness of the country to scientists around the world, and is planting the seeds of a U.S. scientific decline that threatens future economic and technological leadership in a challenging global environment. A new breed of enlightened leaders must reverse this trend, reducing the attacks dramatically while *actively supporting science* with the funds needed to regain its preeminence in the country and world.

Attacks on the press and other news media are another real and nefarious problem. The government has shown an increased proclivity to create "pseudo-events" and news stories for public consumption, as Chapter 6 indicated. Management-by-fear has allowed government officials to classify, reclassify, or hide information under the guise of a battle on terrorism; conceal spending from public scrutiny, e.g. for classified or "black" programs; and take other steps to reduce the press' and public's right to know and to dissent with what is really going on in such areas as spying, torture, and control of information. Chapter 6 also pointed out the dangers of increased consolidation in the news industry and the power that increasingly is in the hands of fewer decision makers to decide what news is fit to read, listen to, or see.

Cures and changes here will be hard to come by, but they must be implemented. The government *shouldn't be allowed to create "pseudo events" and control information* under the espoused need to wage war and protect the nation, and a watchdog press must analyze and challenge government claims and communications to preserve the integrity and validity of the news. It's necessary to consider carefully the *impact of increased consolidation* of the news media and assess the public costs associated with it before quickly acceding to private corporate interests. It's imperative that *oligopoly and increased concentration* in the news or communications industry be carefully examined and controlled. Government and the citizens of the U.S. should nurture and support the *independence of the PBS* as a watchdog organization concerned with accurate, non-partisan reporting of information. An independent press and other elements of the news-communications industry must renew the role of being the critic and "tocsin" or alarm bell of the nation, a role espoused by the founding fathers and one desperately in need of resurrection and support today.

The problems facing the country are looming larger, time is running out, and the need for effective leadership and followership is acute.

Display Leadership ..., Finally

Chapter 7 pointed out some of the basic characteristics or qualities of effective leaders and argued that U.S. leaders in the White House and Congress are sorely deficient when benchmarked against them. Problems or shortcomings included poor planning, a lack of strategic thinking, overly strong concern with earmarks and personal gratification, myopic views of problems and trends, poor organizational skills, spendthrift habits, horrific financial mismanagement, and an inability to confront and deal with critical onerous dependencies (e.g. in oil) that have existed for ages. U.S. leaders' actions—and inaction—are hurting the country's standing and credibility in the world while, simultaneously, negatively affecting the common good at home. Their cozying up to powerful lobbies is actually hurting the democratic process in the U.S. and creating a form of management oligarchy that is disenfranchising a large number of citizens in the political process. Other management problems were noted throughout the book but there's no need to repeat them all, as the point by now hopefully is very clear: U.S. leadership is sorely deficient and it's leading to myriad problems that will hurt the country economically, socially, and politically in the near future. The time has come for action and real leadership before it's too late.

This book has attempted to sound the alarm that all is not well with America, Inc. It has argued vehemently that major troubles are looming and that U.S. leaders must wake up, forgo personal aggrandizement, and act to preserve the country's viability in a changing and threatening world. Gross mismanagement must finally be recognized, addressed, and corrected. *There are major warnings in this book, and they recently have been underscored boldly by* David Walker, Comptroller General of U.S., a non-partisan figure in charge of the Government Accountability Office.[1]

Walker states emphatically and without political dressing that the country is on a "burning platform" of mismanagement and unsustainable policies and practices fueled by fiscal deficits, chronic healthcare underfunding, and huge military commitments. The country, he argues, is "on a path toward an explosion of debt," exacerbated by spiraling health care costs, plummeting savings rates, and increased dependency on foreign lenders whose potential capriciousness could dramatically increase the problems and risks facing the country. Add huge and spiraling military budgets and the looming cost of demands to fix the psychical infrastructure of the nation—bridges, highways, airports, water and sewage systems—and the financial picture becomes even darker and more ominous.

Walker actually draws parallels with the collapse of the Roman Empire, citing such striking similarities between the country's current condition and those that helped sink Rome, including an over-extended military, the irresponsibility or ineptitude of the central government, and a declining political civility at home. Without significant change, the implication is that the U.S. could surely and inexorably follow Rome's path to a loss of power and prestige in the world.

These are tough words, but they mirror and reinforce the points made emphatically in this book. A major crisis is brewing in America, Inc., and U.S. leaders must finally wake up and eliminate the problems of mismanagement and poor organizational design laid out in preceding chapters. This is not a political rant or a false or exaggerated pseudo-event or warning. The issues being raised are real and dangerous and they pose a threat to the continued viability and prosperity of this nation.

◆   ◆   ◆

It's time, finally, for U.S. leaders to act responsibly and do the things effective leaders must do. It's time to recognize that there are solutions to the problems, dependencies, and threats laid out in this book, and that they can be implemented if U.S. leaders in the White House and Congress finally show the necessary resolve to act as effective managers and agents of change.

It's time too for U.S. citizens and the news media to demand change and scream for reform before conditions deteriorate beyond the point of repair. Poor leadership is only supported and encouraged by poor followership and meek and mild media, especially the press. People get the leadership they deserve; the citizens and stakeholders of America, Inc. deserve better, but they must demand it in no uncertain terms. Doing nothing will only increase the likelihood of America, Inc.'s facing serious threats to its viability as a going concern.

Endnote

1. Jeremy Grant, "Learn From the Fall of Rome, U.S. Warned," *The Financial Times*, August 14, 2007.

978-0-595-48434-8
0-595-48434-4

Printed in the United States
204205BV00001B/218/P